Edible & Medicinal
Flowers

Margaret Roberts

Photography by

Phyllis Green

THE SPEARHEAD PRESS

Published by
The Spearhead Press
A division of David Philip Publishers
208 Werdmuller Centre
Claremont
7708

First edition, first impression 2000

ISBN 0 86486 467 1

Photographs on pp. 15, 19 and 45 courtesy Floraprint Southern Africa.

Cover design by Fishfinger Designs
Design and typesetting by Alicia Arntzen, Lebone Publishing Services
Reproduction by Castle Graphics, Johannesburg
Printed and bound by Interpak, Natal

ACKNOWLEDGEMENTS

It has been an extraordinary time growing this book! Unusual in that the last days of the twentieth century saw the actual fruition of many years collecting, trialling and growing every plant that is within the pages of this book, and the writing of the text. A mammoth task indeed, with the harshness of the climate, the rugged mountainside terrain, erratic water supply, searing heat and bitter winter winds, hail storms, veld fires and all else in between, and the true frailty of every tiny seed that has survived and established itself. It is amazing that this bouquet of nature's most exquisite creations is printed, bound and published – a diary of the great evolvement of a garden.

I stand back in the quiet, warm evenings, drenched in the scent of a thousand flowers and never stop marvelling at nature's bounty and the joy of recording it. And with the unending, back-breaking work that the Herbal Centre gardens entail, it is with a heart full of gratitude that I say thank you to the garden and studio staff who helps us when a crop needs to be picked and processed, and for all the long hours tending the plants and making a garden possible, this vast and breathtaking garden that stands well established and rich in its floral diversity. It is there for the visitors – a testament.

To Phyllis Green, the professional photographer of all my magazine articles, who has become more and more enchanted with the flowers, for the many hours given of her free time, the many miles she travelled to find the flowers in perfection, and to have had the privilege of teaching so willing a pupil the medicinal values of each flower she so expertly photographed, my thanks over and over for sharing all the beauty with me.

For my youngest child, Sandra, who has become a part of the Herbal Centre, for her incredible support, excitement, enthusiasm and sheer hard work, from cooking and testing the recipes, to lifting my work load so consistently, from styling the food photographs with Phyllis, to the long hours of tiny details and then feeding us all with elegance, style and such infectious enjoyment, and, for being a lifesaver, my gratitude forever.

For Reneé Ferreira, my editor, who has supported me through the birth pangs of this unusual book and who has shaped it, trimmed it, nurtured it, fertilised it and often pruned it and weeded out around it, for the long hours, my heartfelt thanks.

For Nicholas Combrinck my publisher, my thanks for being so enthusiastic, supportive and approachable. To have a publisher who not only gives an author carte blanche, but who addresses every thought, idea and concept so willingly and so eagerly, is rare and special, and brings out the best in us all – may there be many more shared ideas ahead.

I hope that this book will become an inspiration to the reader to create a medicinal flower garden that I guarantee will uplift and fascinate you all the days of your life. May it grow beautifully.

The Herbal Centre
De Wildt
South Africa
Spring 2000

CONTENTS

Introduction iv

MEDICINAL FLOWERS

RECIPES

INTRODUCTION

This book is an extraordinary collection of the flowers that I have used and studied over the years for their remarkable healing properties. I have grown each one in my herbal gardens and over the years have experimented with them endlessly in cooking, medicinally and cosmetically, until each one has come to feel like a treasured friend.

Flowers are an integral part of our lives and are associated with some of the most poignant moments of human experience, such as celebration and grieving. Their beauty and scent are woven into our consciences from early childhood, whether we realise it or not, and form associations that evoke in us memories of which we as adults are only dimly aware. I still find myself growing flowers that were part of my childhood, and using them with the same passion I had as a child in my first garden. My soul still stirs with the scent of wisteria on a spring evening, the exotic, haunting fragrance of gardenia like the one that grew outside my bedroom window as a child, the heart-rending scent of orange blossom that I associate with taking my children to boarding school so far away from our farm, and the scent of jasmine that recalls the aching grief I felt during my beloved father's last days.

Through the greatest troubles and the most devastating experiences of life, solace can be found in the planting of a garden of memories. I have made new gardens during the darkest times of my life and found the strenuous effort of digging, raking and planting not only steadied and calmed me, but helped to remind me that life has to go on. Flowers bring memories of happy experiences, love, friends and laughter flooding back as well, and help to make life worth living again.

I am convinced that gardening and cooking are the world's greatest hobbies, and what greater joy can there be than to create a garden of health? The most important aspect of this is to grow the plants organically, which means using neither chemical fertilisers nor chemical sprays, and instead gardening with compost, leaf mould and natural mulches, and using natural sprays. To become stringently organic is the only way for our bodies, our minds, our environment and ultimately our planet to heal.

The most valuable part of the garden is the compost heap, no matter how small, so always make sure you make space for this in your garden. It is this natural feeding that boosts your flowers to produce enough beauty and health-giving minerals and oils to change your life.

Making your own compost with an elder tree nearby, a row of comfrey and a row of yarrow, is so simple. Throw every weed you pull up, every raked leaf, the chopped up clippings from pruning and all the vegetable peelings from the

kitchen onto the compost heap, alternated with grass clippings, a few spades of manure and a good weekly watering, and you will be rewarded with a rich heap of compost as precious as gold in two months.

Grow insect-repelling plants as companion plants or space them around the garden to ward off insects. Ones to choose include rue, southernwood, both the annual and perennial basils, khakibos and marigolds (both these belong to the Tagetes family and are very pungent), pennyroyal, jewel or Corsican mint, tansy, curly tansy, yarrow, the sages – especially Cleveland sage – lavender, myrtle, winter savory, wormwood and pyrethrum.

Flowers often give a more delicate taste and texture than the leaves, and it is worth using them for their beauty alone, quite apart from their ability to restore the energy and vitality of which we have been robbed by our frenetic modern lifestyles. The recipes in this book are easy to prepare, and it is my hope that through them you will come to experience the extraordinary ability of flowers to heal, uplift, restore and revitalise.

Margaret Roberts

HERBAL CENTRE, DE WILDT
North West Province
Summer 2000

MEDICINAL FLOWERS

ALMOND BLOSSOM

Prunus dulcis ● *Prunus amygdalis*

I once lived next to an orchard that had a long double row of sweet almond trees that I would wander through in the evenings, watching with fascination as the seasons unfolded. The winter branches would be dark and gnarled artistically, transforming into a breathtaking flurry of delicate, fragrant palest pink blossom in spring, followed by the lush green leaves of summer and the furry encased fruits of midsummer. Due to the heat and dryness of the mountainside, our crop of fruit was never very much to speak of, but my love of the delicate beauty of the blossom led me to create the most exquisite cosmetics, and I learned to cook with the flowers.

MEDICINAL USES

The delicate blossoms contain small amounts of B vitamins, particularly biotin and niacin, vitamin E and traces of several amino acids. The petals and nuts contain calcium, magnesium, iron, phos-phorus, potassium, sodium and zinc. Because the blossoms and the nuts are so rich in the B vitamins, it is a superb energy food. The ancient Phoenicians used the petals in honey as a tonic and sprinkled them into gruels and stews to give muscular strength to soldiers. They also used crushed petals as a poultice over skin spots and, mixed with oil, for dry skin and sunburn.

Crushed petals on an insect bite will soothe and a tea made of the whole flower makes a refreshing mouthwash and gargle that clears up mouth ulcers and sore inflamed gums and, as a bonus, sweetens the breath. To make **almond blossom tea** add ¼ cup almond blossoms and 1 sprig of peppermint or spearmint to 1 cup boiling water. Leave to stand 5 minutes, then strain and drink.

CULTIVATION

The tree grows up to 6 metres in height, rather like a peach tree, and needs full sun and deeply dug, richly composted soil. They must have deep weekly waterings, twice a week in the hot dry months. Trees should be planted 4 metres apart. They are not self fertile so plant three or four varieties together, or ask a neighbour to plant one type and you the other to ensure fertilisation. Almond trees thrive with pruning and restraining, they do well as hedges, as topiaries and as patio plants in extra large tubs, providing they are constantly well fed. I spray mine with a seaweed foliar feed all through the year, and clip and train the supple branches to shape the trees, and I am rewarded with masses of blossom and a nice collection of nuts for all my trouble. They give me so much pleasure that I look forward to spring with great eagerness every year. Underplant with chives, garlic chives, lucerne and red clover, and you'll find it will increase the yield of fruit.

CULINARY

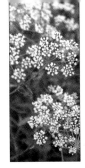

ANISE

Pimpinella anisum

Anise is native to the eastern Mediterranean areas as well as western Asia and North Africa, where it still grows wild as a wayside weed. Because it is so short lived, it often appears in spring and again in late summer, drawing bees and butterflies to it in droves with its sweet liquorice fragrance.

Astonishingly, anise has been cultivated in Egypt for over 4 000 years. Pharaonic texts show that even then it was used as a digestive herb, diuretic and for toothache. The Greeks used it too. Dioscorides wrote in the first century that anise seed 'warms, dries and dissolves, facilitates breathing, relieves pain, provokes urine and eases thirst'. Modern medical science has merely proved that these ancient uses of this marvellous herb were indeed correct.

MEDICINAL USES

Anise seed, and to some extent the leaves and flowers, helps with all digestive ailments – from colic to bloating, nausea to flatulence, heartburn to tummy rumblings – for all ages, from infants through to the very elderly. Both the seed and flowers are antispasmodic. Just chewing a few seeds or flowers will ease period pain, asthma, bronchitis and coughing (it helps to dry up phlegm and is a known expectorant), and for whooping cough there is nothing better.

Doctors are now looking at anise flowers and seeds to help irregular heartbeat and ease anxiety. Stress is ever increasing in our frenetic fast-lane lives and with anise's extraordinary antispasmodic effect, it can be relied upon to ease tight chest pains and distressed breathing. Sit quietly, try to take several deep breaths and slowly sip a cup of **anise health tea** (see recipe on p. 137). It is also excellent for a child writing exams, especially with a sprig of peppermint in the tea to boost concentration and promote clear thinking. For a tension headache this tea often gives immediate results and for a chill, a shock or severe agitation this remarkably soothing tea is definitely worth trying.

Anise flowers in the diet and a tea of the seeds also helps breast milk production and reduces acidity, so it really should be used far more than it is.

CULTIVATION

Anise is an attractive, short-lived annual growing up to 50 cm in height with pretty, feathery flowers typical of Umbelliferae, often mistakenly called lace flowers. It is a rewarding plant to grow as it demands nothing more than good, well-composted soil, full sun and a twice weekly watering. It thrives on neglect, gives a swift return on its easily and quickly raised seeds and is a delight to the eye and palate with its fragile beauty, tender buds and leaves and pungent seeds. When growing anise in the garden, I have found the more one picks, the more flowers are produced.

CULINARY

Anise Health Tea, p. 137
Anise Apple Dessert, p. 122
Anise Pasta Confetti Salad, p. 88

ANISE HYSSOP

Agastache rugosa ● Korean mint

This free-flowering perennial is native to Korea, parts of China, Laos and parts of Russia, growing wild on mountain slopes and along the roadsides. Cultivated as a medicinal plant in China, its name Huo Xiang was first mentioned in the ancient Chinese pharmacopoeia as far back as AD 500. Its uses as a warming, stimulating herb are still employed today in Chinese medicine and scientific studies all over the East prove it to be quite exceptional for treating viral infections, ringworm, fungal infections, digestive disorders, morning sickness, nausea, vomiting and abdominal bloating.

MEDICINAL USES

A **lotion** made of the leaves and flowers is used in Chinese medicine to treat ringworm and fungal infections, and is easily made by boiling 1 cup of fresh leaves and flowers in 2 cups of water with 10 cloves for 10 minutes. This is left to cool and then once strained is used to dab frequently over the area or as a wash. A **tea** made of anise hyssop flowers and a leaf or two, is warming and relaxing and aids the circulation. It has been found to help with digestive tension, nervousness, anorexia and fear. This is particularly helpful for extreme shock where the person is literally shaking from head to toe. A few sips of anise hyssop tea sweetened with honey, will quickly restore calm and speed up the circulation to remove toxins from the body.

For flu and other viral infections anise hyssop tea with 2 000 mg of vitamin C at the first sign of aching muscles, sore throat and fever is often so effective that the infection dwindles to nothing. Anise hyssop is also a valuable emergency treatment. For a fungal infection on the skin, the Chinese used a paste made of boiled anise hyssop leaves and flowers, mashed with a neutral cream, for example aqueous cream or petroleum jelly. This was spread on a cloth, which was placed over the area and held in position with a bandage.

CULTIVATION

Growing anise hyssop is so easy as all it needs is full sun and well-dug, well-composted soil and a deep twice-weekly watering. It is tall and hardy, growing to about 50 cm in height with a mass of fragrant mauve plumes about 2-4 cm long, much loved by bees and butterflies. Cut back the tall flowering stems when they start to look untidy at the end of summer but remember the more you pick the more they grow, so I find I can pick the long sprays three or four times during the summer and new fresh stems quickly appear. Propagation is from rooted cuttings taken from the base of the perennial clump during autumn. If these are kept warm and protected throughout the winter, by late spring you'll be able to plant out quite a show.

CULINARY

Anise Hyssop Party Punch, p. 137
Anise Hyssop and Mushroom Stir Fry, p. 108
Pork Pot Roast with Anise Hyssop, p. 108

ARTICHOKE

Cynara scolymus ● Globe artichoke

Greatly esteemed by the ancient Greeks and Romans, the artichoke was used both a food and a medicine and finds its place in the pharmacopoeias of the world from the earliest times. Dioscorides in the first century AD recommended using its mashed roots as a deodorant, applying it as a scrub to the armpits and feet to fend off offensive odours!

The Italians are considered to be the best artichoke growers and fields of the beautiful silvery grey leaves, fat juicy buds and thistle-like purple flowers grace the landscape everywhere you go. As a garden plant it is eye catching and a row in the vegetable garden will give three or four years of spring-flowering heads.

MEDICINAL USES

Ongoing medical research is extremely interesting in that well-documented results show this unusual plant to be very beneficial taken during the early stages of late onset diabetes, and an extremely good food for diabetics as it significantly lowers blood sugar levels. It is also a good diuretic and although all parts of the plant are medicinal, it is the young flower buds and the leaves that have the highest levels of beneficial constituents for high cholesterol, gall bladder ailments, nausea, indigestion and abdominal bloating, distension and flatulence. All parts of the plant are bitter and stimulate digestive secretions, which in turn help to cleanse the liver and move toxins out of the system, protecting against infection.

Liver tonic: This ancient Mediterranean recipe uses 2 tablespoons fresh artichoke juice – made by liquefying 1 cup chopped leaves with ½ cup hot water and then straining – to 1 cup of wine or hot water, to be taken as a liver cleanser and high cholesterol treatment. 1 cup is taken daily.

Caution: Women who are pregnant or breast-feeding should avoid the globe artichoke as it contains a substance that curdles milk.

CULTIVATION

Native to the Mediterranean region, this much loved plant thrives in warmth, sun and rich, deep, loamy soil. They need richly composted, deeply dug moist soil, the richer the better, and full sun. It is propagated by seed, which should be sown 1½ metres apart in rows. They grow over a metre in height with their beautiful flowers during spring and early summer. After it has flowered, new shoots will appear at the base, which in turn will mature the following season into new flower-bearing plants. Although the artichoke is considered to be a perennial, it is often planted as a biennial or renewed every 3 to 4 years. Cut the flowering head back after reaping the unopened flower buds and mulch well.

CULINARY

Pickled Artichokes, p. 146
Artichokes with Mint and Yoghurt, p. 88
Artichoke Dip, p. 88

BANANA FLOWER

Musa species

The banana tree or palm is a huge-leafed, exotic tropical plant that can grow up to 3-4 metres in height, with a magnificent sheath of leaves at its crown. Each mature shoot produces an exquisite flowering stalk, which hangs under the protective canopy of giant leaves. Ideally it needs hot, moist, tropical air but will survive and even produce fruit against a sunny wall where it is protected against cold winds.

The banana is thought to have originated in Indo-Malaysia and Eastern Asia. The ancient Egyptians are known to have eaten the Abyssinian banana, *Musa ensete*, and numerous varieties were recorded in the tropical and semi-tropical regions of the world over the centuries.

MEDICINAL USES

The ancient Egyptians used banana leaves, fruit and the flowering sheath as a wound dressing, often mashing the fruit and applying it as a poultice over rashes, infected scratches, grazes and burns, covered by either the skin or the leaf which was warmed in hot water. Today many surfers across the world use mashed banana pulp on sunburnt shoulders and noses. Hikers rub aching heels and corns and blisters with the inside of a banana skin and use the flowering bract, magenta in colour and spongy and crisp when young, as a heel guard, pressed into the shoe to ease cracks in the heel.

In Hawaii the flowering bracts are boiled in twice the quantity of water with a few ripe banana skins as a **hair rinse** for scalp problems, oily hair and hair that falls out. Boil for 20 minutes, cool and strain. Use as a scalp massage and hair rinse. Sceptics wonder how it could possibly help, but just look at the Hawaiians' beautiful glossy, thick hair!

CULTIVATION

Growing bananas is a fascinating hobby. Viable buds can be cut away from the parent plant and propagated in full sun in moist, richly composted soil, and a stem will flower and fruit in about 15 months. Once the main shoot has fruited, it can be cut out to allow space for the next shoot to emerge. The clump or 'stool', as it is known botanically, can live for 60 or 70 years, sending up new fruit shoots continuously, but commercial growers keep the clump going for usually no more than 8 to10 years, replacing it with new stock.

Apply a fresh load of compost annually, carefully digging it in around the plant so as not to damage the emerging shoots. I dump a barrow load in January on top of the clump as well and give it a twice weekly deep watering. They really need moisture, so spray the leaves with a hose often during dry hot periods. The best varieties to grow in South Africa, all of which have edible flowers, are *Musa cavendishi*, *M. c. williams*, *M. grand nain selec American*, and *selec Israeli*.

CULINARY

BERGAMOT

Monarda didyma ● Bee balm ● Oswego tea

pains and acts as a sedative that disperses fears and frights and helps to regulate the sleep pattern. Taken with chamomile tea – add one flowering head or 1 leaf to chamomile tea – bergamot also helps to calm and unwind, digest rich food and ease the day's tensions.

Tie a handful of bergamot leaves and flowers in a face cloth, toss under the hot tap and use it in the bath to wash away oiliness and grime from the skin. For a refreshing **skin tonic** boil 1 cup of bergamot leaves and flowers in 1½ litres of water for 10 minutes. Cool and strain. Use as a splash or spritz, or add to the bath for itchy, dry skin and sunburn.

For digestive problems, colic, nausea, bloated distended stomach, flatulence and belching, make the **standard brew** tea (see p. 137) with bergamot flowers and leaves and add 4 cloves per cup. Sip slowly and chew one of the cloves gently every now and then. A teaspoonful of this brew can be given to a fretting baby and to children who have eaten too many sweet things.

CULTIVATION

Growing bergamot is easy and rewarding and it is so loved by the bees and butterflies that no garden should ever be without it. It needs full sun and well-composted soil, and in midsummer it is spectacular with its bright flowering spikes about 80 cm to 1 metre in height. Once they are spent they need to be cut off and the plant tends to look a bit lost, so it is best planted in a mixed border. It forms a cushion-like perennial clump that needs to be divided every three or four years. Do this in winter by thrusting two forks back to back in the centre and splitting it in that way. Plant out into well-composted soil and by midsummer you'll have tall spikes of fragrant bright flowers.

Bergamot originated in North America and the great swathes of red bergamot flowers in the grasslands around the Oswego River near Lake Ontario earned it its name of Oswego tea. The Cherokee Indians as well as the Chippewa, Fox and Ojibwa Indians were the first to use it to ease digestive and respiratory symptoms. Its superb health benefits became more widely known after the famous Boston Tea Party in 1773, when the citizens of Boston rebelled against taxes imposed on tea and the monopoly given to the East India Company and, disguised as Indians, raided three British ships in Boston Harbour, tossing a shipload of English tea overboard. Bergamot or Oswego tea became the fashionable tea to drink.

MEDICINAL USES

For the elderly, bergamot is a most comforting tea taken last thing at night. The recipe for **bergamot health tea** can be found on p. 137. It helps settle the digestion, eases muscular aches and joint

CULINARY

Bergamot Health Tea, p. 137
Roasted Okra with Bergamot Flowers, p. 109
Bergamot and Peach Jelly, p. 123
Bergamot Cream, p. 123

BORAGE

Borago officinalis

A hairy weed native to the Mediterranean regions, borage is a robust and prolific annual that grows with ease all over the world. An ancient, much revered herb, it has an important place in both food and medicine. Through the centuries its calming and stress-relieving qualities have been well recognised, and the crusaders took it on their pilgrimages to give them courage and induce calmness of mind. In Elizabethan times borage flowers were added to drinks like claret cup to prevent drunkenness, and yet to add merriment. Traditionally the flowers were made into syrups and wines and taken for coughs and colds and for anxiety and fear. This is why borage has always been so important through the ages for treating grief and depression.

MEDICINAL USES

A tea made of borage leaves and flowers will reduce high temperatures by inducing sweat and will act on flu and colds quickly and reliably. Being rich in potassium and calcium this tea is both a tonic and blood purifier. To make **borage tea** add ¼ cup fresh flowering tops and leaves to 1 cup boiling water. Stand for 5 minutes then strain and sip slowly. With its high mucilage content it soothes respiratory ailments, chronic coughs, bronchitis, pleurisy and tight chests and whooping cough, easing and breaking down mucous. Make 1 cup of borage tea a day, no more, and divide it up and take a little throughout the day.

Borage has also a comforting emollient action, due to its soothing saponins and tannins, which is helpful for sore, inflamed skin. It can be made into a **lotion** by boiling 1 cup of borage leaves and flowers in 3 cups of water for 10 minutes. Leave to cool, then strain and pour into a spritz bottle and spray frequently over the area or dab on frequently as a lotion. It will soothe eczema, psoriasis, sunburn, rashes and itches.

Caution: Like comfrey, borage contains pyrrolizidine alkaloids, so it should not be taken too often internally. The flowers and the seeds, from which borage oil is made, are the safest parts of the plant.

CULTIVATION

The exquisite blue, star-shaped flowers make a wonderful show in summer and attract bees and butterflies to the garden. They have a fresh, cucumber-like flavour and can be added to cordials, Pimm's cup, salads and desserts. The plants are prolific and benefit from picking, both leaves and flowers. Borage readily seeds itself and needs space in the garden, as it can grow up to 80 cm in height and about 60 cm in width. It needs richly composted, well-dug soil in full sun and thrives with a good twice weekly watering. Even in the dry area where I live it seems to survive against all odds, sending up its blaze of beautiful blue and reseeding itself everywhere, even in winter. The tiny seedlings are easily transplanted.

CULINARY

Borage Sangria, p. 137
Hearty Borage Winter Health Soup, p. 88
Borage Fritters, p. 89

BUCKWHEAT

Fagopyrum esculentum

Although buckwheat is not truly a grain, it is classified as such in most cook books. Sometimes called Saracen corn, it originated in Asia and was brought to Europe by the crusaders. Today it is still widely grown, primarily for its amazing mineral and vitamin content and its astonishing high rutin content. Rutin is of the utmost importance for the strengthening of the walls of blood vessels, for the treatment of high cholesterol and for varicose veins, thread veins and the capillaries in the retina of the eye. The creamy white flowers are equally rich in rutin. They are tender and appetising served on all sorts of savoury and sweet dishes.

MEDICINAL USES

Buckwheat is exceptionally rich in bioflavonoids and this is why it is essential in treating circulatory problems, cold hands and feet, chilblains and haemorrhoids. It also strengthens the inner wall of the tiniest capillaries and disperses small bruises

that appear for no apparent reason. Buckwheat contains all eight essential amino acids, which helps to tone the whole body. It is rich in vitamin C, calcium, magnesium, betacarotene, phosphorus, zinc, manganese, folic acid and potassium, making it an excellent all round tonic for the whole body and for circulation and the heart in particular.

Buckwheat restores health and vitality to those in deep depression due to its remarkably high vitamin and mineral content. Post-flu depression and postnatal depression respond immediately to buckwheat tea. Arthritis and gout in the crippling inflammatory stages respond equally well to buckwheat tea and buckwheat flour and groats in the diet. To make **buckwheat tea** pour 1 cup boiling water over ¼ cup fresh flowers, leaves and stem. Stand for 5 minutes and strain. Take 1 cup daily for 2 weeks, then give it a break for 4 to 5 days and start up again.

Caution: Medical science suggests that those with allergies or those who have cancer should not eat buckwheat, as it is high in vegetable protein and can cause a reaction.

CULTIVATION

Modern research has found this humble plant to be one of the most important medicinal plants known to mankind and as it is so easy to grow and delicious to eat, no garden or cook should ever be without it. It needs well-dug, well-composted soil in full sun. Seeds can be sown directly into the soil, which needs to be kept moist for the first few weeks. Tender whole seedlings can be pulled up and eaten even in the earliest stages. Sow the rows 30 cm apart and sprinkle the heart-shaped seed thinly in shallow drills. It will quickly grow to about 60 cm in height. You can grow two to four crops a season, starting in early August, as it is such a fast-growing annual.

CULINARY

Buckwheat Cake, p. 123
Buckwheat Flower Salad, p. 89
Buckwheat Flower Stir Fry, p. 109

BURDOCK

Arctium lappa

This rather strange and unusual herb originated in Europe and parts of Asia where it is much respected both as a food and a medicine. It grows in temperate regions throughout the world and is being commercially propagated in China for its medicinal seeds. Both Western and Chinese medicine have researched and documented the medicinal uses of burdock and its ancient uses are being scientifically proven. It is a superb skin treatment for recurring ailments like weeping eczema and psoriasis, and allergic rashes. It has a cleansing effect on the whole body from the liver to the blood circulation, kidneys to respiratory organs, and has antibiotic, antiseptic and even diuretic properties.

MEDICINAL USES

Once widely used in cleansing, detoxifying remedies, burdock has been used through the centuries to lower blood sugar levels, break up kidney stones and as a treatment for acne, boils and abscesses. Crushed flowers and buds pounded to a pulp and warmed were applied to the area – even over the kidneys – and held in place with a large, warmed burdock leaf and bound with bandages. Burdock tea is excellent for easing the itch and heat in measles and to soothe and relax muscle spasms. It also appears to have anti-tumour action and will reduce the swelling and discomfort in mumps. To make **burdock tea** pour 1 cup of boiling water over ¼ cup fresh buds and flowers and a small piece of leaf and stem. Stand for 5 minutes, then strain and sip slowly. Burdock contains a rare and precious ingredient arctiin, which is a smooth muscle relaxant. Make a **burdock cream** for sprains, strains, stiff muscles, arthritic joints, rashes, eczema and psoriasis and apply frequently:

> 1 cup burdock flowers, buds, pieces of leaf and stem
> 1 cup good aqueous cream
> 1 teaspoon vitamin E oil

Mix the chopped herbs well into the aqueous cream. Simmer for 15 minutes in a double boiler with the lid on. Cool and strain. Discard the burdock and mix in the vitamin E oil. Pour into a sterilised screw-top glass jar and store in a cool place. Apply frequently.

CULTIVATION

I have established burdock as an easy to grow biennial and in the heat of the African sun it flourishes just the way it does in bitter winter winds and frost. It needs a deeply dug, rich, well-composted loamy soil in full sun and I find it takes afternoon shade quite happily. It needs a deep watering twice or even three times a week and thrives if the leaves are sprayed. In its second year it will send up a flowering head of many small, rounded capsules with a small crown of purple stamens and masses of burs, hence its name. These hook into everything and so get transported everywhere for germination.

CULINARY

Burdock Bud Syrup, p. 138
Burdock Flower and Leaf Tea, p. 138
Burdock Flower Cleansing Soup, p. 89

CALAMINT AND EMPEROR'S MINT

Calaminta ascendens ● *Micromeria* species ● *Calaminta officinalis*

Calamint originated in Europe and Asia, from the British Isles eastwards towards Iran. It flourishes in poor soil and is a familiar sight along roadsides. It was greatly esteemed in ancient times for its medicinal properties and the Greeks used it to clear coughs and ease digestive disorders, while leaf poultices were used to treat bruises and sprains. Calamint tea induces sweating and in medieval times it was revered as a detoxifier and cleanser, and was used as a treatment against the plague. Modern scientific research has verified the presence of a powerful oil rich in pulegone in the plant and research is still being conducted into its use as an expectorant in respiratory ailments. Just taking a deep breath and inhaling the pungent peppermint-like aroma is enough to open sinuses and clear a blocked nose. Calamint was believed in days gone by to have magical protective properties and bunches of fresh calamint were hung in the doorways of homes to protect the occupants, giving rise to the name 'protection plant'.

MEDICINAL USES

Calamint has only been cultivated since the 17th century and once you have it in your garden, it will always reseed itself. The sprays of tiny white flowers last well in water and if crushed and tucked under the pillow will ensure a good night's sleep as the strong peppermint aroma opens the nose and clears the sinuses.

For colic, wind and indigestion, a **tea of calamint** is still favoured in Europe today: pour 1 cup boiling water over ¼ cup fresh flowering sprigs. Let stand 5 minutes, strain and sip slowly. Use the same tea for a fretting child or a colicky baby, giving 1 teaspoon of the warm tea at a time. For a cough, tight chest, flu or a bad cold, use the same brew but add the juice of 1 lemon and 3 teaspoons of honey. It will encourage sweating and so bring down a fever, act as an expectorant and clear the nose and lungs.

For an excellent **treatment for blocked nose and sinuses**, pour 3 litres of boiling water over 2 large cups of fresh flowering sprigs in a large bowl, then, making a towel tent over the head, bend over the steaming bowl. Keep the eyes shut and inhale the steam deeply. It will open the nose, loosen phlegm and act as an expectorant.

CULTIVATION

Calamint and Emperor's mint are confusingly similar in appearance and fragrance, and medicinally are used for the same ailments, yet they are not related at all. Both are delightfully fragrant and pretty creeping perennials with slightly hairy, oval, thumbnail-sized leaves and tiny white or mauve flowers, but the difference lies in the propagation. Calamint has a creeping rootstock that can be divided at any time of the year once the soft flowering spikes have been cut back, while Emperor's mint sows itself freely all around the mother plant. Both take sun and light shade.

CULINARY

CALENDULA

Calendula officinalis

regulates menstruation, aids gastric disturbances, colitis and fevers and infections, it is detoxifying and also mildly oestrogenic. Quick relief for the above ailments can be obtained by drinking a **tea** made by pouring 1 cup boiling water over ¼ cup fresh calendula petals, leaving it to stand for 5 minutes, then straining. The same tea, cooled, can be used as an excellent **lotion** for skin problems such as acne, eczema, oily skin, psoriasis, rashes, grazes, stings, bites and even sunburn.

A **massage oil** can be made by warming equal quantities of calendula petals and almond oil for 15 minutes, stirring all the time. Strain and bottle. This is one of the most comforting oils for chilblains, haemorrhoids and broken capillaries, massaged into the affected area frequently during the day. A teaspoon or two of this marvellous oil added to the bath will soften the skin, moisturise dry patches and is soothing and calming for anxiety, nervous tension and menstrual pain.

Calendula cream is equally easily to make and no home should ever be without it. It is antifungal, antiseptic, anti-inflammatory and astringent. Heat 1 cup petals in 1 cup good aqueous cream in a double boiler for 20 minutes. Stir frequently. Strain and discard the petals. Mix in 2 teaspoons vitamin E oil, pour into a sterilised glass jar and seal. Keep in a cool place.

CULTIVATION

Growing calendulas is remarkably easy. Sow the seeds in late summer and plant out the little seedlings in well-dug, richly composted soil in full sun about 25 to 30 cm apart. Keep them moist until they have settled, after which they'll need a watering two or three times a week. You will be rewarded with masses of flowers all through the winter and well into spring and early summer.

Calendula is often confusingly called 'marigold' in overseas herbal books. South Africans know marigold (*Tagetes* sp.) as that strongly smelling, pungent insect-repelling mainstay of our summer gardens. It is often planted amongst vegetables to keep them insect free. Do not in any way use any *Tagetes* species for medicine or cooking.

Calendula officinalis has no insect-repelling properties, but this old-fashioned winter flowering herb is an amazing medicinal plant, its therapeutic properties having been well documented since the earliest times. In a 12th century Herbal it was suggested that merely looking into the brilliant bright orange calendula flowers would clear up eye ailments, improve the eyesight and clear the head!

MEDICINAL USES

Calendula has anti-inflammatory properties, relieves muscle spasm, prevents haemorrhages, is astringent, antiseptic, helps to heal wounds,

CULINARY

Calendula Omelette, p. 90
Calendula Curry, p. 110
Calendula Custard, p. 123

CALIFORNIAN POPPY

Escholzia californica

That this glorious orange flower is edible will come as a great surprise to many, I am sure! I learned about its remarkable healing properties from an American Indian visitor to my herb gardens, who inspired me to know and grow more of this old-fashioned plant that has been so taken for granted. Centuries ago American Indians used the flowers, and to some extent the leaves, as a painkiller, particularly for toothache. A leaf and a couple of petals would be well chewed and the tooth packed with the softened leaf. It has tremendous analgesic, antispasmodic, calming and sedative properties, and is valuable in treating both physical and psychological problems in children as it is gentle and safe.

MEDICINAL USES

Although closely related to the opium poppy (*Papaver somniferum*), it has a very different effect in that it is not narcotic and it does not disorientate like opium poppy.

Researchers are looking at the promising effect it has on bedwetting in highly strung children, difficulty in sleeping and establishing a good sleep pattern, and anxiety, nightmares, sleep-walking and panic attacks.

The easiest way of taking Californian poppy as a medicine other than in cooking, is as a comforting tea. Combined with chamomile to enhance relaxation and encourage sleep, it is an easily assimilated and very gentle medicinal nightcap that is completely safe for children. To make **Californian poppy tea** pour 1 cup boiling water over 3 petals and 1 small leaf of the Californian poppy and add 1 tablespoon fresh chamomile flowers. Stand for 5 minutes, strain and sweeten with a touch of honey. For a child under one give ½ cup, for children over 1 years old and adults sip the full cup slowly just before going to bed.

Note: Both chamomile and Californian poppy flower at the same time of the year.

CULTIVATION

Usually treated as an annual, the brilliantly coloured flower of the Californian poppy with its finely cut grey-green leaves is a gorgeous sight in spring. It thrives in any soil as long as it is well-drained, and has adapted to withstand all sorts of climates across the world so far from its native habitat in western North America. It needs full sun and thrives on a twice weekly watering, slightly more in hot weather, and then can literally be forgotten about! It benefits from picking – the more you pick the more flowers it produces. Sow seed in autumn in boxes and keep warm and protected and moist throughout winter. Transplant in late winter to a well-dug, well-composted bed in full sun, spaced 40 cm apart. The mature height is about 30 cm.

CULINARY

CAPE SORREL

Oxalis pes-caprae ● Suring

S orrel is the common name confusingly given to several species of plants with acidulous sap. *Oxalis pes-caprae* has beautiful, brilliant yellow flowers in late winter and is not to be confused with the *Rumex* species of sorrel. Indigenous to the Cape of Good Hope and used in traditional Cape cooking, Cape sorrel is an easy to grow plant that has become a prized hothouse plant overseas, where it obligingly blooms at a completely different time of year to its native cousins. Several tribes use fresh Cape sorrel as a salt substitute for bland foods, and eaten with freshly caught, grilled fish on the beach, Cape sorrel makes a succulent, never to be forgotten addition to a glorious meal.

MEDICINAL USES

Sailors in the sixteenth and seventeenth centuries calling at the Cape collected the tender, juicy, swollen roots of the Cape sorrel as a treatment for scurvy, and ate the leaves and flowers as well. The swollen root was dried and taken on long voyages, when it could easily be rehydrated by soaking it in water and used medicinally. The leaves crushed and applied to burns, scratches and grazes are still used as a first-aid treatment in rural areas of the Cape today. Warmed in hot water, the leaves can be bound over a boil or suppurating sore as a **poultice** to bring it to a head, held in place with a crêpe bandage and replaced frequently by fresh warmed leaves.

Sorrel flowers pounded with water and made into a paste spread on acne spots and pimples and left to dry there, will quickly clear the spot of redness and help to dry it up. Teenagers should eat a few flowers every day during its spring flowering to clear their skins of oiliness and pimples, and the juice of the flowering stems can be dabbed onto the spots to hasten the healing.

CULTIVATION

It grows prolifically on waste ground, tolerating icy winds and salt spray as easily as it does desolate, hot, sandy areas. It requires no care or attention at all, except perhaps a weekly watering during its winter flowering period. It thrives on the Cape's winter rainfall and stoically withstands the cold, wet conditions, offering a blaze of uplifting colour before the other spring flowers appear. Its flowering period is often brief, however, for by late spring the heat shrivels the flowers and eventually it all but disappears underground, leaving only a few dried leaves to mark the spot where it grew. In the garden with regular watering it can go on well into summer, but its dormant period is late summer to midwinter. With well-dug, well-composted soil in full sun it will flourish in the garden, but always be sure to mark the spot where it grows or in its dormant period you may be apt to forget that it's there and plant something else on top of it. It is a herb well worth growing.

CULINARY

Yellow Sorrel Salad, p. 103
Sorrel Salad Dressing, p. 103
Cape Sorrel and Pickled Fish, p. 118

CARAWAY

Carum carvi

serve a tiny bowl of caraway seeds on each table to chew on between courses or between mouthfuls. Interestingly, caraway's antispasmodic, diuretic and expectorant qualities have been confirmed by medical research and to add to its benefits, the seeds and leaves sweeten the breath, improve appetite, counter heart irregularity and ease menstrual cramps. The **standard brew** for all the ailments is ¼ cup caraway flowers and 2 teaspoons seeds in 1 cup of boiling water. Stand for 5 minutes, then strain and sip slowly. If used as a mouth wash and gargle, it will clear bad breath, gum ailments and tighten the teeth, it is believed! A teaspoon or two of this tea will calm and quieten a restless baby, ease indigestion and restore a feeling of well-being to the elderly.

Caraway is a most extraordinary herb and added to the dog's food will help against wind and bad breath. Caraway is now being medically tested as a heart and pulse regulator and as a treatment for severe menstrual pain. The flowers and seeds are an expectorant and tonic, and are added to some patent medicines, particularly for treating chronic coughs.

CULTIVATION

Cultivated primarily for its seeds, but also for its flavour-filled leaves, roots and flowers, caraway makes a charming garden plant with the typical lace flower that indicates its Umbelliferae family origins. The flowers have the same effects as the seeds, though not as strong, and can be used in fruit salads, salads and stir fries with such delicious results you'll become as infatuated with this easy to grow annual as I am. It needs a sunny position and loose, light soil and grows as a quick annual two or three times a season during the warm months, scattering seed everywhere. I sow the seed straight into the ground three times during spring and summer and give it a good dressing of compost three times a year.

The word caraway has its origins in the ancient Arabic word for seed, *karawya*. The ancient Egyptians used it in medicine and as a flavouring and Isaiah speaks of the cultivation of caraway in the Bible. Archaeologists have found seed in little clay containers in diggings on Mesolithic sites, dating from thousands of years BC. It originated in Central Europe, Asia and North Africa, where it is found on waste ground and grasslands. Its tendency to self seed prolifically meant that it became widespread, and naturalised further afield. Caraway is one of the most ancient herbs and is still extensively cultivated across the world for food as well as medicine. It is now cultivated worldwide on a large scale.

MEDICINAL USES

Caraway is a much respected antispasmodic, the seeds soothe and work directly on the digestive tract, easing spasms, colic, bloating, flatulence and heartburn. In some Middle East eating-houses they

CULINARY
Caraway Egg and Potato Salad, p. 90
Caraway Fish Curry, p. 110
Caraway Flowers and Peach Pashka, p. 124

CARNATION

Dianthus caryophyllus ● Clove pink

The carnation is an ancient herb, revered through the centuries for its exquisite clove-like scent and remarkable medicinal value. Native to southern Europe and India, it was a common feature of European monastery and cottage gardens and in Elizabethan texts it was referred to as the gillyflower.

The original species, *Dianthus caryophyllus*, has sadly become almost extinct through the centuries, giving way to the hybridised forms of carnation with little scent and even less medicinal value. Today carnations are available in a vast array of colours, from red, pink, salmon and magenta through to white and yellow, and even striped and flecked, but it is the old-fashioned clove-scented variety, usually in pink, that is used herbally. The species *D. carthusianorum*, *D. plumarius* 'Doris', *D. deltoides* (Maiden pink) and the Allwoodii pinks, which are a cross between *D. caryophyllus* and *D. plumarius*, can also be used herbally.

MEDICINAL USES

For about 2 000 years the bright petals of *Dianthus* have been used medicinally to soothe, calm and quieten nervousness and anxiety, to treat kidney and bladder ailments, skin ailments like eczema, and constipation.

Carnation cleansing cream: Our grandmothers made a beautifully scented simple cream, which they used daily to cleanse off grime and oiliness and to moisturise dry skin areas and cracks around the lips. Here is the modern version: In a double boiler simmer 1 cup of good aqueous cream and 1 cup of fresh carnation petals stripped of their calyxes. Mix in 2 tablespoons of glycerine and 1 tablespoon almond oil. Simmer for 15 minutes with the lid on, stirring every now and then. Pour through a sieve and quickly stir in 2 teaspoons of vitamin E oil. Pour into a sterilised jar with a screw-top lid.

Carnation lotion: This is a great favourite to refresh and soothe fraying tempers on a hot day. Add 1 cup of carnation petals stripped of their calyxes, 10 cloves and 1 stick of cinnamon to 1 litre of boiling water. Simmer for 10 minutes with the lid on. Cool, strain and pour into a spritz bottle. Add a few drops of carnation essential oil if liked. Shake well and spray over face, neck and arms frequently.

CULTIVATION

Carnation is a short-lived perennial that needs well-drained soil. Propagation is easy, either by sowing seed or by taking stem cuttings in spring. Merely strip off the little leafy tufts that form along the flowering stem and, leaving the small 'heel' still attached, strip off the lower leaves and press the cutting into wet sand. Keep it shaded and moist and it will quickly send out tiny roots.

CULINARY

Carnation Tonic Wine, p. 138
Mango Nectar with Carnation Petals, p. 139
Carnation Pickle, p. 146

CARPET GERANIUM

Geranium incanum ● Wild geranium ● Bergtee ● Vrouetee ● Creeping geranium

While all the plants previously known as geraniums are now correctly known as pelargoniums, only one small, rather unobtrusive plant is still called geranium, and that is South Africa's pretty, feathery-leafed groundcover, the carpet geranium. This much loved indigenous plant has been used for centuries by most South Africans and is now sold in nurseries around the world as far afield as Australia. In Europe and Britain, where it is known as creeping geranium, it is used in hanging baskets and window boxes, where its silvery feathery leaves and small bright magenta flowers tumble and cascade attractively. I look on the carpet geranium as a childhood friend. My grandmother grew great swathes of it in her terraced seaside garden in Gordon's Bay in the Cape when I was a child and we used it in so many ways. We drank a pleasant tasting tea of it most mornings, and dipped the flowers, wet with rain or dew, in icing sugar and served them as sweets to our friends.

MEDICINAL USES

Traditionally, a tea made of leaves and flowers eased bloating, diarrhoea, excessive and irregular menstruation, colic, indigestion and flatulence. It is called *vrouetee* because this is the best tea for expelling the afterbirth, starting milk flow for the newborn and easing cystitis and other bladder infections in women. To make the **tea** steep ¼ cup of flowers in 1 cup boiling water for 4 to 5 minutes. Strain and sip slowly.

Carpet geranium is also an age-old lotion used for washing itchy dry skin and rinsing hair that gets oily very quickly. Mixed with oats it makes a superb scalp treatment for dandruff, flaky scalp and psoriasis of the scalp, soothing and softening the irritated area. For the **lotion** boil 2 cups of *Geranium incanum* leaves, sprigs and flowers in 2 litres of water for 10-15 minutes. Strain. Use as a lotion or rinse.

For the **oats scalp treatment** add 1 cup of oats (the large flaked non-instant kind) to 1 litre of the geranium lotion and simmer for 5 minutes until the oats start to soften. Remove from the heat and cool until pleasantly warm. After shampooing and rinsing the hair, carefully spread handfuls of the warm oats and geranium lotion onto the scalp, massaging it in well. Wrap hair in a towel and relax for 10 minutes, then rinse thoroughly with warm water to which a little apple cider vinegar has been added.

CULTIVATION

It is unfussy as to soil type and requires little more than a place in the sun, the odd spadeful or two of compost every now and then, and never much more than a weekly watering. Pull off rooted tufts to propagate, and keep them shaded and moist until they are established. Undemanding and needing no attention, this pretty groundcover deserves much more space in our gardens.

CULINARY

Carpet Geranium Comfort Tea, p. 139
Crystallised Carpet Geranium Flowers, p. 124
Pear and Carpet Geranium Stir Fry, p. 124

CHAMOMILE

Matricaria recutita ● *Chamaemelum nobile*

Two species of chamomile are used medicinally and they have identical properties. German chamomile, *Matricaria recutita* is a spring annual with small, daisy-like white flowers and fine feathery leaves, while *Chamaemelum nobile*, often called lawn chamomile, is a perennial which is lower growing (about 10 cm in height) and spreading, with similar flowers and leaves. Both are indigenous to Europe and both are superb medicinal plants whose flowers, fresh or dried, have been valued for centuries for their amazing healing properties.

MEDICINAL USES

Chamomile is cultivated in Europe for homeopathic medicine and current research confirms its ancient uses: it is excellent for digestive problems such as acidity, gastritis, bloating, colic, hiatus hernia, peptic ulcer, Crohn's disease and irritable bowel syndrome. For pregnant women it helps morning sickness and eases sore nipples in lactating mothers (drunk as a tea or put on as a lotion). Tense, aching muscles and menstrual cramps are quickly soothed by a cup of hot chamomile tea. It also soothes away stress, anxiety, panic attacks, and is anti-allergenic, effective against hayfever, asthma, eczema and skin rashes. It reduces catarrh and, used as an eyebath, relieves eye strain.

Chamomile flowers contain an aromatic oil, which gives it its typical scent, and possess powerful antiseptic and anti-inflammatory properties. A superb **gargle**, **douche** and **eye wash** can be made using fresh or dried flowers: boil 1 cup fresh chamomile flowers or ¾ cup dried chamomile flowers in 1½ litres of water. Simmer gently for 10 minutes. Strain and add 1 cup of cold water. Mix well. Use as a douche or wash to clear any infections, irritations and itchiness. For tired, red, irritated eyes use as a gentle eye bath – soak a clean face cloth in the warm brew, cover the eyes with it and lie down for a few minutes. Use as a gargle for dry, strained throat, especially if you are a public speaker or a singer. Store excess in the fridge and warm it a little each time you use it, but never in a microwave.

CULTIVATION

Growing annual chamomile is easy. Sow seed in mid-autumn where it is to grow in full sun in well-dug, well-composted soil. Keep it moist – I sprinkle a light cover of leaves over the area – and water lightly twice a day until the tiny, feathery seedlings push through. When they are big enough to handle you can, in the very early stages, transplant them, but after that they do not like to be moved. Chamomile is essentially a cool weather plant and will flower prolifically in spring, reaching a height of 25-30 cm. If left to go to seed it will come up year after year.

CULINARY

Chamomile Tea, p. 139
Chamomile Syrup, p. 139
Chamomile Fruit Jelly, p. 124

CHICORY

Cichorium intybus

whole urinary tract. As a treatment for gout, rheumatic conditions and general aches and pains of the joints, chicory was once considered to be a herb particularly appropriate for the elderly and was also used as a gentle laxative for children. A **tea** of leaves and flowers – ¼ cup mixed leaves and flowers with 1 cup boiling water poured over it and left to stand for 5 minutes, sweetened with a touch of honey if desired – is the way to treat any of these ailments and usually no more than 1 cup a day will do the trick. The tea is slightly laxative and safe for children, made as a standard brew and ½ a cup given at a time to children under 10 years of age.

Mothers in medieval France and England grew chicory in their cottage gardens, which they used for purging and for flushing out the bladder, and today's research verifies these uses. It literally washes out bladder and colon, clears infections, acts as a strong tonic and increases the flow of bile. Around AD 23-79, chicory juice mixed with strong vinegar and a little rose oil was used to treat headaches. Today doctors find that a tea made of the flowers and a leaf or two, aids digestion, clears toxins from the body and flushes the kidneys. If that same tea is used as a wash or added to the bath during an attack of cystitis, it soothes any external discomfort and itch gently.

Caution: Excessive and continued use may impair the function of the retina in the eyes due to its exceptionally powerful action.

CULTIVATION

The chicory root stump or crown may be dug up and trimmed before flower production, then stored in a warm, dark place to develop young buds called chicons. These are eaten in salads, or as a vegetable. Witloof is the variety to use, sown in rich, well-composted soil, in full sun, in rows 20 cm apart.

CULINARY

Chicory and Tuna Salad, p. 90
Chicory Stir Fry, p. 110
Pickled Chicory Flowers, p. 146
Chicory and Pear Dessert, p. 125

A deep-rooted, hardy perennial that sends up a beautiful blue flowering branch in summer, chicory was once a common sight in Europe and Western Asia along roadsides and in marshy places. It has now become naturalised all over the world. Records of herbal uses of chicory date back to the first century. In about 60 AD Pliny the Elder made a mixture of chicory juice, rose oil and vinegar to treat headaches, and modern research into chicory's detoxifying properties would indicate that he was on the right track. Since the earliest times chicory root has been roasted dry and ground to make a coffee substitute, or peeled, scrubbed and either boiled as a vegetable or roasted with onions and potatoes.

MEDICINAL USES

Chicory has a mildly bitter taste and the root is much the same medicinally as the root of the dandelion, *Taraxacum officinale*, having a cleansing action on the liver, stomach and kidneys and the

CHIVES

Allium schoenoprasum

There is much speculation today about where this remarkable plant originated, but Marco Polo found it on his travels to China, where it had probably been in use for a few thousand years, and brought it back to the west. Today it is widespread and one of the most popular culinary plants. A member of the onion family along with garlic, leeks and spring onions, chives contain sulphur, which accounts for their pungent smell and flavour.

MEDICINAL USES

Chives have marvellous medicinal properties and from the earliest times were used as a treatment for chest ailments, bladder and kidney infections and to cleanse the blood. Modern research verifies their age-old uses: chives lower blood pressure and cholesterol, build up resistance to infection, treat respiratory disorders and assist the whole digestive tract and urinary system. All the Allium

family contain mild natural antibiotics, and although chives do not contain as much as garlic, for example, its benefits are still quite astonishing.

A strange and pungent recipe that our great grandmothers made for fighting colds, was to slice an onion and a few chive leaves and flowers, cover them with brown sugar and leave them to stand 4-6 hours well covered. The juice was strained off and a teaspoon taken at a time. To soothe a sore throat, lemon juice was added to the mixture.

Chives chopped with onions and mixed with a little grated fresh ginger root, lemon juice and a little chopped parsley, and spread onto a finger of bread, was given to any child suffering from a cold, a cough or a dose of flu. All these ingredients fight coughs and colds and boost resistance.

Chives also ease and promote digestion and, sprinkled onto food, they stimulate the appetite. Chopped flowers with grated carrots, celery and parsley are a favourite **health booster salad**, and with dandelion flowers and leaves will fight flu and colds exceptionally well. A large daily helping of all these superb health-boosting, immune-building herbs will go a long way to helping us cope with the pressures of modern living.

CULTIVATION

Chives, garlic chives and wild garlic all need well-dug, richly composted soil in full sun with a deep watering twice a week. Chives die down in winter and then can be divided into small clumps and replanted. Wild garlic and garlic chives can be divided at any time of the year. Plant chives 20 cm apart as a path edging as they grow only about 20 cm in height. Wild garlic and garlic chives need 40 to 50 cm between them and they will reach about 50 cm in height with their pretty flowering heads.

CULINARY

Chive Blossom Vinegar, p. 146
Chive and Garlic Chive Health Salad, p. 91
Creamed Spinach and Chive Flower Supper
    Dish, p. 111

CLOVER

Trifolium pratense

It may come as a surprise that both white and red clover (*Trifolium repens* and *T. pratense*) are herbs with astonishing medicinal value that have been greatly esteemed for centuries. Medieval Christians associated clover's three-lobed leaves with the Holy Trinity, and monks in Europe grew it in their physic gardens to cure all manner of ailments, from kidney stones to conjunctivitis, arthritic pains and dry coughs.

Clover is native to Europe and Asia and is used all over the world in animal fodder. It is an excellent companion plant for pasturing crops as it replenishes the soil with both nitrogen and boron – a mineral often found lacking in over-cultivated soil – as well as other trace elements.

MEDICINAL USES

In around 1930 doctors were using red clover flowers as an anti-cancer treatment and some are still prescribing it for breast, ovarian and lymphatic cancer. It was once widely used for treating bronchitis, whooping cough, arthritis and gout, and as a soothing treatment for psoriasis and eczema, taken both internally and applied externally as a lotion. Crushed clover flowers have been used for years by country children to soothe bee stings and insect bites, rubbed on the area.

Crushed red clover flowers and leaves can be used as a **compress** over arthritic joints and gout-inflamed areas. Soak the flowers and leaves in hot water, draining, bind in place with a crêpe bandage and leave it on overnight. Together with a cup of clover tea even the most severe aches will be soothed. To make the **tea** pour 1 cup boiling water over ¼ cup red clover flowers and leaves, stand 5 minutes, strain and sip slowly. For a cough, bronchitis and whooping cough mix in a good squeeze of lemon juice, 2 teaspoons of honey and a pinch of ginger powder. The cooled tea also makes a superb eye wash for conjunctivitis and irritated red eyes.

As a **douche** to soothe vaginal itching, boil 2 cups of flowers and leaves in 2 litres water for 15 minutes with the lid on. Stand aside and cool, then strain. Add ½ cup apple cider vinegar and use it lukewarm as a douche or use as a wash lotion externally. Its emollient qualities immediately soothe the irritated area.

For an **ointment** for bites, itch, rashes, eczema and psoriasis, simmer 1 cup red clover flowers in 1 cup good quality aqueous cream in a double boiler for 20 minutes, giving it an occasional stir. Strain, pour into a sterilised jar and seal. Keep refrigerated.

CULTIVATION

Clover is a short-lived perennial and is terribly easy to grow. Little tufts can be pulled off the mother plant and planted out in moist soil. All it requires is richly composted soil in full sun and a deep watering twice a week, and it offers an abundance of honey-scented flowers in return.

CULINARY

Cauliflower and Clover Cheese, p. 111
Lentil and Clover Risotto, p. 111

CORIANDER

Coriandrum sativum

Coriander has been used as a medicinal and culinary herb for over 2 000 years. Native to Europe and the Middle East, it is mentioned in the Ebers papyrus, dating back to about 1500 BC, in Sanskrit texts and in the Bible, where it is one of the bitter Passover herbs. The Chinese recorded using it during the Han Dynasty, between 202 BC and AD 9.

All parts of the plant have a pungent aroma and may be used in cooking. The broader lower young leaves, called *danya*, are much loved in Indian cuisine. In parts of Europe the root is eaten as a tasty vegetable, and the seed can be used in curries, chutney, soups, sauces, vinegars and vegetable dishes. The pretty lacy mauvish-white flowers, so typical of the Umbelliferae family, can be added to salads, stir fries, fruit salads and stewed fruit. The Romans combined coriander seeds with cumin and vinegar and used it as a preservative for meat, very similar to the blend of spices we use for making biltong!

MEDICINAL USES

This strongly aromatic annual is an exceptional remedy for colic, flatulence, digestive upsets, gripes and bloatedness. Apart from being a superb antispasmodic, it is a wonderful remedy for anxiety attacks and tension, drunk as a tea. It also cleanses the breath after eating garlic – merely chew a flower or two or a few seeds – and helps rheumatic aches and pains, both as a tea and as a lotion. Make **coriander tea** by pouring 1 cup of boiling water over either ¼ cup of fresh leaves and flowers or 1 teaspoon of dried seeds, leaving it to stand for 5 minutes and then straining it. Sip slowly for all the above ailments.

The ancient Chinese made a **lotion** by boiling 1 cup fresh coriander leaves, flowers and twigs in 1 litre of water for 10 minutes or, if there is no fresh green plant available, 3 tablespoons of seeds in 1 litre of water for 15 minutes. Strain and pour into a sterilised bottle. Soak a cloth in the lotion and bind over an itchy rash, inflamed areas and painful, aching joints or use as a spritz to cool the inflamed area and to remove the itch from insect bites.

CULTIVATION

Growing coriander is simple and rewarding, since three or four crops can be achieved before the first frosts of winter. It needs full sun and a light, well-drained soil with a good dressing of compost. It requires a good watering twice a week and thrives in heat and dryness. Sow the seed directly into the ground where it is to grow, about 20 cm apart, keeping the soil moist and protected with a thin layer of dry leaves until the seedlings are strong enough to withstand the full sun. They grow up to 60 cm in height.

CULINARY

CORNFLOWER

Centaurea cyanus

The cornflower is indigenous to Europe and now grows wild in all temperate regions, often in cornfields, which gave rise to its name. The exquisite blue flowers and the leaves are both used medicinally, and the use of the flowers in cooking is an ancient practice that ought to be revived. The brilliant blue petals can be added to cakes, fritters, biscuits, tarts, custard, and cheese and pasta dishes.

Monks in twelfth century England, Ireland and later Wales and France made cornflower wine, which was used to treat a wide variety of ailments, ranging from stomach problems, kidney and bladder ailments, tremors, vertigo and liverishness to flu, chest ailments, coughs and excessive mucous. A cornflower infusion was used as a tonic after a severe illness, and even given to children. Modern research verifies these ancient uses, as the petals and leaves have been found to contain small amounts of natural antibiotics.

MEDICINAL USES

An infusion of the glorious blue flowers is still used in French herbal medicine as an eyewash for eye ailments, and a poultice of petals is applied over the eyes to ease eye strain and strengthen the eyes. The flowers are also made into a bitter **tonic tea** to improve resistance to infection and to ease rheumatic conditions such as aching joints and stiffness. Pour 1 cup of boiling water over ¼ cup of leaves and flowers, stand for 5 minutes, then strain. Drink 1 cup a day.

Cornflowers steeped in hot water for 5 minutes and then spread on a cloth and applied as hot as can be tolerated, make an excellent **poultice** for an inflamed rheumatic joint or a swollen stiff ankle. In France cornflowers are still called 'casselunette', which means break the glasses, as a cornflower wash or poultice is believed to strengthen the eyes. For an **eye lotion**, pour 1 cup of boiling water over 1 tablespoon of fresh petals. Stand for 8 minutes. Strain. Use as an eye bath to revive tired eyes.

CULTIVATION

I have found cornflowers to be best grown as a winter annual. I sow the seed in late summer and plant the seedlings out in full sun, 50 cm apart, before winter. It grows quickly and establishes itself well in lightly composted, well-drained soil with a good watering twice a week. The plants grow to about 50 cm in height and the more flowers you pick, the more are produced, right through winter and spring, until they succumb to the hot weather in midsummer. The flowers retain their exquisite royal blue colour and are beautiful in bath preparations as they soothe and soften the skin.

CULINARY

Butterscotch and Cornflower Sauce, p. 125
Strawberry and Banana Dessert with
　Cornflowers, p. 125
Cornflower Pasta Salad, p. 91

CRAB APPLE BLOSSOM

Malus floribunda ● *Malus pumila*

Crab apples grow wild in the hedgerows of Britain and Europe and have been used in both medicine and cooking since ancient times. Recipes for cider using crab apples date back many hundreds of years, and although the sour fruits are pretty inedible, they do make delicious jellies.

Some crab apple species are grown as garden ornamentals, their lovely white, pink and cerise flowers heralding spring and drawing bees and butterflies. The fruits of these ornamentals vary in colour from dark russet to crimson, orange to golden yellow, and the flowers from white to deepest crimson. I have seen a row of large cement urns planted with crab apples pruned into lollipops down a suburban driveway and marvel at their attractiveness in every season: their show of blossom in spring, their neat greenness in summer, their flush of bright fruits and glorious coloured leaves in autumn, and their bare sculptured shapes underplanted with a blaze of mauve and yellow violas in winter.

MEDICINAL USES

In the ancient herbals the crab apple was revered as a medicine for boils, abscesses, splinters and wounds, and for coughs and colds and a host of other ailments ranging from acne to kidney ailments. Many dishes made with apples and apple blossom are of medieval origin and the crab apples, roasted, drenched in honey and dried, were used by the monks and physicians as treatment for diarrhoea, dysentery and gallstones. In the spring they gathered the blossoms and preserved it in vinegar for drawing poultices and for beestings and other insect bites.

Crab apple blossom vinegar: In a bottle of white grape vinegar, press in as many blossoms as it can hold. Keep in a dark place for 7 days. Strain and repeat with more fresh blossoms and buds. Strain after another 7 days and keep near at hand for the summer's insect bites! For a wasp or hornet or bee sting, immediately soak a pad of cotton wool in the crab apple vinegar and hold it in place over the sting for 10 minutes. Keep dabbing with more vinegar for the next 30 minutes and you'll find that it hardly swells at all. Use the same vinegar frequently dabbed on to mosquito bites to relieve the itch.

CULTIVATION

Planted as a hedge or as a specimen shrub or small tree, crab apples do well in richly composted soil in full sun, and can be espaliered against a wall or clipped into a charming topiary. They do exceptionally well in colder areas, but also adapt to seaside gardens and even more tropical gardens. Because they are so slow growing, they make perfect container subjects and it seems a pity that they are not used more in landscaping as they need so little attention. Prune in late winter.

CULINARY

Crab Apple Verjuice, p. 139
Crab Apple Blossom Sponge Fingers, p. 125
Lemon and Crab Apple Blossom Jelly, p. 147

24

DAHLIA

Dahlia juarezi ● *Dahlia rosea*

With its glorious range of colours the dahlia is spectacular in the summer border, but it is only relatively recently that it has become a garden ornamental rather than a food crop. The Mexicans had been using it for several centuries for both food and medicine before it was introduced to Europe in 1789 by the superintendent of the Mexico City Botanic Gardens, who sent the first dahlia seeds to the botanist Cavanilles of Madrid. He named the plant *Dahlia pinnata*, in honour of Dr Andreas Dahl, a botanist and pupil of the famous Swedish botanist Carolus Linnaeus.

The tubers, rather than the flowers, were the part of the dahlia that was eaten and they are still eaten today by the Tunebo Indians in British Columbia. Their rather pungent taste was not popular with the Europeans, however, and they all but disappeared until Napoleon's wife, the Empress Josephine, became the first person in France to grow them in her world-famous gardens at Malmaison.

MEDICINAL USES

The dahlia petals as well as thinly sliced tuber were used by the Aztecs and later the Mexicans as excellent skin treatments. Crushed and warmed and placed over rashes and grazes and infected scratches, the petals formed a soothing **poultice** that was also used over insect stings and inflamed rough areas of the skin.

The petals were used to soothe tired feet and were used in a **foot soak**. Boil 2 cups of petals and 1 cup of sliced tubers in 2 litres of water for 10 minutes. Leave to stand for a further 10 minutes, strain and use as a wash, soaking the feet in it for a few minutes or use the water to wash sunburned skin and rashes.

The exquisite and spectacular tree dahlia, *Dahlia imperialis*, with its 3 metre high cascades of lilac single flowers that never fails to draw the eye in all its autumn glory, has been used through the centuries as a poultice. Crushed petals placed over an itchy sore spot on the skin give quick relief and for a pimple place a small piece of crushed moistened petal over it. It will soothe and quickly bring it to a head.

All the dahlia varieties are edible, though the tubers are not very palatable, and although the petals are not very tasty either, they can be used as an attractive decoration, for example on rice and mealie dishes in the Mexican style.

CULTIVATION

Dahlias come in a dazzling array of colours and make for a spectacular display in summer. Most of the single and pompon dahlias come from *Dahlia rosea* while the cactus varieties originate in *Dahlia juarezii*. They can be planted from August to November.

Tubers set into richly composted soil in full sun give a display that lasts all summer long, needing no attention except to cut back, dig up and store tubers in early winter.

CULINARY

Mexican Mealie and Chilli Dish, p. 111
Cream Cheese and Dahlia Dip, p. 92
Sun-dried Tomato and Dahlia Bread, p. 92

DANDELION

Taraxacum officinale

This common weed with its astonishing array of health benefits is proof indeed that a weed is a plant out of place! It originated in Europe but is now widespread all over the world, its name deriving from *dents de lion*, meaning teeth of the lion, a reference to its jagged leaves. It is astonishing to think that a plant with such remarkable medicinal properties, and which was actually an official medicine in the sixteenth century, could have become largely forgotten, but happily it is once again the subject of a resurgence of interest and research.

Dandelion is primarily a detoxifier and a diuretic and Arab physicians way back in the eleventh century recommended it as a treatment for liver and kidney ailments. In the thirteenth century physicians of Myddfai in Wales named dandelion as a cure-all cleanser. Those ancient physicians were amazingly accurate, as modern research has shown it to be one of the most important and effective of all herbs for detoxifying the body.

MEDICINAL USES

Dandelion is one of the best bile stimulants known, it helps to break down gallstones, soothes chronic rheumatism, clears gout, eases painful and stiff joints, and also aids fever, constipation, insomnia and, surprisingly, hypochondria. It helps to detoxify the body after a hangover, after over-indulging or eating junk foods, and helps clear up acne and boils.

To take dandelion medicinally, eat three fresh leaves daily in a salad. The younger the leaf the less bitter it is. Add a sprinkling of flower petals from two flowers for the betacarotene content as well as the vitamins, minerals and amino acids the petals contain.

Dandelion flowers and young leaves in spring are considered to be the ultimate spring tonic, flushing the toxins from the body and clearing pollution build-up. **Spring tonic wines** were made across Europe and still can be found today in rural areas. This wine is diuretic and digestive, and a simpler version is to boil 2 cups of flowers in 2 litres of water with 1 cup of honey, 10 cloves, 2 star anise and the juice of 4 lemons. Simmer gently for 15 minutes with the lid on. Cool, strain and add 1 litre of good wine if liked. Refrigerate. Take a wine glass daily.

The milky latex in the stems and at the flower base is an excellent treatment for removing warts, corns and verrucas. Apply the juice frequently, at least twice a day. Repeat every day until the wart or corn or verruca subsides.

CULTIVATION

I brought back dandelion seeds from England thirty years ago and as it is such an undemanding and robust perennial and self seeds everywhere, I am never without it. It is unfussy as to soil type, thrives in any sunny position, transplants easily and the rewards from the bright yellow flowers and jagged-toothed leaves are enormous. But do be sure you have the right species before eating it.

CULINARY

Dandelion and Bacon Salad, p. 92
Dandelion Flower Omelette, p. 92
Dandelion and Beetroot Salad, p. 93

DAY LILY

Hemerocallis species

The Chinese first cultivated the day lily for both food and medicine thousands of years ago. By the twelfth century it had been introduced to the New World, where it became established in the gardens of the rich. Much reverence and mystery was associated with the flower owing to its short life span – each exquisite flower blooms only for a day. The three petals came to symbolise the Trinity, while the three sepals represented yesterday, today and tomorrow, symbolising the transience and brevity of life. The flowers will last without water for a day and so over the centuries have often been used in religious ceremonies and to decorate shrines, fonts and places of worship in many cultures across the world.

Pliny the Elder advised the use of a tea made of the dried flowers for easing the pain of childbirth. In the late nineteenth century day lilies were thought to have pain-killing abilities and so were taken in the form of a tea to relieve rheumatism, aching joints, toothache and cramps.

MEDICINAL USES

The earliest medicinal uses of the day lily were as a **tea**. Add 1 fresh flower to 1 cup of boiling water. Leave it to stand for 5 minutes, then strain. Add a touch of honey and sip slowly. The tea is a great comfort for aching muscles and strains and sprains and was often used as a lotion, bandages being soaked in it to bind over sprains and bruises.

Crushed petals were used over a bruise, warmed and bound in place. For toothache the tea without the sweetening of honey is still used today to ease the pain and clear mouth infections, swilling it round the mouth several times during the day. For a **mouthwash** add 1 teaspoon of cloves to the tea recipe above. Cloves are excellent as a disinfectant and as a painkiller for toothache.

CULTIVATION

Perennial, undemanding and so easy, these lilies can be the backbone of a garden – or even vegetable garden – and what makes them infinitely appealing is they need no attention other than a deep twice weekly watering, a few barrowloads of compost twice a year and the occasional division. Plant them about 75 cm apart in well-dug, richly composted soil and apart from the odd tidying up of dry leaves and stems, they can largely be left to themselves. They flower prolifically and I have counted nine or ten blooms on a stem, each opening one day after the other. You will be rewarded with a splendid display all summer long.

They take full sun and light shade equally well and adapt to all types of soil. Divide the clump every three or four years in winter by pushing two forks into it back to back and then forcing them apart. Cut off the long leaves, leaving only about 10 cm, and replant in newly composted soil, watering in well. They cross pollinate easily, so within a few seasons you may find you have a new colour.

CULINARY

Day Lily Stir Fry, p. 112
Golden Day Lily and Yellow Peach Salad, p. 93
Steamed Day Lilies and Asparagus, p. 112

DELICIOUS MONSTER

Monstera deliciosa ● Ceriman ● Swiss cheese plant

MEDICINAL USES

Discard the little top of each scale as there are tiny hairs of calcium oxalate on each section that can cause a burning irritation to the skin and tongue. Cut away the top and use only the ripened tips at the centre of the flower. The inner pulp and very ripe bits of the flowers are used as a treatment for skin spots, pimples, dry flaky skin on the heels and elbows and rough spots on the toes. Sticky and soothing, leave it on as long as possible, then wash it away with tepid water to which a dash of apple cider vinegar has been added.

The soft young outer covering of the flower, the spathe, is still used in Mexico today as a comforting poultice over a sprain or bruise. Pressed open and softened in water, it makes a soothing dressing that is often used to hold other herbs in place over a wound or contusion.

The leathery little plates can be loosened off the ripe fruit and the creamy inner core rubbed onto sunburned skin.

CULTIVATION

It has an extraordinary growth habit, climbing by means of masses of aerial roots. On an indoor plant restricted to a pot these roots can dangle rather untidily, but do not cut them away as the plant draws moisture from the air by means of them and they help it to survive. It continues to fruit at erratic intervals during the warm months and I have found it to do so readily if sprayed with water every week and if its aerial roots are lead down into a bed of rich, moist compost which I replenish twice a year. It needs shade and protection and if it is in a greenhouse or on a verandah, it will benefit from a partner. As my grandmother said, they need to chat to one another so far from their jungles!

This familiar house plant belongs rather surprisingly to the Arum family. Originating in the jungles of Mexico and Guatemala, it is one of about 30 species of tropical climber belonging to the genus *Monstera*.

The delicious monster produces incredibly tough, woody, multi-jointed stout stems that bear huge, perforated leaves up to a metre long at intervals along the nodes. In its third year the flowering spike will appear if conditions are suitably moist. The inflorescence is a tough, creamy, arum-like flower with a bisexual spadix enclosed in a creamy white spathe. The rind that covers the spadix is covered in pale green hexagonal scales or plates, and the flower takes a year to ripen. As this happens, so the rind disintegrates and small pieces fall away, each with a succulent, exotic-tasting tip. Finally the scented, edible white pulp, which is the centre of the flower is exposed, and it is this flower heart with its flavour of guavas, pineapple, granadilla and banana that is simply food for the gods.

CULINARY

ECHINACEA

Echinacea purpurea ● Purple cone flower

Echinacea is undoubtedly one of the world's most important medicinal plants. Over recent years it has drawn increasing respect from the medical profession, as its ancient uses in traditional herbal medicine are being verified by scientific research. It is native to North America, and is now cultivated on a large scale throughout the world.

The Sioux and the Comache Indians have been using it for centuries for the very ailments for which we use it today: bronchitis, pneumonia, viral infections, acne and boils, animal and insect bites and stings, fever blisters, earache, flu, coughs and colds, sore throats and tonsillitis, skin allergies and infections, fungal infections, kidney and bladder infections, mild asthma, toothache and abscesses. It is a natural antibiotic, it boosts the immune system, it is anti-fungal, anti-allergenic, anti-inflammatory and detoxifying. With all these amazing properties it is little wonder that it is being researched for its ability to combat the HIV virus, and echinacea could be set to become the plant of the new millennium.

MEDICINAL USES

For allergic rhinitis, echinacea tea taken with 3-4 tablets of the biochemic tissue salt Natrium muricatum (available from your local pharmacy), will immediately soothe and open up the nose and stop the streaming. One of its key actions is that it is an exceptional anti-allergenic plant.

Echinacea tea: Use ¼ cup flower petals, leaves and root and pour over this 1 cup of boiling water. Stand 5 minutes, strain and sip slowly. During an acute infection take 2 cups a day, for chronic infection take 1 cup on alternate days. For chilblains make a cup of tea to drink and cool a second cup as a lotion to apply externally to the sore fingers and toes. Dip pads of cotton wool into the lukewarm tea and apply to the area.

For post-viral fatigue syndrome, commonly known as ME, take 1 cup of echinacea tea daily and include the petals of the flowers in the diet. Echinacea tea is being researched, with favourable results, as a treatment for asthma, particularly allergic asthma, and hayfever, cold sores or fever blisters caused by the *Herpes simplex* virus (see also Elder Flowers).

CULTIVATION

Echinacea is an easy to grow perennial. It thrives in well-dug, well-composted soil and, being a prairie plant, it can do with very little water and needs no care or attention other than cutting off the spent flowers in midwinter. It grows up to 40 cm in height with bright pink, daisy-like flowers and the clumps need to be spaced 50 cm apart as they spread rapidly. The cushion of tough, coarse leaves gives rise to tall flowering spikes in midsummer. The plant dies down in winter, almost disappearing from sight. Cover with compost in spring and soak it well.

CULINARY

American Indian Savoury Echinacea Spread,
  p. 93
Echinacea Pane Bagno, p. 93
Echinacea and Melon Fruit Salad, p. 126

ELDER FLOWERS

Sambucus nigra

The elder is a sprawling, multi-stemmed deciduous shrub or small tree that is indigenous to Europe. It has been much revered through the centuries for its medicinal powers and it was believed to have magical protective properties. One of the most popular traditional beliefs was that it kept witches away, and in Europe elder trees were often planted close to the house. The purplish black berries, which follow the flowers in midsummer, are particularly high in vitamin A and C, and for centuries have been made into a glorious wine or syrup for coughs, colds and bronchitis.

MEDICINAL USES

Elder is a renowned antiviral herb which helps to reduce fevers, fight flu and colds and boost the immune system. The flowers are used to tone the mucous linings of the nose and throat, helping to reduce catarrh and alleviating sinus problems, allergic rhinitis, hayfever, coughs, sore throat, post nasal drip and chronic earache. They also stimulate the circulation and help to ease arthritis by encouraging sweating and urine production, which in turn remove acidity and toxic waste products from the body.

Research has found that the flowers help to break down the *Herpes simplex* virus, which is marvellous news for sufferers of fever blisters or cold sores. To rid the body of the *Herpes simplex* virus try a **tea** made of equal quantities elder flowers, echinacea petals and black peppermint (*Mentha piperita nigra*). Use enough to fill ¼ cup and pour over this 1 cup boiling water. Leave to stand for 5 minutes, then strain and take 1 cup every alternate day for 2 months and then thereafter once or twice a week for 4 to 6 months. In persistent cases, continue for a further 3 or 4 months, taken twice a week.

Elder flower cream: Simmer 1 cup elder flower heads and 1 cup aqueous cream in a double boiler for 15 minutes with the lid on, giving it an occasional stir. Strain, discard the flowers and add 2 teaspoons vitamin E oil. Mix well. Store in a sterilised jar. Apply to rough skin, dark spots, freckles and pimples.

CULTIVATION

The elder is an undemanding shrub that requires little more than a sunny position. It will tolerate most soils but thrives in well-composted soil. It is propagated by cuttings in the spring. It can be clipped back in winter to prevent it from becoming too sprawling and untidy. It can reach a height of about 4 metres, but is easily trimmed to form a hedge and can even be confined to a large tub, providing it has full sun and well-composted soil.

CULINARY

Elder Flower Lemonade, p. 140
Elder Flower Fritters, p. 126
Elder Flower and Rhubarb Dessert, p. 126

EVENING PRIMROSE

Oenothera biennis

The evening primrose is a hardy biennial which is native to North America, where it is a common weed. It has been used for centuries to treat a wide variety of ailments and modern research is verifying these age-old uses. The Ojibwa, a North American Indian tribe, were the first to discover its medicinal qualities, and they used it to treat asthma and chest ailments, as a poultice and lotion for bruises and skin disorders, as a tea for fear, nervousness, panic attacks and anxiety, and for ageing women. It was brought to Europe around 1614 as a botanical curiosity and today it is recognised as one of the world's most important medicinal plants.

Leaves and flowers have long been added to soups, stews and teas, and American Indians pickled the buds in oil and salt for the winter. Just eating one of the clear yellow flowers in the garden in the evening gives you a scented mouthful that sets you wondering about this remarkable easy to grow plant.

MEDICINAL USES

Evening primrose oil is used extensively for premenstrual tension, multiple sclerosis, as an anti-coagulant, antispasmodic and in the treatment of wounds, skin eruptions, gastric irritation such as irritable bowel syndrome, coughs, colds and menopausal hormone correction. It contains the important gammalinolenic acid, GLA, which has been proven to lower blood pressure by preventing the clumping of platelets, as well as cholesterol levels. It aids weight loss and is used as a treatment for eczema, taken internally as well as an external lotion and wash. To make an **infusion**, simmer 3 cups leaves and flowers in 1½ litres water for 15 minutes. Cool and strain. It has also been found to be effective in the treatment of hyperactive children. To make a **tea**, pour 1 cup boiling water over ¼ cup fresh flowers and leaves. Let stand for 5 minutes then strain and sip slowly.

CULTIVATION

The evening primrose will tolerate any sort of soil and is as undemanding as any weed, merely requiring a sunny position. The leaves are arranged in rosettes in the first year, and these can be eaten like spinach, and along the stem in the second, when fluorescent yellow flowers that scent the night air are also produced. New flowers open every evening, only to fade and shrivel in the hot sun the following day during summer. Masses of seeds form in the capsules of the spent flowers, and it is these seeds that contain the remarkable evening primrose oil that is used for such a wide variety of ailments. It seeds itself prolifically all over the garden, and once you have it you will find seedlings popping up everywhere. Root it out after the seed spire turns brown and scatter the seeds. The plant grows to about 1 metre in height.

CULINARY

FALSE ACACIA

Robinia pseudoacacia ● Robinia ● Apiary tree

Originally from North America, this often overlooked tree has become naturalised in Britain and Europe, where it edges fields and resiliently endures heat and drought, snow and frost, and long periods of rain. This was probably one of the first plants to be used by the perfume industry. It was originally planted by bee farmers, which is why it was often called the apiary tree, as honey from these flowers was so sought after for its exquisite fragrance and delicious taste! Brought to South Africa and Australia by the colonists because of its extraordinary medicinal properties, it can still be found in old gardens and along roadsides.

MEDICINAL USES

In medieval times the false acacia, also known as robinia, was used by the monks to make a sweetly scented mead, which was taken to relieve stomach ache and colic and to relax and alleviate muscle spasm, aching joints and stiff necks. False acacia has been identified as one of the herbs the crusaders took with them in their medicine chests, along with yarrow to staunch bleeding and borage for courage.

A tea made of the flowers is still used today all over the world as a gentle, natural laxative and for a stronger action tiny pieces of bark are added. For the **standard brew tea** use ¼ cup fresh robinia flowers and pour over this 1 cup boiling water. Stand for 5 minutes, strain and sweeten with a touch of honey. Sip slowly. This antispasmodic tea is also a natural emetic and laxative.

For a severe chill and to warm up the body and soothe stiff muscles and ease throbbing chilblains, try the following **winter warming drink**. Simmer ½ cup dried flowers, ½ cup honey, 1 tablespoon grated lemon zest and 1 cinnamon stick in 1½ cups water for 10 minutes. Strain and add ½ cup brandy. Stir well and drink as hot as can be tolerated. Sip slowly and feel the cold melt away.

Crushed robinia flowers are quickly soothing over insect bites and stings. Mixed with a little apple cider vinegar they will take the swelling down if applied immediately. Hold in place with a crêpe bandage.

Note: Dry the spring and early summer flowers for winter use, as their glory is short-lived.

CULTIVATION

This attractive tree will reach a stately 8 to 10 metres in height and its spread is about 5 metres, offering deep shade. Propagation is by the thick stolon-producing root, which can often be a nuisance as it is difficult to get rid of once it is established. False acacia can be used to form a magnificent hedge, which with its spiny branches is impenetrable.

CULINARY

False Acacia Syrup, p. 140
False Acacia Liqueur, p. 140
False Acacia Flower Fritters, p. 127

FEIJOA

Feijoa sellowiana ● Pineapple guava ● Brazilian guava

This fascinating shrub is unusual in that it is a monotypic genus, which means that it is the sole representative of its genus. It was discovered in 1819 by a German explorer named Sellow, who found it growing abundantly in Brazil and named it after Don de Silva Feijoa, a San Sebastian botanist, and himself. It was introduced into Europe only around 1890, by Edourd André, a French horticulturist who found that it thrived in his garden on the French Riviera. From there it was introduced to Australia, New Zealand and California in around 1900.

Very little is known about the feijoa and there has been virtually no research done on it, which is surprising because not only is it prolific and easy to grow, but its small, green fruits which appear in abundance in late summer are exotically sweet and succulent to eat. They resemble miniature guavas, with white, fragrant, guava-flavoured flesh. Its attractive, dense grey-green foliage makes this evergreen shrub an asset to any size garden.

MEDICINAL USES

In its native Brazil, Uruguay, Paraguay and Argentina, the feijoa is used to treat certain thyroid conditions as it is rich in iodine. The flowers and fruit are made into a **tea**. Add ¼ cup of mixed flowers and fruit to 1 cup of boiling water, stand 5 minutes, then strain and sip slowly. This same brew is used to treat dysentry and diarrhoea, but with extra flowers added – 2 tablespoons flowers or 1 tablespoon flowers and ½ tablespoon fruit. Steep for only 5 minutes in boiling water, then strain. Sip a little at a time. Repeat until the condition subsides.

In Paraguay fresh, crushed flowers and the ripe fruit are applied to rashes, mild burns, insect bites and stings and itchy, inflamed areas.

A **lotion** made of the flowers is used to soothe sunburned skin. Boil 1 cup of flowers can be 1 litre of water for 10 minutes, then cool. Strain and spray or splash over the area. Slices of the fruit can also be used as a poultice.

CULTIVATION

The feijoa adapts remarkably well to any soil and temperature and can be found growing in the most unlikely spots, but flourishes best in warm, protected, richly composted sites. It needs full sun and a deep weekly watering, and clipped, trained and controlled it makes a most charming topiary, a luscious espalier against strong wires on a sunny wall, a neat hedge or an attractive container plant, and can be trained over arches. Left alone, it can reach 6 metres in height and spread, but pruned and controlled it is a perfect shrub for a small garden and is beautiful in all seasons. Underplant with tansy to prevent the fruit from being stung and hang a tin with molasses and water and fruit peels in the tree as fruit fly bait.

CULINARY

Brazilian Feijoa Conserve, p. 127
Feijoa Fruit Salad, p. 127
Buttered Banana and Feijoa Breakfast Dish,
    p. 94

FENNEL

Foeniculum vulgare

The ancient Greeks and Romans considered fennel to be a sacred herb and used it for slimming – just the way we do today – and in Anglo-Saxon times both the seeds and flowers were eaten on fasting days to still hunger pangs. It was also used as a tonic herb, and Roman warriors took it to keep in good health when they went off to battle. Once a favourite strewing herb, especially during the Middle Ages, its pleasant aniseed-type fragrance helped to clear the air of bad smells.

MEDICINAL USES

Both the seeds and flowers are a palatable and useful digestive remedy, and taken as a tea or chewed after a heavy meal will alleviate flatulence, heartburn and colic, aiding the whole digestive process and easing the feeling of fullness. See p. 140 for the recipe for **fennel tea**.

Fennel is a circulatory stimulant and anti-inflammatory, it promotes milk flow in nursing mothers, it is a mild expectorant, a superb diuretic, and an excellent slimming herb.

Fennel flower antacid: A combination of three incredibly digestable herbs makes this the most comforting antispasmodic, and for settling abdominal distention and bloating it is quick acting and immediately soothing. If you do not have flowers, you can use the seeds alone. Mix together 1 tablespoon each of the following: fennel flowers, fennel seeds, caraway flowers, caraway seeds, anise flowers, anise seeds. Place in a screw-top jar and shake well. (Pull the flowers off their stems.) The flowers will dry naturally in the mixture if the lid is kept off. Pour 1 cup of boiling water over 1 dessertspoon of the mixture and stir well. Let it draw for 5 minutes, strain and sip slowly.

Fennel facial steam: For clearing spots, cleansing oily skin and removing blackheads and acne, this ancient beauty aid is still popular today. Pour 1½ litres of boiling water over 2 cups fennel leaves and flowers. Making a towel tent over the head, hold the face over the steaming bowl for a few minutes. Rinse in tepid water to which a dash of apple cider vinegar has been added. Pat dry. Do this once a week for problem skins.

Caution: Fennel is a uterine stimulant. Avoid too much during pregnancy. Small amounts in cooking are quite safe.

CULTIVATION

Fennel is a hardy perennial that is easy to grow. It needs richly composted soil in full sun and a deep watering twice a week. The pretty yellow umbrels of flowers are much loved by bees and butterflies. The mature flowering stems scatter a mass of seed. The seedlings can be transplanted when they are 6 cm tall into well-dug, well-composted soil about 80 cm apart in full sun.

CULINARY

FRUIT SAGE

Salvia dorissiana ● Giant woolly sage

There are hundreds of species belonging to the genus *Salvia*, but very little has been written about this spectacular variety with its huge, shocking pink flowers, large leaves and unmistakable fruity scent and flavour. A cousin to *S. elegans* and *S. officinalis*, it endeared itself to gardeners in centuries past, but as more and more hybrids have become available it has sadly been all but forgotten. There is little evidence of its uses in ancient herbals other than as a strewing herb, and because of its fruity fragrance it is sometimes confused with pineapple sage, with its masses of tiny red flowers. If it were not for one little cutting brought into South Africa with a few other botanical specimens for research, fruit sage would not be available today, and I hasten to resurrect it, as from the tiny cutting in the Herbal Centre trial gardens it has become queen of the winter garden and a favourite in the nursery. It grows 1½ to 2 metres in height and width, with great sprays of thumb-length, brilliant pink, fragrant flowers whose fruity nectar is adored by sunbirds.

MEDICINAL USES

The genus name *Salvia* derives from the Latin *salvere*, meaning 'to save', and is aptly named, as all species have amazing medicinal properties. Among other things sage is a valuable digestive aid, a herbal remedy for both animals and humans, and burning sage will clear toxins and bad air and odours.

A tea made of the flowers is an excellent digestive that eases a feeling of fullness, slight nausea, colic and flatulence, and helps you relax. To make **fruit sage tea** pour 1 cup boiling water over ¼ cup flowers. Leave to stand for 5 minutes, then strain and sip slowly. It is a most useful relaxing herb and a bunch of leaves and flowers tied up and tossed into the bath will do more to help you unwind than anything else I know. The soothing oils seem to ease aching muscles and rashes and dry, itchy skin. A leaf placed in the shoe on a long walk will ease tiredness and soothe blisters, and crushed flowers placed over an insect bite and bound in place will take away the redness and itch. A **poultice** of the leaves placed for a few seconds in hot water and then patted dry and immediately placed over a bruise, a pulled muscle or a strain, will comfort and soothe and help to relax a tired, aching joint.

CULTIVATION

Grow fruit sage in full sun in a large, compost-filled hole. It needs protection during very cold winters and should be neatly pruned back after the early spring flowering period is over. It needs space but can also be potted into large tubs and clipped and trained. On a hot patio the huge velvety leaves are a wonderfully handy insect repellent. Rub the leaves onto chair legs, table tops and benches to keep flies and mosquitoes away. Your guests will be intrigued by the fruity scent.

CULINARY

Fruit Sage Dessert Whip, p. 127
Baby Carrots with Fruit Sage and Honey, p. 95
Roast Pork and Fruit Sage, p. 112

35

FUCHSIA

Fuchsia species ● *F. corimbiflora* ● *F. magellanica* ● *F. denticulata* ● *F. racemosa*

The fuchsia is native to central and southern America and parts of New Zealand. In 1690 a French missionary priest, Charles Plumice, discovered a fuchsia in Mexico and sent it excitedly back to France, naming it after the celebrated Bavarian botanist, Leonard Fuchs (1501–1566). Nearly all trace was lost of the plant for the next century, but a few specimens were taken to Kew by a Captain Firth. Years later, in 1793, an avid gardener, James Lee, spotted a flowering fuchsia on a window sill in London and begged a cutting from the lady who lived there, to whom it had been given by her sailor son. Lee raised the first plant from that, took more cuttings and established a small nursery which marked not only the beginnings of his fortune, but a new fashion in potted plants.

MEDICINAL USES

No proper research has been done on the fuchsia's medicinal and culinary values, but in southern America the crushed petals and the juice from the berries have long been used to treat skin ailments, freckles, small blisters and rashes. The flowers of the New Zealand tree fuschia (*F. arborescens*) are eaten and used crushed on bites, scratches and grazes, the pinky juice relieving itching and taking away the redness. They are also used in washing water to soothe inflamed blisters and sunburn.

In rural parts of Scotland, *F. magellanica* flowers are crushed and wrapped round a corn or callous on the foot and kept in the shoe all day. Fresh flowers can be reapplied at night, held in place by a bandage, and by the next morning the painful corn is something of the past.

Fuschia jelly: The flowers and berries are used to make a superb jelly that includes lemon juice and apple juice and a dash of brandy, and is taken for sore throats, tonsillitis and to strengthen the voice. Simmer 1 cup each flowers and berries with 1 cup of sugar, 1 cinnamon stick, the juice of 1 lemon, 2 cups water and a peeled, chopped apple for 10 minutes. Cool and strain, then add 2 tablespoons gelatine dissolved in a little hot water. Allow to set in the fridge. This is also soothing for sore throats and the early stages of a cold. Take 1 tablespoon at a time and hold it in the mouth as long as possible.

CULTIVATION

Cuttings can be easily taken, needing little attention other than keeping them shaded and moist in boxes filled with sand. Once planted out in semi-shade or full shade, they will give years of pleasure and ask little in return other than a deep watering twice a week, or daily if they are in tubs or hanging baskets, and a dressing of peat and wood ash (not coal ash) over their roots in winter. Plants should be pruned back in spring, and can take quite vigorous pruning if they are well established, but they do need winter protection.

CULINARY

Fuchsia and Potato Mash, p. 95
Cold Chicken and Fuchsia Salad, p. 95
Fuchsia Ice-cream Topping, p. 127

GARDENIA

Gardenia jasminoides

The exquisite gardenia, with its waxy white, heavily fragrant flowers and glossy green leaves is native to China, where it has been revered for its medicinal, cosmetic and fragrant properties for over 2 000 years. The Chinese add fresh flowers to the bath and tie them into muslin with a handful or two of salt to use as a scrub to soften and cleanse the skin. Gardenias were cultivated for the empresses of Japan in centuries past to wear in their hair, for corsages as well as in the bath. In the cooler months they were cultivated in tubs in greenhouses to ensure their bounty of flowers.

Gardenia flowers are still used in cooking in many rural areas today, and can be added to sugar, drinks, fruit salads, desserts and syrups. To scent tea in the ancient Chinese way, tuck a fresh gardenia flower into a tin of loose tea leaves, close the tin securely and leave it for 4 to 5 days, or until the flower dries, while it imparts its heavy, beautiful fragrance to the tea leaves. Flowers tucked into raw rice, oats or sago will impart the same sweet, heady scent.

MEDICINAL USES

In traditional Chinese medicine a soothing **lotion** was made to wash sores, grazes and insect bites. Boil 2 cups mixed flowers, leaves and roots in 2 litres of water for 15 minutes with the lid on. Cool a little, strain and use as a wash. Drink a little of this infusion for flu, to lower the temperature, and to cleanse the liver. Interestingly, ancient Chinese drawings depict the gardenia root, fruit and flowers being used to treat snakebite.

In Indonesia, where the gardenia is extensively grown, the leaves and flowers are made into a **tea**. Add ¼ cup chopped leaf and flowers to 1 cup boiling water, leave to stand for 5 minutes, then strain. This can be taken to ease tight, asthmatic breathing, lower a fever, calm heart palpitations, lower high blood pressure and to ease stress, fear and anxiety. Take ½ cup in the morning and ½ cup in the evening. Sipped slowly, the warm tea sweetened with a little honey is comforting and relaxing.

CULTIVATION

The gardenia is beautiful enough to be a focal point in a frost-free garden, demanding little more than a large hole filled with good alkaline leaf mould or lime-free compost well mixed with peat. It prefers a partially shady spot but will also thrive in full sun, providing it has a bit of afternoon shade. A deep weekly watering is all that is required and the dead heading of its spring to late autumn flowers. It will do well in a large tub, where it can be kept neatly trimmed into a ball shape. In the open ground gardenias will reach a height of up to 2 metres and about 1 to 1½ metres in width and they benefit from the occasional dressing of peat to keep the leaves from turning yellow.

Propagation is by soft wood cuttings in spring and hard wood cuttings in late summer. They provide a mass of blooms and cut flowers floating in a shallow glass bowl will scent a room for days.

CULINARY

Gardenia Milk Shake, p. 140
Gardenia Chocolate Mousse, p. 128
Gardenia and Litchi Fruit Salad, p. 128

GARLAND CHRYSANTHEMUM

Chrysanthemum coronarium • Chop suey greens • Edible chrysanthemum

MEDICINAL USES

A **tea** from the leaves and flowers is a gentle diuretic that helps with cystitis and water retention. To make the tea use ¼ cup flowers and leaves and pour over this 1 cup boiling water. Leave to stand for 5 minutes, strain and drink. One cup a day is sufficient, but in the case of swollen feet, add fennel flowers and leaves and celery leaves and drink 2 to 3 cups through the day.

A **lotion** made by boiling 1 cup of flowers and a few leaves is excellent for oily, spotty skin. Use it as a rinse after washing the face. Fresh crushed flower petals, moistened in hot water, can be applied to spots and pimples.

As a tonic herb the garland chrysanthemum is much loved in China as it is rich in minerals, amino acids and vitamin A, D and E. A thin **soup** made of the flowering tops and celery and parsley is taken as a spring tonic and blood and kidney purifier. Flavoured with a dash of lemon juice, sea salt and cayenne pepper, this soup will also clear up a lingering cold and clear the chest of mucous.

CULTIVATION

It likes well-dug, richly composted soil in full sun and a lot of water – a deep soaking at least twice a week. It does not do well in the heat of midsummer and is best grown as a winter or cool weather crop. It will survive frost and cold winds, but does best in a protected area, where it will reach a metre in height and even in width, with a glorious show of bright yellow daisy-like flowers that go on and on until the heat makes them bolt. The plants benefit from the picking of both leaves and flowers. Sow fresh seed in trays every February for winter planting and transplant the seedlings once they are big enough to handle. Shade and protect the small plants in the beginning and do not let them dry out.

This attractive bright and easily grown annual is popular in oriental cuisine, and has only lately been introduced to the rest of the world. It has been grown for centuries in gardens all over the East, and in China particularly, for use in stir fries and teas, and has marvellous medicinal properties. The ancient Chinese use for this chrysanthemum was as a blood tonic, to help clear toxins from the body and to assist the functioning of the kidneys and bladder. It is a gentle diuretic and also a deodoriser.

The leaves are used extensively in cooking as a chop suey green and big bunches of the pungent, crisp feathery leaves are now sold in markets all over the world. The bright yellow petals are crushed into butter, fat, batters and sauces to lend colour and flavour. Finely chopped raw leaves and flowers sprinkled over stir fries and rice dishes add a rich, full taste and help to clear the body of toxins, an important benefit if one has eaten food that is too rich or spicy.

CULINARY

Garland Chrysanthemum Stir Fry, p. 112
Garland Chrysanthemum Croutons, p. 96
Garland Chrysanthemum and Apple Dessert,
    p. 128

GLADIOLUS

Gladiolus hybrids

The huge variety of gladioli that are cultivated today are believed to have descended from the bright orange parrot flower, *Gladiolus dalenii* (formerly *G. natalensis*), which is indigenous to South Africa and was taken to England in the early 1700s. In 1904 one of the engineers responsible for building the bridge that spans the Zambezi River at the Victoria Falls, Sir Frederic Fox, found the pretty *Gladiolus primulinus* growing wild in the perpetual spray of the falls and took it to the Royal Horticultural Society in England. From there Unwins of Cambridge, a long established seed firm, developed new hybrids using those original corms.

MEDICINAL USES

The Zulu and Sotho people have for many generations used the corms of wild gladiolus ground down to a fine meal to treat dysentery, diarrhoea and stomach upsets, and farmers in

KwaZulu-Natal make an **infusion** of the corms and lower portion of the leaves for coughs and colds. Use 1 dessertspoon corms (peeled and finely chopped) and leaves to 1 cup of boiling water, leave to stand 5 to 6 minutes, strain and drink.

Gardening in the summer heat with scratches and blisters from the secateurs, we all learnt quickly that a crushed flower would soothe a sore spot or stop a scratch bleeding. Zulu flower pickers showed us how to crush and squeeze the petals into a tight ball, which they rubbed over their nails to strengthen them from breaking, and the dark red flowers lent a beguiling pink tinge! Gladiolus petals placed in a jar of water and left in the sun for a few hours make a soothing wash for hot, tired feet.

CULTIVATION

I became intrigued by this easy to grow plant in the early 1960s, when my mother-in-law grew an acre or two of the most breathtaking hybrids for the local florists in Rustenburg. They withstood the heat and drought admirably and we sprayed for thrips twice weekly, which we found damaged the buds. Using Jeyes fluid according to the instructions on the container is the preferable method, but every year the new corms must be planted in a different area to prevent the build-up of Jeyes fluid residue in the soil. Water was lead into a furrow from the dam above, flooding the rows once a week. Every winter the corms were lifted, cleaned, stored and replanted in early September in soil rich with compost and manure.

In my herb garden I grow the wild orange gladiolus for medicinal purposes and find it multiplies quickly and easily. Space them 25 cm apart and stake if the flowering spike becomes too heavy.

CULINARY

Stuffed Gladiolus Flowers, p. 96
Gladiolus and Bean Stew, p. 113
Gladiolus and Avocado Open Sandwich, p. 96

GOLDEN ROD

Solidago virgaurea ● *Solidago canadensis*

Most species of golden rod are native to North America and were reputedly spread across the world by soldiers and gypsies. It has been used medicinally since ancient times and is cultivated today for herbal and homeopathic medicine. The North American species, *Solidago canadensis*, was brought over to Britain in 1648 by John Tradescant. The European and Asian variety, *S. virgaurea*, also known as Aaron's rod, was once called woundweed because it reputedly had wonderful healing properties. Its generic name, *Solidago*, comes from the Latin *solido*, meaning to join or make whole. Today there are many cultivars that have been hybridised from those original species. Both these varieties are the best for medicinal purposes.

MEDICINAL USES

It is the flowers that have the medicinal value and these can be dried in the shade on brown paper and stored in airtight jars for winter use. They have diuretic, antiseptic and anti-inflammatory properties, and are an important anti-oxidant. They are effective for urinary tract ailments, from cystitis to more serious conditions such as kidney stones and nephritis. They also help to relieve backache caused by kidney conditions, and ease arthritis. Golden rod's saponins act specifically against the *Candida* fungus, which causes oral and vaginal thrush, and it is a valuable herb for chronic sinusitis and nasal catarrh. It has a mild yet thorough action and is helpful in treating gastro-enteritis and diarrhoea in both adults and children. Recent research has found it to significantly reduce hot flushes during menopause. With this amazing array of healing properties we should all be growing golden rod! As a general tonic and as a treatment for any of the above ailments, a cup of **golden rod health tea** (see recipe on p. 141) taken once a day for a few days is wonderfully soothing. For acute conditions up to 3 cups can be taken through the day, for chronic conditions no more than 1 cup. Make it fresh every time.

CULTIVATION

Solidago virgaurea, the European variety, is a clump-forming perennial with long, slender-toothed leaves and multi-branched stems about 75 cm long with tiny yellow flowers that brighten the autumn border. A wasteground weed, it will grow in any soil as long as it is in full sun, and all it needs is a barrow of compost every spring, a deep weekly watering and literally no attention other than cutting back the spent flowering spires in winter and the occasional division of the clump.

Solidago canadensis is the tall flowering variety and forms a spectacular clump. Its flowering spires reach over a metre and a half and, like *S. virgaurea*, it requires a deep weekly watering, full sun and a good amount of compost each spring.

CULINARY

Golden Rod Health Tea, p. 141
Golden Rod and Celery Health Drink, p. 141
Golden Rod Soup, p. 96

GRANADILLA FLOWER

Passiflora edulis ● *Passiflora* species ● Passion flower

Native to America and first recorded in Europe around 1699, the granadilla flower is also known as the passion flower, and is traditionally associated with Christ's Passion. Spanish monks first noted its symbolism, but it was a botanist and physician in the sixteenth century, Monardes (after whom bergamot, *Monarda didyma*, is named), who first recorded in writing the symbolic interpretation of the flower.

The pillar or column in the centre of the flower, representing the cross, holds three stamens, representing the Holy Trinity. The five anthers under the stamens indicate the five wounds, which nailed Christ to the cross. Beneath the three stigmas is a small, swollen seed vessel, denoting the sponge soaked in vinegar that was thrust at Christ's mouth to quench his thirst. The three stigmas also represent the three nails that pierced his hands and feet, and the calyx the halo. The corona of fine tendrils is usually purple: this depicts the crown of thorns, stained by

Christ's blood, and the 10 petals that surround the flower are 10 of the 12 disciples, excluding Peter who denied him and Judas who betrayed him. The digitate leaves suggest the hands of the persecutors and the long green tendrils along the stem the whips that lashed him in the hands of the persecutors. The colour purple is that of the robe thrown over Christ in mockery, and the white the purity of his love.

MEDICINAL USES

It is fascinating to know that the fruit, leaves and flowers of the granadilla have been used through the centuries to calm nervousness, to soothe, tranquillise and quieten, and to allay fears and anxiety. For those suffering from insomnia and panic attacks this may prove to be particularly useful. The delicious fruit is a digestive aid. There are about 400 different granadilla species and a number of them have a similar sedative action. *Passiflora incanata* and *P. quadrangularis* have been found to contain serotonin, one of the main chemical messengers within the brain.

Calming tea: Use 1 granadilla flower, calyx and stem removed, and pour over this 1 cup boiling water. Leave to stand 5 minutes. Strain and sweeten with a touch of honey.

CULTIVATION

The vine needs full sun, a deep, richly composted hole, and a fence or support to grow up. It needs to be protected from winter frost and I usually replace my vines every four or five years. Keep it lightly tied up and trimmed, apply a seaweed foliar feed every six months and water deeply twice a week, and you'll be rewarded with an abundance of flowers and fruit.

CULINARY

Passion Flower Nectar, p. 141
Passion Flower Cake Topping, p. 128
Passion Flower Tropical Fruit Salad, p. 129

HAWTHORN

Crataegus oxycantha ● *Crataegus monogyna*

In the Middle Ages hawthorn was a symbol of hope. It is an ancient herb, indigenous to the British Isles and Europe, where it still grows in hedgerows today. It is a charming tree, spectacular in spring with its heady white blossoms, glossy green leaves in summer and brilliant red berries in autumn and early winter.

Medicinally, only two species, *Crataegus oxycantha* and *C. monogyna*, may be used. Many hawthorn species with red berries are for sale in nurseries, so it is important to get the correct species if you are planning to use them in a home remedy.

MEDICINAL USES

It is used principally for circulatory and heart ailments such as angina, heart strain and coronary disease, as it has antispasmodic and sedative properties and it is an effective vasodilator. It normalises both high and low blood pressure by regulating the action of the heart. Excellent for stress and heart tension, it helps hearts weakened by age, and is also helpful for nervous heart problems, irregular heartbeat and arteriosclerosis. Historically it has also been used for removing kidney and bladder stones, for treating diarrhoea, and as a diuretic. The bark has been used to treat malaria and other fevers and although the tiny red berries are not very appetising, they are perfectly palatable and, like the flowers, are important for heart ailments and circulation.

Crushed hawthorn flowers and buds or crushed hawthorn berries are excellent in a **cream** for poor circulation and chilblains. Simmer 1 cup of flowers, buds or fruit to 1 cup of aqueous cream in a double boiler for 20 minutes. Strain and add 10 drops rose geranium oil and 2 teaspoons vitamin E oil. Store in a sterilised jar and use as a massage cream on hands and feet after a hot bath.

Make a sage flower and hawthorn flower **tea** for easing menstruation and menopause problems. Use ¼ cup fresh mixed sage and hawthorn buds and flowers and a leaf or two of each. Pour over this 1 cup boiling water, leave to stand 5 minutes, stir well and then strain. This will ease bloating, premenstrual tension, regulate oestrogen flow and slow down a racing heart.

CULTIVATION

It is slow growing, reaching about 8 metres in height if left unchecked, or it can be pruned and trained to form a superb hedge or boundary, or trimmed as a specimen tree. All hawthorns do best in cold areas, withstanding icy winters, frost and even snow, but are also able to adapt to hot areas. In Europe a new hawthorn called *Crataegus azarolus*, or azarole, has been hybridised, the fruit of which is more appetising and makes a good jam.

CULINARY

Hawthorn Flower Tea, p. 141
Hawthorn Pancakes with Lemon Curd, p. 129
Chicken and Hawthorn Flower Stir Fry, p. 113

HOLLYHOCK

Althaea rosen

The common hollyhock is native to China and was taken to Europe in the sixteenth century, where it became a much loved cottage garden plant. Known as the Holyoke or Beyondsea rose, it was grown far and wide for its medicinal properties, as a dye, as well as for its edible flowers. Monks in Europe used the darker red petals of the spectacular flowers to colour wine and medicines, and the flowers were added to batters, soups and stews as a health giving, soothing tonic.

MEDICINAL USES

The hollyhock has a soothing effect on the mucous membranes and is useful for treating coughs, colds and bronchitis. Hollyhock species have been used since 300 BC to treat earache due to chronic catarrh, and hayfever with catarrh and allergic rhinitis.

Hollyhock counters excess stomach acid, peptic ulcer pain and soothes and eases gastritis, irritable bowel syndrome, diverticulitis, colic and even diarrhoea. A warm, comforting tea made of hollyhock flowers will ease cystitis and frequent urination and, used as a lotion, will soothe skin inflammations, rashes, boils and even abscesses. The leaves and the root are also used, and its close cousins, the marsh mallow, *Althaea officinalis*, and the common *Malva sylvestris*, are used in the same way. To make **hollyhock tea** use 1 hollyhock flower and pour over it 1 cup boiling water. Leave to stand 5 minutes, strain, sweeten with honey and add a squeeze of lemon juice. Sip slowly. Take 1 cup daily as a treatment for all the above.

In the sixteenth and seventeenth centuries hollyhock tea was popular for easing irregular menstruation, for spongy gums used as a gargle and as a tea, and to dissolve 'coagulated blood from falls, blows and knocks'. As a **lotion** used for washing and as a **douche** it has a soothing effect on tender, inflamed skin. Boil 4 to 6 flowers in 2 litres of water for 10 minutes, strain and add ½ cup of apple cider vinegar.

CULTIVATION

The hollyhock is easy to grow, and seeds are available in nurseries and in seed catalogues the world over. All that is required for a spectacular spire of breathtaking flowers is a well-dug, richly composted spot in full sun. Sow the seeds directly into the ground where they are to grow, 75 cm apart, and keep them moist and shaded. With their long tap root they do not like to be transplanted, but very small plants can be relocated quickly, provided they are immediately submerged in water once they are removed and then kept moist and shaded in their new positions for a week or two. The hollyhock is supposedly a biennial, but I find it mostly does as an annual. In warm areas the tall flowering spire is quick to mature and during midsummer makes an eye-catching display in the border.

CULINARY

Hollyhock Summer Fruit Salad Pancake, p. 129
Hollyhock Scones, p. 129
Hollyhock and Green Bean Salad, p. 96

HONEYSUCKLE

Lonicera species ● Woodbine

Also known as woodbine, honeysuckle is a perennial evergreen climber, native mainly to Europe and the Caucasus, but some varieties are also found wild in north Africa, North America and western Asia. There are numerous varieties, all of which are exquisitely fragrant, and all with similar medicinal properties. The genus was named in the sixteenth century by a German physician, Lonicer, who strongly advocated its medicinal properties. Monks in Europe had been using it for centuries to treat chest ailments, hayfever and homesickness. Most commonly used varieties are *Lonicera caprifolium*, the pink flowering, more bushy *L. pericymenum*, and in old gardens the winter flowering winter sweet, *L. fragrantissima*, a shrubby variety that has tight, stalkless clusters of creamy white flowers on bare branches.

MEDICINAL USES

Honeysuckle flowers have emollient, expectorant and antispasmodic properties and, crushed and pounded in a gentle **cream**, make a soothing, pain-relieving treatment for aching, swollen haemorrhoids. Simmer 2 tablespoons of flowers and 2 tablespoons of aqueous cream in a double boiler for 20 minutes. Strain and add 1 teaspoon vitamin E oil.

For a heart tonic, asthma, hayfever and rheumatism, an ancient remedy was to take honeysuckle tea and eat honeysuckle flowers once a day for a period of 10 days. To make the **tea** use ¼ cup fresh flowers and pour over this 1 cup boiling water. Stand 5 minutes, strain, sweeten with honey and sip slowly.

Recent research has found honeysuckle flowers, and to an extent the leaves, to be outstanding in the treatment of colitis.

Made into a **lotion** it quickly soothes skin inflammations, aches and dry rashes. Boil 2 cups flowering sprigs in 2 litres of water for 10 minutes. Cool and strain. Use as a splash, lotion or as a spray in a spritz bottle for sunburn, rashes and eczema.

CULTIVATION

I grow honeysuckle over fences and arches, or place shaded benches nearby where one can sit and enjoy the glorious scent. It goes on undemandingly year after year, scenting the hot summer days and nights with its heady fragrance. An arch of honeysuckle over a gate was an old tradition in rural gardens. Easy to grow, all it needs is a deep, well-composted hole, a good strong support and a deep weekly watering. I tie in and wind in the tendrils continuously and every winter tidy up the thick growth. New plants can be propagated by merely pulling up rooted runners and replanting them, keeping them moist until they take off. Honeysuckle is tolerant of adverse conditions, and will thrive in spite of heat, drought, bitter winter winds and even neglect.

CULINARY

Honeysuckle Energy Drink, p. 141
Honeysuckle Fruit Salad, p. 130
Honeysuckle Syrup, p. 141

HYSSOP
Hyssopus officinalis

Native to southern Europe, hyssop is a lovely, free-growing perennial that is a tough yet persistent roadside weed, particularly in the Balkans and Turkey. It loves sunny places and does well in barren, poor soil, preferring the roadsides to the garden! The beautiful blue flowers, which are borne in late summer, are much loved by bees and butterflies.

Once considered nature's cure-all, hyssop has been a much revered herb since the earliest times. It was used by the ancient Greeks for purifying temples and for the cleansing of lepers. It is mentioned in the Bible: 'Cleanse me with hyssop and I shall be clean' (Psalm 51 v. 7). Over the centuries some have thought this could have been oreganum, marjoram or winter savory, but it is now believed that it is probably the same hyssop we know today, as modern research has found that the mould that produces penicillin grows on hyssop leaves. This could have acted as antibiotic protection for lepers when they were bathed in hyssop.

MEDICINAL USES

The diverse uses of hyssop have earned it a rightful place in folk medicine through the ages that has been verified by modern day research. It was prescribed in ancient times for asthma, stomach aches, nasal catarrh and pleurisy. Now it is found to relax peripheral blood vessels and to have significant antiviral properties, particularly with the *Herpes simplex* virus. It is expectorant, anti-catarrhal, anti-inflammatory and anti-spasmodic. It eases chest colds and asthma, clears bronchitis and urinary tract inflammation and is used with figs for constipation. To make **hyssop tea** use ¼ cup flowering sprigs and pour over this 1 cup boiling water. Stand 5 minutes, then strain. Sip slowly. Sweeten with a little honey if liked.

Caution: Do not take hyssop during pregnancy or nervous irritability, as strong doses can induce muscular spasms.

CULTIVATION

I don't find hyssop particularly easy to grow, but it does do well if it likes the spot. It is a short-lived perennial, and full sun, lightly dug soil and not too much attention or water seem to be all it requires. You'll be rewarded with 30 cm high flowering spikes and an equal spread. All it ever needs is for the spent flowers to be cut off from time to time. New cultivars in Britain range from white through to pale blue and pink flowering spikes and all seem to have similar properties. Propagation is by seed and by small cuttings taken from around the base of the plant. In the hot area where I live, I find it does best with afternoon shade. Hyssop will thrive in the cooler areas of the country with a yearly dressing of compost as it takes light frost and cold winds well.

CULINARY

Hyssop Green Salad, p. 97
Hyssop Meal-in-One Chicken Dish, p. 113
Poached Nectarines and Hyssop, p. 130

JASMINE

Jasminum officinalis ● *Jasminum multipartitum*

This exquisite plant with its sweetly scented, star-shaped flowers was introduced first to Britain and then Europe from the East via the ancient trade routes in around 1548. The Chinese first used the flowers as a flavouring in tea centuries ago, and later in perfumery.

There are about 300 *Jasminum* species throughout the tropical and subtropical regions of the world. Chinese jasmine, *J. polyanthum*, is a favourite in our South African gardens, heralding spring in headily fragrant billows of pink buds opening to starry white flowers. The beautiful Arabian jasmine, *J. sambac*, native to south east Asia, is also added to ordinary tea and used in Buddhist ceremonies. *Jasminum multipartitum* is indigenous to South Africa and its flowers are used in traditional medicine.

All the jasmines grown today have some medicinal or culinary use. *J. officinalis* is the best species for the perfume industry and for medicinal uses.

MEDICINAL USES

Jasmine oil is used to lift depression and ease stress, and has a calming and soothing effect. Ancient Indian and Chinese doctors, herbalists and religious sects used jasmine as a sedative to treat a number of ailments and as a muscle relaxant, usually in the form of a **tea** (see p. 143) or added to oil as a massage for stiffness and soreness. Later jasmine infusions were added to the bath to release tension and to oils and creams for dry and sensitive skins.

Because jasmine oil is so remarkable as an antidepressant and for anxiety-related sexual problems in both men and women, it is superb as an aromatherapy massage oil. A few crushed jasmine flowers rubbed into the temples will ease a tight throbbing headache.

Caution: Avoid jasmine oil during pregnancy as it is a uterine stimulant.

CULTIVATION

It is only recently that the summer flowering medicinal jasmine (*Jasminum officinalis*) has become available to gardeners in the southern hemisphere, and its more fragile, trainable growth makes it a popular plant for growing up fences and columns, and for pruning and clipping into bushes. It has the additional advantage of flowering all through the summer. Just three flowers in a room will impart a marvellous scent, soothing, calming and uplifting.

Growing your own jasmine is so easy that no garden should be without it. All the jasmines take full sun to partial shade and require no more than a good watering twice a week and a dressing of compost twice a year. Tidying and pruning off the spent flowers is essential to prevent new growth from climbing over the old wood, forming untidy nests.

CULINARY

Jasmine Syrup, p. 142
Jasmine Tea, p. 142
Jasmine and Strawberry Dessert, p. 130

JUDAS TREE

Cercis siliquastrum ● *Cercis canadensis* ● Red bud tree

The Judas tree is a small, attractive tree that originates in Asia and the Mediterranean regions, so named because legend has it that Judas hanged himself from a tree of this species.

Tough, resilient, drought resistant and even to a large extent frost resistant, it used to be a garden favourite and was commonly available at nurseries, though sadly seems to have gone out of fashion. Its pinky-mauve, almost magenta-coloured pea-shaped flowers are strikingly beautiful in spring, when the bare branches are covered in masses of brilliant blossoms, which withstand the early spring winds. The tough camel's foot type leaves give dense shade in summer.

Cercis canadensis or red bud tree, a North American native, is its close relative. Both grow to about 5 to 8 metres in height and form attractive, wide, shrubby trees that make superb focal points in a small garden as their growth habits are gently twisted and contorted to form a mass of fascinating branches.

MEDICINAL USE

Once used to treat anaemia and lack of energy, the Judas tree was an important ingredient in the convalescent's diet, as well as for periods of overwork and stress, or for students writing exams. It has been used through the centuries to treat kidney stones, respiratory ailments and swollen feet during pregnancy. It is a gentle diuretic and will clear a runny nose and ease a tight chest and laboured breathing. The flowers are rich in carotene, high in vitamins and minerals and have been found to help dissolve fatty deposits in the blood and liver when combined with parsley. A soothing **cream** will heal skin rashes, infected sores and fungal conditions. Boil 1 cup Judas flowers in 1 cup good aqueous cream in double boiler for 20 minutes. Strain through a fine sieve. Discard the flowers and add 3 teaspoons of vitamin E oil to the cream. Stir well and pour into a sterilised jar. Massage into nails or affected areas.

To make **Judas flower health tea** use ¼ cup fresh flowers and pour over this 1 cup boiling water. Stand 5 minutes and strain. Sweeten with a little honey and add a squeeze of lemon juice.

The American Indians used the red bud to treat ailments ranging from toothache to bladder infections, spotty skin to splitting toe nails, using crushed flowers as a poultice or lotion and adding them to teas.

CULTIVATION

To plant a Judas tree, all that it requires is a deep, well-watered hole filled with compost in a sunny position. Sink the plant into it without disturbing the roots. After that water the sapling well once a week, making sure that it has a big 'dam' around it to hold both compost and water. Do not plant anything close to its trunk. It needs no pruning.

CULINARY

Judas Tree Pickle, p. 147
Judas Tree Stir Fry, p. 113
Judas Tree Flower and Mulberry Jelly, p. 130

LAVENDER

Lavandula angustifolia

Native mainly to the Mediterranean area and cultivated throughout the world, this hardy herbaceous plant was used by the early Romans in their bath houses as a strewing herb and as a beauty aid. The varieties within species are breathtaking in their colour, shape and fragrance and eminently worth collecting. The main species include *Lavandula dentata* or French lavender, *L. stoechas* or Spanish lavender, *L. latifolia* or Dutch lavender, *L. allardii* or blind lavender and the huge *L. angustifolia* group, or English lavenders, which have the best flowers for cooking purposes.

MEDICINAL USES

Burn lavender stalks and a few flowers in the fireplace to disinfect and deodorise and perfume the room. Sprigs of lavender rubbed onto kitchen counters will discourage flies. Skin ailments respond beautifully to lavender's antibacterial properties and throughout history lavender has been used for its calming and soothing effect.

Lavender oil and lotions help ease sore throats, rheumatic aches and pains, depression, headaches and sleeplessness.

Lavender tea: Add ¼ cup fresh flowers to 1 cup boiling water, stand 5 minutes, then strain. It is excellent for nervous anxieties as well as a wonderful deodoriser and underarm wash – all that was needed to keep fresh in medieval times.

Crushing fresh lavender flowers and inhaling the rich scent and rubbing crushed leaves and flowers on the temples, immediately soothes a pounding headache and relieves dizziness and fainting fits. Rub fresh lavender sprigs on children's pillows to stop restlessness and add a small bunch of fresh flowers tied up in muslin to the bath to help wind down after a hectic day.

Lavender massage cream: This soothing cream is ideal for dry skin, cracked heels, rheumatic aches and pains, sore tired feet and to calm irritable children. Simmer 1 cup fresh lavender flowers in 1 cup aqueous cream in a double boiler for 15 minutes. Stir occasionally. Strain out the flowers, cool for 10 minutes then add 1 tablespoon almond oil and 10 drops pure lavender essential oil. Spoon into a sterilised jar and keep well sealed.

CULTIVATION

I find growing the large English lavender, *L. angustifolia* Herbal Centre Giant, the most rewarding of all the lavenders for the southern hemisphere. All lavenders require full sun and are quite unfussy as to soil type, but do need well-drained, light soil and a good watering once a week. All lavenders should be cut back after flowering to encourage new growth of flowers and usually need to be replaced every 4 to 5 years. Allow enough space for the bush to spread; the Herbal Centre Giant needs a metre in height and width. Propagation is by cuttings or seed.

CULINARY

Lavender Biscuits, p. 130
Lavender Cheese Squares, p. 97
Cajun Potatoes with Lavender, p. 97

LINSEED

Linum usitatissimum ● Flax

Linseed is an ancient plant that has been cultivated since at least 5000 BC as a source of flax or linen fibre. Flowers and seeds took secondary place to the fibre content of its stems at that time, but the Greeks were well aware of its extraordinary medicinal content. Pliny the Elder (AD 23-97) wrote about linseed's virtues: 'What department is there to be found of active life where linseed is not employed? And, in what production of the Earth are there greater marvels to us than this plant?'

MEDICINAL USES

Flax is becoming one of the new century's wonder plants and medical research is concentrating on this easy to grow plant. New evidence proves that the seeds and flowers contain enzymes that hugely benefit the whole urinary system, including the kidneys. The seeds are rich in mucilage and unsaturated fats, and are a world-renowned remedy for constipation, digestive irritation and sluggishness. A **poultice** of crushed flowers and warmed seeds relieves painful boils. Crushed flowers moistened with milk have been used as a soothing poultice for rashes, grazes and sunburn since the Middle Ages. 'Flax flower tea' is still used in country districts in Europe today as a **lotion** and a **soak** for tired aching feet. Gently boil 1 cup of flowering tops in 1 litre of water for 10 minutes with the lid on. Stand aside and cool until pleasantly warm.

Placing crushed flax petals on a spot or pimple helped to soothe the inflammation, the gypsies found. They dried the blue flowers for winter use and used them in a tea for chilblains, chills, circulatory problems, cold feet and for treating coughs, sinusitus and the aches and pains of rheumatism. Here is the recipe for **Gypsy Linseed Tea for Chest Ailments and Rheumatism**:

> 2 tablespoons linseed
> 2 tablespoons fresh flax flowers or
>   1 tablespoon dried flowers
> 1 litre cold water
> 6 cloves
> Rind of ½ lemon

Simmer covered for 15-20 minutes. Strain and add the juice of 2 lemons and about 3 tablespoons of honey and a pinch or two of cayenne pepper. Take ½ a cup 3 or 4 times during the day. Warm it up each time, but not in a microwave!

CULTIVATION

Linseed is an easy and fast-growing annual that enjoys full sun and deeply dug, well-composted soil. Sow the seeds by scattering them over an area, then raking them in and soaking the ground with a gentle spray. Mulch the ground with a light layer of leaves to help keep it moist until the seedlings are sturdy, watering twice weekly. In no time you'll be able to pick the small, heavenly blue flowers.

CULINARY

Flax Flower Chocolate Sauce, p. 130
Spaghetti and Tomato with Linseed, p. 114
Flax Flower and Potato Soup, p. 97

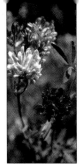

LUCERNE

Medicago sativa ● Alfalfa

Lucerne is one of the oldest of all cultivated plants. The ancient Arabs called it the 'father of all foods', and used it as a feed for their magnificent horses who were fleet of foot, brave and supple. Today this long-lived perennial is grown all over the world as fodder for horses and cattle. It makes a pretty garden subject, too, as its mass of mauvy blue flowers attract a host of butterflies in early summer.

MEDICINAL USES

Nutritional experts rate lucerne as one of the most important food supplements known to mankind. It is rich in silica, manganese, calcium, iron, potassium, magnesium, sodium and vitamins A, B, C, E, K and the rare vitamin U, as well as being the only plant in the world other than comfrey that contains vitamin B12.

A **tea** of leaves and flowers – ¼ cup fresh leaves and flowers steeped in 1 cup boiling water for 5 minutes – is of tremendous benefit to those under extreme stress or suffering from a loss of energy, over-exhaustion, anxiety and panic attacks. A cup taken daily for a week and then on alternate days will do much to relieve modern day tensions and ease desperation.

Eating fresh leaves, flowers and the tiny, thread-like alfalfa sprouts gives an immediate energy boost, flushing toxins from the body and helping to absorb vitamins and minerals. One winter the Herbal Centre garden staff put this to the test. Half the staff ate a large **daily salad** of lucerne sprigs and flowers, dandelion leaves and flowers (see p. 26), buckwheat leaves and flowers (see p. 9), celery and parsley leaves, landcress and a squeeze of lemon juice. They sometimes added nasturtium leaves and flowers, chopped chives, clover leaves and flowers, and pansies and borage flowers for variation. Needless to say not one of the 'salad eaters' got a cold or flu that winter and every one of the 'non-salad eaters' did!

Lucerne is vitally important for convalescents who need easily assimilated nutrients and should be added daily to their diet in the form of teas, soups and the fresh leaves and flowers in salads. It also has substantial oestrogenic activity, which is good news for treating symptoms of menopause and irregular menstrual cycles.

CULTIVATION

Lucerne is very easy to grow and requires very little attention other than cutting back the long flower-bearing branches 3 or 4 times a season to encourage the tender new shoots. It needs full sun and compost-enriched soil. Because it is cut so often for baling as cattle food, it needs constant feeding, so a good dressing of compost twice a year is important. Water twice weekly in summer and every 10 days in winter.

CULINARY
Lucerne Energy Drink, p. 142
Iced Avocado and Lucerne Soup, p. 98
Lucerne Flowers and Vegetable Tempura, p. 98

MINT

Mentha species

The *Mentha* genus comprises an incredibly rich diversity of species, which originated in Europe but have now spread all over the world. I have chosen just a few of my favourite species to write about here, all with edible flowers and all differing slightly in taste. Apple mint, *Mentha suaveolens*, is perfect for mint sauce and more tasty, I find, than most other mints; black peppermint, *M. piperita nigra*, has a strong peppermint flavour and is excellent for stimulating the brain; eau de cologne mint, *M. piperita* var. *citrata*, as its name suggests, smells and tastes of eau de cologne, and is best with fruit salads and desserts; spearmint or garden mint, *M. spicata*, is most delicious with ice-cream; and chocolate mint, *M. spicata* var. *piperita*, has delectable chocolatey overtones.

MEDICINAL USES

All the edible mints are anti-inflammatory, antiseptic, antibacterial, antispasmodic, anti-

flatulent and effective stimulants. A **tea** made of a thumb-length sprig in 1 cup of boiling water eases digestion and provides relief from abdominal discomfort and stomach upsets. During exam time a cup of peppermint tea works wonders to help concentration and ease nervous energy. For menopause peppermint flower tea will relieve hot flushes and help ease digestive problems, take away a bloated feeling and help heartburn and a rapidly beating heart. Peppermint tea will also relieve cold and flu symptoms. Chew a sprig of any mint and the flower to sweeten the breath and use the mint tea as a gargle and mouthwash to clear mouth and gum infections.

Mint **lotion** will soothe itchy, inflamed areas, mosquito bites and rashes, and if added to the bath will soothe sunburn, windburn and chapped winter skin. Boil 3 cups mint flowers and leaves, especially peppermint and spearmint, in 2 litres of water for 10 minutes. Stand aside to cool. Then strain and pour into a spritz bottle and spray the area or dab on with cotton wool pads soaked in the brew or add to the bath for a relaxing soak. For a **foot bath** add 3 or 4 drops of peppermint essential oil and soak the feet for 10 minutes. This will soothe tired feet beautifully.

CULTIVATION

All mints need moist, rich soil and do best in partial shade in damp areas, but will also flourish in full sun as long as their roots are in water or very moist soil. Propagation is by roots pulled off the mother plant and immediately planted into wet soil. The mints constantly seek new ground, so it is a good idea to edge the bed with plastic or plant the mint in tubs to prevent them from spreading uncontrollably. Provide a rich dressing of compost twice a year to prevent the mint bed from becoming depleted.

CULINARY

Chocolate Mint Mousse, p. 131
Watermelon and Mint Dessert, p. 131
Mint and Mushroom Supper Dish, p. 114

MORINGA

Moringa oelifera ● Drumstick tree

This small, dainty shrub-like tree with its creamy white, sweetly scented flowers and light green, fern-like foliage is attractive enough to be a focal point in a tropical or subtropical garden. It is native to India, where it has long been cherished and respected not only for its dainty appearance, but for its importance as a nourishing staple food. In many Indian households the moringa is on the daily menu in some form or other: the leaves are cooked with tomato and onions as spinach, the pods are used in traditional sauces and chutneys, soups and stews, and the flowers in stir fries and puddings. All parts of the tree are rich in protein, vitamins and minerals, including calcium, phosphorus, vitamin C, iron and folic acid, as well as betacarotene, which is essential for healthy vision.

MEDICINAL USES

Medicinal uses of the leaves and flowers have been well recorded in India's pharmacopoeias. They stabilise blood pressure, purify the blood and build strong bones and teeth, due to their high calcium content. An acknowledged remedy for dysentery and diarrhoea is the juice of the leaves followed by coconut water, and leaves added to carrot juice are an effective diuretic.

The roots are used as a heart medicine and to bring down fever; oil from the seeds is used for gout and rheumatism; the gum from the trunk helps dental caries and gum ailments; a poultice of leaves soothes glandular swellings and headaches; leaves and flowers help prevent infections of all kinds, especially throat, chest and skin; and the juice of the leaves will clear blackheads and pimples. What a plant!

Add ¼ cup dried powdered moringa seeds to 1 bucket of river water to clear it of organic pollution.

CULTIVATION

The moringa needs full sun and does well even in a neglected corner, pushing up its pretty fragile branches against all odds. In a deep, well-composted hole a specimen of my own has grown 4 metres in height in one year.

Propagation of the moringa is by seed. Once the pod ripens, it splits to reveal about 10 winged seeds. Rub the seeds on a stone to weaken the casings and plant the seeds in individual bags in moist sand. Germination takes about 2 months. The moringa has a long tap root and the seedlings do not like to be disturbed once established, so when planting them out into their final positions in full sun, be very careful how you slit the bag and lower the plants into the hole. Make a big 'dam' around the sapling and flood it with water once or twice a week until it is well established. Thereafter a weekly watering will ensure a crop of abundant leaves and flowers. The moringa can grow 3 metres in one year.

CULINARY

MULLEIN

Verbascum thapsus ● Verbascum ● Aaron's rod ● Our lady's taper

This beautiful tall biennial, native to Europe, once enjoyed pride of place in many gardens but in modern times has sadly been all but forgotten. In its first year it forms a large rosette of huge, downy, soft grey-green leaves, which medieval advice recommended for those suffering from cold feet to line their slippers on bitter winter nights! In the second year a tall spire of brilliant yellow flowers and a mass of tight buds is produced. This can reach well over a metre in height and makes mullein an eye-catching border plant. The flowers appear all summer long until finally the spike dries off, scattering a multitude of seeds everywhere. In days gone by the tall flowering spike dried and dipped in tallow was burned as a taper, usually in funeral processions but also on feast days and in religious ceremonies.

MEDICINAL USES

From the first century mullein was used as an expectorant to treat coughs and pleurisy. A syrup of honey and mullein was also made for coughs and added to fruit dishes for children with colds and bronchitis. A poultice of warmed leaves was used to ease muscular aches and rheumatic pains and an ointment made with leaves and lard was found to be excellent for haemorrhoids and varicose veins.

Mullein cough syrup: This is excellent for all chest conditions, bronchitis, pneumonia and chronic catarrh. Make fresh batches frequently. Simmer 1 cup flowers and a few small leaves, taken off the flowering spike, in 3 cups water with the rind of ½ a lemon for 15 minutes with the lid on. Strain, discard the leaves, rind and flowers. Add 3 tablespoons lemon juice and 3 tablespoons honey. Mix well. Drink ½ to ¾ cup at intervals through the day – about 5 times a day.

Modern science has proved that this easy to grow plant is indeed amazingly beneficial for a wide variety of illnesses, including respiratory ailments, hayfever, sinusitis, feverish chills (it promotes sweating), eczema and earache. For all these ailments the leaves and flowers can be taken as a **tea** once or twice a day. Pour 1 cup of boiling water over ¼ cup of fresh leaves and a couple of flowers, stand for 5 minutes to infuse and then strain. It is also useful as an antiseptic wash for wounds and infected grazes and scratches.

CULTIVATION

Mullein requires full sun and is unfussy as to soil type. Although it prefers well-drained, compost-rich soil, it will grow easily in the most inhospitable places and needs no attention whatsoever other than a good weekly watering. Transplant the seedlings when they are still small but just big enough to handle as they have a long tap root that does not like to be disturbed. Both flowers and leaves can be dried for winter use, although I find the plant survives the frost and strong cold winds well.

CULINARY

Mullein and Carrot Lunch Dish, p. 114
Stuffed Marrow with Mullein Flowers, p. 115
Strawberry and Mullein Mousse, p. 131

MUSTARD

Brassica alba ● *Brassica nigra*

Both black and white mustard have been grown as a crop since medieval times and are still widely cultivated across the world for use both as a condiment and medicinally. From its native Middle East and Mediterranean areas, it has spread in popularity through India, China and Burma across to America. Mustard is rich in minerals, including high levels of phosphorus as well as calcium, iron, potassium, and vitamins A, B and C. It is no wonder that mustard is being researched for its ability to boost the immune system.

MEDICINAL USES

Mustard seeds, leaves and flowers are a marvellous circulatory stimulant as well as being a noteworthy alkaline food. Mustard greens – the flowers and young tender seeds included – compare very favourably with other leafy green vegetables with the added advantage that they do not have a high oxalic acid content, which robs the body of nutrients. Its alkaline content aids digestion and mustard is both a good antispasmodic herb and a diuretic. It has been used for centuries to treat bronchitis and pleurisy, it is believed to have antiseptic properties, as well as helping arthritis and rheumatism and urinary ailments. The old-fashioned mustard **foot bath** recommended in our grandmothers' day at the first sign of a feverish cold or flu, really worked. The remedy involved soaking the feet for 10 minutes in hot water in which 2 tablespoons of mustard powder had been dissolved.

Eating the leaves and flowers fresh in a daily salad is an excellent tonic, but for treating constipation, bronchitis and pneumonia there is no better medicine than a **mustard soup**. Simmer 2 cups mustard flowers and leaves, 1 cup chopped celery, ½ cup parsley and 1 cup beetroot leaves in 1 litre of water for 10 minutes. Liquidise and season only with lemon juice.

For an **immune-building drink** combine 1 cup of grape juice, 1 cup mustard flowers and leaves, ½ cup parsley, 1 carrot and 1 apple in a liquidiser. Blend until smooth and drink twice a day.

CULTIVATION

Mustard is such an easy crop to grow, it seems a pity that so few gardeners consider it. It is a fast-growing annual that needs fertile soil in full sun, rich in humus. Growing mustard and cress on wet cotton wool was one of the most rewarding experiences I ever had as a child and one which modern children seem to hardly know. Making your own mustard can provide enormous pleasure. Keep on sowing new rows so you can reap the seeds and use the new crops, flowers and leaves at the same time. The plant can literally be eaten when only 1 centimetre high and as a garden subject its bright yellow flowers will bring you not only pleasure and good health, but butterflies too!

CULINARY

Homemade Mustard, p. 147
Mustard Flower Pickle, p. 147
Mustard Flower Vegetable Curry, p. 115

MYRTLE

Myrtus communis

Myrtle is an ancient, much respected herb, which was dedicated in ancient times to Venus, the Roman goddess of love and carried in bridal bouquets to symbolise love and constancy. Native to warmer, temperate climates of southern Europe, it has been used for over 2 000 years as a flavouring, a perfume, a cosmetic and a medicine. The more one grows myrtle the more impressed one becomes as the entire plant is usable. In Chile myrtle seeds and dried flower buds are used to make a type of coffee, and the flowers are used in pickles. The aromatic leaves and stems are important ingredients in pot pourris, as well as being good insecticides.

MEDICINAL USES

Myrtle buds and flowers have been found to contain quite high quantities of vitamin C, malic and citric acid and an array of minerals. Both leaves and flowers are astringent and antiseptic. The leaves have a marvellous skin-cleansing action and soothe skin rashes, oiliness and problem skins. An excellent **skin lotion** can be made by boiling 2 cups flowering sprigs in 2 litres of water for 10 minutes. Cool and strain. Use as a toner, soaked on pads of cotton wool, or as a spray to keep the skin smooth and moist. This same lotion makes an excellent wash for oily, spotty skin. Being both antiseptic and astringent, this soothing lotion quickly clears up rashes, spots and infected bites. Recent research has revealed that myrtle contains a substance that has a substantial antibiotic action, so this explains why it is so quick to clear up infection and why it so effective in treating acne and, taken as a tea, urinary disorders.

A **poultice** of flowering sprigs soaked in hot water and then bound over a sprain or bruise as hot as is comfortable will immediately disperse the haematoma and lessen the tension and swelling over the sprain. For many years I have made a beautiful myrtle vinegar which, in my physiotherapy practice, I found to be helpful for sprains and bruises. To make the **myrtle vinegar** fill a bottle with flowering myrtle sprigs and top it up with white grape vinegar. Stand in the sun for 10 days. During that time strain out the old sprigs and replace with new ones twice so that the minerals and vitamins contained in myrtle leach into the vinegar. Finally rebottle and press one myrtle sprig into the bottle for identification. Add to the bath or use on a warmed cloth over bruises and sprains to effectively ease the pain.

CULTIVATION

Myrtle is easily cultivated, but slow growing. It grows 1 to 3 metres in height and with its evergreen, glossy leaves, can be placed in an eye-catching position in the garden as it never has an off period. It makes a superb, tough hedge and takes clipping and pruning beautifully. It needs full sun and well-composted soil to really thrive, and a deep weekly watering. Propagation is by cuttings, which root easily.

CULINARY

Myrtle Pepper, p. 147
Myrtle and Cheese Spread, p. 98
Apple and Myrtle Stir Fry Dessert, p. 132

NASTURTIUM

Tropaeolum maju

Afamiliar summer annual all over the world, the nasturtium originated in South America, particularly Bolivia and Peru. It was introduced to Spain in the sixteenth century and was recorded by the well-known herbalist Gerard in London in the 1590s. With its pleasant peppery taste it has become a favourite herb the world over. Today nasturtium seeds are marketed around the world and beautiful cultivars abound, from the more compact bush nasturtiums to double-flowered varieties, in a breathtaking array of colours. The bright orange sprawling nasturtium that we all grew up with is happily still around, but the colours of the latest varieties now include brilliant yellow, cream, wine red and every combination and shade in between.

Along my pergola walk this season I was delighted to count twenty-one different colours and combinations, all of which were self sown from a single packet of seeds sown two summers previously.

MEDICINAL USES

All parts of the plant may be used. As a child I was taught to eat a nasturtium leaf at the first sign of a sore throat, another an hour later and a third an hour after that. Only many years later did I learn that nasturtium is high in vitamin C and a natural antibiotic. It is still used today in South America as a treatment for bladder and kidney ailments, for coughs, colds and flu, and for sore throats and bronchitis. It contains a variety of vitamins and minerals and through the centuries has been used to treat scurvy and blood disorders.

In ancient South America nasturtium was taken as a hair growth stimulant. Now medical science has proven that the juice from the flowers and buds stimulates the tiny capillaries of the scalp! A **nasturtium, nettle and rosemary hair rinse** can be made by boiling 1 cup of each herb in 2 litres of water for 15 minutes. Cool and strain. Massage into the scalp and rinse the hair. Keep the excess in the fridge. The French decoction is 1 cup nasturtium flowers and buds and ½ cup leaves in 1 litre of water. Simmer for 15 minutes in a closed pot, strain and use as above.

CULTIVATION

Growing nasturtiums is child's play and a rewarding crop for children to grow themselves. Merely loosen a bit of soil in full sun and press the big seeds into it, keep the soil moist, and within a few days the succulent little seedlings will appear. They thrive literally anywhere and in any soil, although if the soil is too rich you'll have masses of leaves at the expense of the flowers. In a protected area nasturtiums are biennial, but as they seed themselves with such ease, I pull out the old plants and let the new young ones take over.

CULINARY

Nasturtium Salad Vinegar, p. 148
Nasturtium Cheese Dip, p. 99
Grilled Aubergine Salad with Egg and
    Nasturtium Flowers, p. 99

ORANGE BLOSSOM

Citrus species

Citrus trees have been in cultivation since the first centuries of civilisation. Originating in China and south east Asia, the earliest species moved westwards via the trade routes to India, then Arabia and finally to the Mediterranean. Roman records from Palestine in the first century mention citrus, and from then on citrus trees were cultivated both in Italy and the rest of the Roman world. In 1002 citrus trees were established in Seville in Spain, and the famous Seville orange, valued for its bitter taste in marmalade, is still cultivated today. Lemons had been cultivated in Egypt by the tenth century and from then on citrus trees were established in warmer regions around the world.

MEDICINAL USES

All citrus fruits are high in vitamin C and – particularly lemons – are excellent for treating excess acidity in the body. They ease constipation, clear catarrh and blocked noses, and their high vitamin A and betacarotene content makes them

vitally important for our daily health. Calcium, phosphorus and magnesium are present in the fruit, and to some extent in the flowers.

To make **orange blossom water**, simmer 1 cup orange blossoms and 4 orange leaves in 1½ litres of water in a pot with a well-fitting lid for 15 minutes. Stand aside and cool, then strain. Add 2 tablespoons apple cider vinegar and pour into a sterilised bottle and cork well. Shake for 1 minute. Use as a skin tonic to clear oily skin, to brighten tired skin and dab it frequently onto spots, rough areas and open sores. Orange blossom is astringent and contains a skin softening oil that is effective in refining coarse, oily skin.

Orange blossom has been found to be sedative, antispasmodic, and an excellent remedy for depression, anxiety, nervous debility, grief, fear and insomnia. A tea made of fresh orange blossom will aid sleep and act as a natural tranquilliser. To make **orange blossom tea** use 1 tablespoon fresh flowers, or ½ tablespoon dried flowers, and pour over this 1 cup boiling water. Stand 3 to 5 minutes, strain and sip slowly for any of the above ailments and for poor circulation, as a natural blood cleanser, for premenstrual tension, fatigue, palpitations and stress.

CULTIVATION

Any number of varieties of citrus are now available to gardeners around the world, from tiny kumquats, calamondins and chinottas, which do exceptionally well in tubs and make enhancing patio plants, to tangerines, limes, rough-skinned lemons, ruby grapefruit and blood oranges. They are evergreen, easy to care for and incredibly rewarding to grow. A deep watering twice a week is imperative, and it is important to apply a good dressing of compost every 4 months and to check for pests and leaf curl.

CULINARY

PANSY AND VIOLA

Viola lutea ● *Viola tricolour*

'*Pansies with their happy faces, grow with joy in sunny places.*' No garden is complete without an edging or planting of pansies and violas. The exquisite garden pansy (*Viola x Wittrockiana*) hybrids available today probably derived from *Viola tricolour*, *Viola lutea* and possibly *Viola altaica*, whose beautiful markings were so admired by gardeners and botanists during the nineteenth century that pansy societies were founded to hybridise and improve the species. The array of species available today is breathtaking in its variety of colours and markings, and there is a huge selection in terms of seed available. The tiny heartsease, *Viola tricolour*, the forerunner to the beautiful viola and pansy hybrids we know today, originated in Europe and Asia, but has now spread all over the world. Violas, or 'little pansies', as they are often known, are an enchanting small-flowering variety which were originally hybridised by James Grive in 1863 from show pansies crossed with *Viola cornuta*, which come from the Pyrenees, and *Viola lutea*.

MEDICINAL USES

The tiny heartsease is an important heart medicine, hence its name, and is also used to treat high blood pressure, indigestion, coughs, colds and rheumatic conditions. It has also been used to treat skin ailments such as eczema, rashes and inflammation. To make a soothing **cream**, pound 1 cup of flowering sprigs of *Viola tricolour* to a paste, mash in 1 cup of aqueous cream until it is fully incorporated, then warm in a double boiler for 15 minutes, stirring frequently. Strain through a fine sieve and mix in 2 teaspoons vitamin E oil. Spoon into a sterilised screw-top bottle. Keep in the fridge. Apply frequently.

A **tea** made of the flowering sprigs of *Viola tricolour* and one or two garden pansies can be used as a treatment for high blood pressure. Add ¼ cup flowers to 1 cup boiling water, leave to stand 5 minutes, then strain. Take 1 to 2 cups daily until the blood pressure normalises, thereafter 1 cup on alternate days or twice every week. Wonderfully versatile, it can also be used to treat coughs and colds, stiff, sore joints, gout and rheumatoid arthritis. To ease rheumatism and aches and pains, add a strong **infusion** to the bath. Boil 4 cups *Viola tricolour* flowering sprigs and pansies in 2 litres water for 10 minutes. Cool for 5 minutes, strain and add to the bath.

Caution: Do not take pansies and violas medicinally for long periods of time as it can cause nausea and vomiting.

CULTIVATION

Pansies require little attention other than well-dug, compost-rich soil, a twice weekly watering and frequent dead heading to ensure a longer flowering period. Plant in early winter as the pansy is a cold weather annual.

CULINARY

Strawberry and Pansy Granita, p. 132
Almond Pansy Macaroons, p. 132
Pansy and Asparagus Cheese Bake, p. 99

PEACH BLOSSOM

Prunus persica

Three hundred years before Christ, the Greek philosopher Theophrastus wrote about the peach, naming it *perske* after Persia, which he thought to be its country of origin, and Dioscorides mentioned the peach in the first century. It is in fact native to China, where a vast number of varieties exist today. It took many centuries for the peach to reach Europe and in 1629 the first peach trees were sent to America, where they flourished, and from there they spread rapidly around the world.

MEDICINAL USES

Organically grown peaches are a superb health food. Rich in vitamins A and C and betacarotene, the fruit – and to a lesser extent the blossom – is alkaline to the body and helps to eliminate toxins. It is important that peaches are eaten fresh rather than tinned or dried, as the sugar and sulphur content are best avoided, and they should be unsprayed and organically grown. Easily digestible, they are

particularly important for the elderly and they combine beautifully with other fruits. In seventeenth century Italy peach blossom was made into a poultice for bruises, rashes, eczema, grazes and stings.

Tea made from the leaves or blossoms is a marvellous detoxifier for the kidneys and the significant calcium, phosphorus and iron content has a tonic action on the blood. Even today in rural areas across the world peach blossom tea and, later when the leaves appear in early summer, peach leaf tea is made to ease kidney ailments and urinary infections and to clear the body of toxins, especially after a debilitating illness. To make the **tea** use ¼ cup of fresh or dried blossom and pour over this 1 cup of boiling water. Stand 5 minutes, then strain. Sweeten with honey if liked or add a slice of lemon or, in case of aching kidney area, a few thin slices of fresh ginger.

Caution: Do not use the ornamental flowering peach, it is only the blossom of the fruit-bearing peach that is used medicinally.

CULTIVATION

It is important to choose a variety of peach that will do well in your area from the vast number of varieties available. I tend to choose the earliest of fruiting peaches as this eliminates the need to spray. Tansy planted under the trees will help prevent insect attack. Peach trees need rich, well-composted soil in full sun and can be pruned into attractive small trees that are perfect even for a small garden. Peaches fruit on young shoots, so pruning is not difficult. Merely shaping the tree in its first few years will ensure a practical, attractive shape in years to come. I am always saddened by the waning in popularity of peach, plum, fig and apricot trees compared to a mere 50 years ago, when every garden had at least one or two varieties of fruit tree. Their brief early spring flowering is a delight to the eye, and the first sign that spring is on the way.

CULINARY

Springtime Peach Blossom Sundae, p. 133
Peach Blossom Spring Fruit Salad, p. 133
Grilled Mushrooms with Peach Blossom, p. 115

PINEAPPLE SAGE

Salvia elegans ● *Salvia rutilans*

The sages are a huge family comprising hundreds of species, some of which are annual, some biennial and some perennial, of which pineapple sage is one. It is a deliciously scented and flavoured sub-shrub which originated in Mexico and other parts of South America. In ancient times pineapple sage was used in sacrificial ceremonies as a gift to the gods. Floors and pillars were rubbed with the branches to impart its exotic fragrance and bunches of pineapple sage were burned on ceremonial fires to ward off evil spirits. Water flavoured with pineapple sage flowers was drunk at ceremonies to cleanse the body before imbibing potent drinks made from prickly pears and other fermented fruits, and also was taken afterwards to help relieve hangovers.

MEDICINAL USES

Like *Salvia officinalis*, pineapple sage, also a member of the great Labiatae family, has antibiotic properties and a **tea** made of the flowers and a few leaves is an effective treatment for chesty coughs, colds and blocked noses. Infuse ¼ cup of fresh flowers and leaves in 1 cup of boiling water, stand for 5 minutes and then strain and sweeten with honey. Lemon juice added to the tea makes an effective gargle and was once popular with chanters and singers in religious ceremonies, who believed it strengthened the voice.

A poultice of crushed flowers will quickly soothe bee stings and mosquito bites and a bundle of flowering sprigs tied in a piece of muslin and tossed under the hot water tap in the bath will soften and soothe sunburned and wind-chapped skin. The crushed flowers were also used as a cosmetic by country girls, who would rub them on their cheeks to give a blush. Mashed into a little boiling water and left to stand until pleasantly warm, the flowers were also rubbed into the nails to strengthen and lightly colour them.

CULTIVATION

Pineapple sage can reach 1 metre in height in favourable conditions. It is frost tender and sun loving, and forms a striking feature in the garden with its abundant multi-stemmed growth. A twice yearly dressing of compost and a deep weekly watering is all it requires. In late winter cut back all the flowering stems to ground level to encourage tender new shoots. The strong, unmistakable pineapple scent is attractive to butterflies and just one blazing bush will draw a host of beautiful multicoloured butterflies to the garden. To propagate pineapple sage, dig out small tufts of rooted new shoots with a sharp spade and transplant immediately into well-dug, well-composted soil 1 metre apart in full sun. Do not let the new little clumps dry out and mulch the ground around them with dry leaves to protect them against changes of temperature.

CULINARY

Pineapple Sage and Grapefruit Health Breakfast, p. 100
Couscous and Pineapple Sage, p. 100
Pineapple Sage and Pineapple Drink, p. 143

60

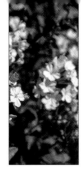

PLUMBAGO

Plumbago auriculata ● Cape leadwort ● Cape forget-me-not

This pretty, blue-flowering, scrambling shrub, which is indigenous to South Africa, has become a treasured hothouse plant all over the world, beloved because of its long flowering period and the sky blue clusters of flowers it so lavishly produces. In its wild state it grows in great swathes on banks and hillsides, which in summer are clothed in magnificent blue. It is enormously obliging, however, and can be trained up trellises, espaliered on a wall or fence, or clipped into a pretty hedge, requiring little more than the occasional pruning and clipping back of spent flowers. A strong individual stem can be staked and side bits constantly pruned to form a beautiful blue topiary ball. It takes three years to reach perfection with regular attention, but the result is well worth the wait.

MEDICINAL USES

Plumbago flowers make a soothing **lotion** to beat the heat, refresh and revitalise hot, greasy skin and it helps to refine large pores and cleanse away perspiration and grime. Boil 2 cups flowering heads in 2 litres of water for 10 minutes. Cool, then strain and add 4 tablespoons of rose-water (see p. 67). Moisten pads of cotton wool with this fragrant brew and use these to wipe the face, or pour into a spritz bottle and spray the face, neck and arms to clear away dust, grime and perspiration and to cool down. It also acts as a refreshing air conditioner especially if used on a long midsummer journey.

The flowers can be used in a wonderfully soothing **cream** for sunburn, burns, spots and rashes. Mix 1 cup crushed flowers into 1 cup aqueous cream, then simmer in a double boiler with the lid on for 25 minutes, stirring well. Strain the cream through a fine sieve while it is still hot and then, as it cools, mix in 4 teaspoons vitamin E oil. Pour into sterilised jars and keep in the fridge. Use fresh crushed flowers over a bruise, held in place with this cream and cover with a cloth, then bind in place and relax for 10 minutes. You'll be amazed at the efficacy of this old-fashioned folk treatment.

CULTIVATION

Propagation is by rooted pieces dug off from the mother plant. New plants should be planted in a sunny position and will tolerate even poor, dry soil, making plumbago a valuable garden plant for dry regions where water is in scarce supply. A newer variety of plumbago called Royal Cape is available at many nurseries, and is being marketed as far afield as England, America and Australia. This variety is particularly suitable for large tubs or training into a small topiary ball, and is especially attractive on account of its astonishing brilliant blue flowers.

CULINARY

Plumbago Fruit Jelly, p. 133
Plumbago and Beetroot Salad, p. 100
Lamb and Potato Pot Roast with Plumbago,
    p. 116

PLUM BLOSSOM

Prunus domestica

Originating in Western Asia and the Caucasus and dating back about 2 000 years, the plum naturalised first in Greece and then throughout the temperate regions of the world. In the fifteenth century plums were grown widely in France and Italy. They were a staple fruit crop in Britain right up until the Second World War, when their popularity unaccountably waned and plum orchards gave way to other more important food crops. From then on plums were found mostly in cottage gardens and old farmyards and sadly many of the early varieties were lost for all time.

MEDICINAL USES

All varieties of plum are rich in minerals and vitamins, but need to have fully ripened before eating to prevent acidity. They are high in phosphorus, calcium and vitamins A and C. Fresh plums have a laxative effect, and dried prunes are an even more potent natural laxative. In ancient Greek medicine plum blossoms were used to treat bleeding gums and mouth ulcers, and to tighten loose teeth. Mixed together with sage leaves and flowers, plum blossoms were used in plum wine or plum brandy as a mouthwash to soothe a sore throat and mouth ailments and to sweeten bad breath. As both the plum and the sage flower in spring, it is easy to see why they would be combined in a gargle or mouthwash.

Plum blossom is so prolific in spring and the trees are in flower for such a brief period, I make **plum blossom vinegar** every spring. Pick 1 cup of blossom when they are fully open, calyx included, and push them into a bottle containing 3 cups of apple cider vinegar. Give it a daily shake. Do this for about 10 days, then strain. Discard the old blossoms and replace with 1 cup of fresh ones. Leave them in the bottle for 10 days and then strain. Use 1 tablespoon of the vinegar in 1 glass of water as a rinse or gargle to clear mouth infections and sore throats.

CULTIVATION

Plums favour a heavier, moister soil than most fruits, but bear well in most positions, requiring little attention other than good, rich soil in full sun, a dressing of compost twice a year, a deep weekly watering and a winter pruning that shapes the tree. In colder areas plums do well trained or espaliered in a fan shape against a wall, and can be pruned vigorously early on, as the branches often sag with the weight of the fruit. Plant tansy under the tree to keep fruit flies at bay.

A plum tree planted near the house will enable you to enjoy its fragrance and beauty all year round. Nurseries these days offer self-pollinating varieties and all species make a charming garden tree, with exquisite white blossoms in spring, and fruit and shade in summer. Judicious propagation has resulted in about 1 500 varieties, including prunes, and commercial plum orchards are happily once again in vogue.

CULINARY

Chinese Plum Blossom Tea, p. 143
Plum Blossom and Pumpkin Supper Dish, p. 116
Plum Blossom and Celery Cheese Platter, p. 100

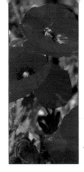

POPPY

Papaver rhoeas ● Field poppy ● Flanders poppy

The bright red field poppy, *Papaver rhoeas*, has grown prolifically across Europe, Asia and the Mediterranean region for thousands of years, where it has been used for both food and medicine as well as symbolically. In the Victorian language of flowers the poppy signifies consolation. In Britain at the end of the First World War the field or Flanders poppy became the flower of remembrance for those killed at Flanders, the red petals symbolising the red of their blood. The Shirley poppy (*Papaver rhoeas* subsp. *Shirley*) is descended from the field poppy and also comes in a wide range of colours that are breathtaking in spring. The opium poppy is quite different to the field poppy and comes in many forms, from fringed petals to double and single flowered varieties in a startling array of petal shapes and colours. The growing of the opium poppy is strictly controlled due to its potent narcotic effects. It is the source of the powerful painkillers codeine and morphine, and morphine's derivative heroin.

MEDICINAL USES

Field poppy seeds sprinkled out of their ripe capsules were once believed to give energy and foresight and so were treasured and stored for use throughout the year.

Field poppy petals placed wet over a pimple or spot or insect bite and left there to dry, will soothe it and take the hot inflammation away. Victorian ladies crushed red field poppy petals to a pulp and rubbed them into their nails to give them a pink colour, and in medieval times the pulp was used on warts.

Poppy petals steeped in vinegar for 10 days make a soothing addition to the bath to ease itches and rashes. To make **poppy petal vinegar** for the bath, take 1 bottle white grape vinegar and carefully push into it as many petals as it can hold. The petals will colour the vinegar pink and deep red as the vinegar blanches them. Keep it in a warm place out of direct sunlight for 10 days. Give it a daily shake, then strain, discard the old petals, rebottle, add 4 or 5 fresh ones for identification and cork well.

Caution: Do not eat or use the opium poppy in medicine. All parts of the opium poppy except the fully ripe seeds are dangerous.

CULTIVATION

All poppies need full sun and light, well-dug soil that is fairly rich, a weekly watering in late winter and spring and a twice weekly watering as spring warms up. Sprinkle the tiny seeds over moist, well-dug, well-composted soil in full sun in early autumn. Cover lightly with small leaves scattered to maintain the moisture. Keep lightly watered daily until they establish and become robust. Thereafter water twice weekly. Collect the seed heads for dried flower arrangements and use the petals lavishly to decorate salads and fruit salads.

CULINARY

Poppy Brandy, p. 143
Red Salad with Poppy Seed Vinaigrette, p. 100
Poppy Petal Muffins, p. 101

PRICKLY PEAR

Opuntia ficus-indica ● Cactus pear

The rather prehistoric-looking prickly pear, or cactus pear as it is now known, is native to Mexico and parts of North and South America, and has become naturalised in most hot, dry countries across the world. It even flourishes in the great beds of volcanic lava near Sicily and in the coastal areas of the Mediterranean. The exotic, egg-shaped flowers emerge along the rims of the leaves in midsummer, their frill of bright petals topping a large, juicy, swollen calyx filled with pulp. All parts of this extraordinary plant are edible, but all are covered in tiny thorns, so careful handling is extremely important.

MEDICINAL USES

The crushed petals are used on insect bites to reduce the swelling and itch. Medical tests have found the petals and calyx to be rich in flavonoids, mucilage, fruit acids and sugars, as well as high quantities of vitamin C. The whole flower is astringent, and in Mexico the peeled, sliced fruit is used to reduce soreness and redness on scratches, grazes and infected wounds. The astringency stops the bleeding and tightens the surrounding tissue. The inner skin that has been peeled from the ripening fruit, thorns carefully removed, is a comforting dressing for wounds, burns, rashes and bites.

Because the whole flower has this extraordinary astringent action, it is used in several countries to soothe and heal the gastro-intestinal tract, for diarrhoea, colitis, irritable bowel syndrome, gastric ulcers, colic, heartburn and flatulence. In many rural areas the whole ripe fruit, which is the entire flower, thorns thoroughly removed, is preserved in a syrup of honey and vinegar for the winter months. In America the fruit is eaten fresh all through the season – which usually lasts 4 months – to treat an enlarged prostrate gland, an effective folk remedy that has often astonished doctors.

The elongated 'stem leaves' from which the other leaves grow can be used as a splint for broken bones. Scrape off the thorns and split the stem leaf in half. Nestle the limb in it and bind in place. A couple of leaves that have been gashed or scraped to release their oily juices, can be tossed into a stagnant pool to get rid of mosquito larvae.

CULTIVATION

It is easily propagated by merely chopping off a leaf and thrusting the stem end into loose, moist soil, where, if it is kept watered, it will sprout strong roots and continue to multiply by bearing more and more fleshy thick leaves. It thrives in heat and drought and withstands wind, hail and storms stoically. Watch out for the brilliant red cochineal bug that was introduced to control the spread of the cactus. Brush the tiny white flecks off with a coarse bristled brush at the first sign. Other than this pest, there is nothing that will cause this remarkable plant to falter in its steady growth.

CULINARY

Prickly Pear Summer Dessert, p. 133
Prickly Pear Salad, p. 101
Prickly Pear Breakfast Dish, p. 101

PUMPKIN, SQUASH AND MARROW FLOWERS

Cucurbita species

All species of pumpkin, marrow and squash are vigorous, easy to grow, rambling vines. An enormous number of cross-bred and closely related species have been grown for millennia in Africa, the Americas and parts of Asia, appearing in Europe only in the sixteenth century, where they developed the huge variety we know today. Marrows and courgettes have more French, English and Italian origins while the tougher, larger pumpkins were grown more widely in the Americas and Africa. Fields of mealies interplanted with pumpkins are a familiar sight in Africa, particularly the huge, flat *boerpampoen* which so resiliently withstands the rigours of the African climate and has always been a standby in times of food scarcity.

MEDICINAL USES

All species flower prolifically and all the flowers are edible. The tender tips of the vines can also be eaten. They are delicious steamed or stir fried and,

along with the flowers, were considered survival foods and were believed to impart strength and fleetness of foot. Hulled pumpkin seeds liquefied with a little milk were traditionally used to treat worm infestations in both humans and animals and this remedy is still used today by rural communities across the world.

The pumpkin, and to a large extent the flower, is rich in vitamins A, B and C, phosphorus, calcium and also contains carbohydrate and protein. It is an alkaline food rich in betacarotene, and the highly nutritious inner kernels of the pips are good for the bladder and kidneys and for prostate problems.

External applications of hot pumpkin over a boil or abscess were an ancient method of bringing a boil to a head, although one should be careful here not to make it too hot. I have used this many times on the farm over suppurating wounds, for animals as well, and I am always amazed at its healing qualities. Rural people spread mashed pumpkin over grazes and scrapes, held in place with a pumpkin flower that has been split open and bound in place with a crêpe bandage. The leaves are not used as they irritate the skin with their prickly texture.

CULTIVATION

All species of *Cucurbita* are annual. Seed should be sown after the last frosts have passed, and all need full sun and well-composted soil. Space 50 cm apart and water often until the plants are well established. Thereafter they need very little attention apart from a twice weekly watering. They can be left to trail or trained over fences and arches. For me no summer is complete without a few vines somewhere in the vegetable garden or even in the back border.

CULINARY

Pumpkin Flower Soup. p. 101
Stuffed Squash Flower Salad, p. 102
Baked Pumpkin with Stuffed Pumpkin
    Flowers, p. 116

ROCKET

Eruca vesicaria sativa ● Rock salad ● Roquette

Rocket has recently undergone a huge revival in popularity, although it has been cultivated since the Middle Ages. It is native to the Mediterranean area and was first prized by the Romans, who used the pungent-tasting leaves lavishly in their banquets and chewed the seeds, believing that their hot, biting taste would give them vigour and energy. Fascinatingly, rocket plants have germinated after the excavation of Roman courtyard gardens, as the seeds have become exposed after centuries of lying dormant. Rocket is still a tremendously popular herb in Italy, and perhaps it is the Italians with their culinary flair who in recent times have reintroduced it to the rest of the world.

MEDICINAL USES

Interestingly, the seeds have been used through the centuries to treat bruises and sprains. Crushed seeds were spread on top of a warmed, folded bandage (warm by wringing it out in hot water)

and held against the skin without allowing the seeds to touch the skin. Crushed petals were also used to treat skin blemishes by pounding them into a pulp and spreading the softened mixture over the area, squeezing the juice so it covered the blemish completely.

Some ancient herbals record that rocket was eaten in Elizabethan times before a whipping to alleviate the pain, and with its very high vitamin and mineral content, including potassium and silica, it is possible that there are some painkilling components in the leaves, although scientific research has yet to verify this.

In medieval times rocket flowers and green seeds were crushed with honey and taken a little at a time as a cough syrup. In some ancient herbal recipes sage and parsley were included in the pungent mixture. To make the **cough syrup**, mix equal quantities of flowers, leaves and honey, crush and pound to a paste. Take one teaspoon at a time. Chew it well and then swallow half a glass of water to wash it all down.

Medieval monks were not allowed to grow rocket in the cloister gardens as it was considered to be a dangerous aphrodisiac! No longer regarded a sexual stimulant, rocket is nevertheless considered to be an invigorating tonic herb in Europe and doctors still prescribe it for those who are overtired and anxious. To make a **tea** use ¼ cup rocket flowers and ¼ cup fresh parsley and pour over this 1 cup boiling water. Stand 5 minutes, strain and sprinkle with ¼ teaspoon cayenne pepper and sip slowly.

CULTIVATION

Rocket is a fast-growing annual and once you have it in the garden it will reseed itself vigorously, often two or three times during the summer. It demands little attention, growing quickly and easily and thriving in well-composted soil in full sun, but also does well in rocky places with poor soil and scant moisture.

CULINARY
Rocket and Chicken Liver Pâté, p. 102
Mushroom and Rocket Soup, p. 102
Potato and Ham Frittata with Rocket, p. 102

ROSE

Rosa species

The rose is without doubt the most loved of all flowers across the world. Roses date back thousands of years, and through the centuries have been revered for both their fragrance and their medicinal and cosmetic properties.

Both the ancient Greeks and Romans used both rose petals and hips in cooking and preserved the petals in vinegar. The Romans used the rose for ceremonial purposes and built the first hot houses to ensure blooms all year round, controlling the temperature with pipes of hot water.

MEDICINAL USES

Rose petal tea has a calming, tranquillising effect. To make the tea, pour 1 cup of boiling water over ¼ cup of fresh, unsprayed rose petals. Leave to stand for 5 minutes. Strain and enjoy. Sweeten with a touch of honey if liked.

Rose-water dates back to AD 980-1037, when the Arab physician Avicenna used it to treat skin ailments and mixed it with honey for use as a cough syrup. Boil the 6 cups rose petals, a small twist of lemon rind and 4 cloves gently in 1 litre water for 15 minutes, with the lid on. Remove from the heat, strain and pour into glass bottles with screw tops. Rose-water may be splashed on the outside of the eyes in cases of conjunctivitis. It has an antisceptic and soothing quality and can be used even on sensitive skins.

Rosa gallica, which is native to the Middle East, was used in the Middle Ages as a treatment for depression and anxiety and to aid circulation. Modern medical research has proven these properties and the precious rose oil, known as attar of roses, is used nowadays in aromatherapy for these very same ailments.

The rose hip forms once the petals have fallen and the swollen calyx ripens, and can be used in cough mixtures, syrups, jellies and jams. Its high vitamin C content as well as fruit acids, and betacarotene, pectin and tannin content boosts the body's immune system and makes an excellent tonic that will give energy and vitality and strengthen the artery walls, thus aiding circulation.

CULTIVATION

There is a rose for every type of garden and for every gardener's taste. My favourite roses, however, are the old-fashioned roses of which the exquisite, fragrant, shell-pink Margaret Roberts is a member (see photograph). Roses ask for very little – all they need is a large, deep hole in the full sun, filled with compost and a sprinkling of the moisture absorbent crystals that will keep the plant from drying out. It requires a deep, twice weekly watering, feeding with an organic fertiliser two or three times a year and a good mulch of compost during the winter. Pruning is essential in midwinter and deadheading should never be neglected to ensure masses of blooms.

CULINARY

Rose Hip Syrup, p. 143
Rose Petal Cream Jelly, p. 134
Rose Punch, p. 143
Rose Petal Syrup, p. 144

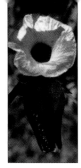

ROSELLE

Hibiscus sabdariffa

Also known as Rosella, Indian sorrel, Jamaican sorrel, Florida cranberry, Oseille rouge and Flor de Jamaica, roselle is a spectacular annual that reaches about 2 metres in height with pretty, pale cream flowers typical of hibiscus. Native to India and across south east Asia, it is believed to have been taken to Africa and the West Indies by slaves. The earliest recording of the plant was by the Flemish botanist M de l'Obel, in 1576, and the edibility of the leaves and flowers was documented in Java in around 1682. It is used primarily as a colouring and flavouring in food, and has been grown sporadically as a commercial crop in various parts of the world.

MEDICINAL USES

It is a rewarding plant to grow as all parts are edible. Roselle's added benefits are its high vitamin C content, numerous amino acids and high iron and potassium content. It is good for coughs, colds and sore throats, and the seeds can be roasted for coffee. It is a good diuretic, it stimulates the digestive processes, it is anti-spasmodic and antibacterial and a good tonic, building blood and boosting the immune system.

A strong **lotion** of roselle flowers and calyxes is beautifully astringent and excellent for refining pores, cleansing oily problem skin and dabbing onto blemishes and inflamed spots. Simmer 1 cup of roselle flowers and calyxes in 2 litres of water with 10 cloves and 1 stick of cinnamon for 20 minutes with the lid on. Leave to cool. Strain. Add 3 tablespoons witch hazel bought from your chemist. Pour into a sterilised screw-top bottle and shake well. Use on a pad of cotton wool as a cleansing lotion after washing the face.

Roselle gargle for sore and strained throats: Boil ½ cup roselle flowers and calyxes in 1 litre of water with ½ cup sage leaves and the juice and rind of 2 lemons. Simmer gently for 10 minutes with the lid on. Cool and strain. Use as a gargle and also sip and swallow a little frequently. You can sweeten it with honey if liked.

One of my favourite teas is the sour-tasting astringent, energising bright red tea made from the brilliant calyxes of the roselle. The fresh or dried calyx makes a magnificent **health tea** (see recipe on p. 144) that soothes a cold, clears a sore throat, stops a cough, opens the nose, and clears up mucous. It is astringent, so full of vitamin C it clears skin conditions like acne, and tastes so refreshing you'll use it as a base for cooldrinks.

CULTIVATION

Roselle is a quick, prolific annual that will do well in just about any soil as long as it is well dug, has full sun and a twice weekly watering. I sow seeds in autumn and keep them protected for planting out in spring – it is very frost tender – and then I sow again in October for a late summer crop.

68

ROSEMARY

Rosmarinus officinalis

One of the world's best loved herbs, rosemary gets its name from the Latin *rosmaris*, meaning 'dew of the sea'. It is native to southern Europe and particularly the Mediterranean area, and has been used by cooks and apothecaries for centuries. Rosemary is traditionally a symbol of fidelity between lovers, as well a symbol of remembrance. It is carried in brides' bouquets and used in wedding arrangements and wreaths, and given to friends to strengthen friendship and commitment.

MEDICINAL USES

Rosemary is an antiseptic, it stimulates the circulation and eases aching rheumatic joints and stiff muscles. It is antispasmodic, antibacterial and a remarkable restorative herb, aiding recovery from long-term stress and chronic illness. It is an energising, uplifting, stimulating herb, associated with raising low blood pressure and lowering and levelling high blood pressure. It is helpful for depression, headaches and premenstrual tension, and is also an excellent anti-inflammatory, astringent, tonic herb and scalp treatment.

Rosemary tea is excellent as an antiseptic gargle and a mouthwash. It tightens the gums and clears halitosis and any mouth infections. Sipped in small amounts, rosemary tea eases flatulence, stimulates the smooth muscles of the digestive tract and the gall bladder, thus increasing the flow of bile. To make **rosemary tea**, steep 1 thumb length fresh sprig of rosemary flowers and leaves in 1 cup boiling water. Let stand for 5 minutes, strain and sip slowly.

Use rosemary **lotion** for acne and skin problems. Boil 1 cup fresh flowering rosemary sprigs in 1½ litres of water for 15 minutes with the lid on. Cool, strain and apply on soaked cotton wool pads after washing the face.

One of rosemary's astonishing effects is that of stimulating hair growth even after chemotherapy. **Rosemary hair restorer**: Boil 3 cups of rosemary leaves and flowers in 2 litres of water for 15 to 20 minutes with the lid on, giving it an occasional stir. Cool, strain and store in the fridge. Use as a rinse after shampooing and massage into the scalp daily with pads of cotton wool soaked in the lotion.

CULTIVATION

Rosemary is a dense, woody prolific shrub that reaches about 1 metre in spread and height. All it requires is a well-dug, richly composted hole in full sun and a deep weekly watering.

Propagation is by cuttings at any time of the year. Take slips about 7 cm long, strip off the lower leaves and root the sprigs in wet sand. Once they have rooted, plant the new plants a metre apart. Other than the occasional clipping into shape, rosemary needs no attention.

CULINARY

Lamb Chops with Rosemary, p. 116
Grilled Rosemary Sosaties, p. 117
Tiramisu with Rosemary, p. 134

ROSE-SCENTED GERANIUM

Pelargonium graveolens

The great *Pelargonium* genus originates in South Africa, and all species are wonderfully fragrant. They were introduced into England in the mid-seventeenth century and from there spread throughout Europe. The scent of the leaves ranges from rose to peppermint, pine to spice, nutmeg to citrus, and chocolate to apple, and just lightly crushing a leaf will release the glorious fragrance. Today pelargoniums are widespread throughout the world and are valued as both pot and bedding plants.

MEDICINAL USES

Rose geranium leaves and flowers are anti-depressant, antiseptic, anti-inflammatory, diuretic, fungicidal and deodorant. In my work as a physio-therapist, I made a massage cream for aching muscles, stiff necks and arthritic aches and pains using geranium. To this day I am never without a jar or two.

Rose geranium massage cream: In a double boiler combine 1 cup of rose geranium leaves and flowers with 1 cup of boiling water, 1 cinnamon stick, 6 crushed cardamom pods, 6 crushed cloves and 2 teaspoons of anise seeds. Simmer for 10-15 minutes, stirring frequently. Cool for 10 minutes and strain. Discard the leaves and spices, add 1 tablespoon almond oil, 1 teaspoon vitamin E oil and 6 drops of rose-geranium essential oil. Mix well and pour into sterilised screw-top jars.

The tiny, exquisitely marked flowers have the same taste and fragrance as the leaves and can be made into soothing, calming teas and drinks that help to lessen the onslaught of the frenetic pace at which so many of us live. A cup of **rose-scented geranium tea** made with a quarter of a cup of fresh leaves, and flowers too if you like, steeped in 1 cup of boiling water for 5 minutes, then strained and sipped slowly, will calm and relax you.

Rose geranium wash: This is excellent for oily and problem skins. Tie a big handful of rose-scented geranium leaves and flowers in a bunch with an elastic band, pour 2 litres of boiling water over it and, holding the bunch by its stems, swish it around in the water for a few minutes. Leave the bunch in the water to cool until pleasantly warm. Then, after cleaning the face with a good cold cream, wash the face with this scented lotion as a final rinse.

CULTIVATION

Growing scented geraniums is easy. Cuttings broken off and rooted in wet sand strike remarkably easily and this can be done at any time of the year, except during the coldest months. Plant them in a sunny position with a little compost in the early stages and keep them protected until they are sturdy. They require no more than a weekly watering once they are established. Cut the plants back at the end of the growing season to prevent them from becoming straggly and untidy and make a mass of cuttings for new plants with the clippings.

CULINARY
Rose-scented Geranium Mousse, p. 133
Rose-scented Geranium Filo Baskets, p. 134
Rose-scented Geranium Mashed Potatoes, p. 103

SAGE

Salvia officinalis

The genus name Salvia is derived from the Latin *salvare*, meaning 'to cure', and sage's medicinal properties have been respected for centuries. It is native to the Mediterranean area and the Romans considered it to be a sacred herb, gathering it with great reverence and ceremony. The Chinese held sage in just such reverence and valued it so greatly that Dutch merchants in the seventeenth century recorded that the Chinese would trade three chests of China tea for one chest of sage leaves.

MEDICINAL USES

An ancient remedy for a sore throat was a gargle made from sage leaves and flowers, and sage was mixed with honey and lemon juice as a remedy for coughs and chest ailments. To make this **cough remedy**, chop 1 tablespoon of fresh sage leaves and a few flowers very fine. Mix in 1 tablespoon of runny honey and 1 tablespoon of lemon juice. For a runny nose, grate in two

teaspoons of fresh ginger root. Mix well. Take 1 teaspoon at a time frequently during the day.

Sage has been found to contain oestrogen, and as such is used to treat irregular menstruation and the symptoms of menopause, including hot flushes and lowered oestrogen levels.

Sage also has some antibiotic properties, which is probably why it is so effective in clearing a sore throat and excess mucous from the nose, throat and chest. It was traditionally used as an asthma remedy, and with its excellent digestive and calming action, it immediately soothes the spasm and anxiety. It is a nerve tonic, and with its natural astringency it helps diarrhoea, abdominal cramps and colic. For all these ailments it should be taken as a tea. The **standard brew** is ¼ cup fresh flowers and leaves in 1 cup of boiling water, allowed to stand for 5 minutes, then strained. Add a touch of honey to sweeten, and a squeeze of fresh lemon juice. The usual dose during infections is 1 cup three times a day. As a general tonic take 1 cup daily, but give it a break of 4 to 5 days every 10 days.

Caution: Sage is best avoided during pregnancy and by epileptics.

CULTIVATION

It takes fairly easily from mature cuttings but does not like wet feet, so once your cuttings have rooted in moist sand, plant them out in individual pots in a well-drained mixture of compost and sand to strengthen. Plant them out 50 cm apart in the garden in a well-drained position in full sun. Water only once a week, as sage will not thrive during long periods of rain or under a watering system. It needs no attention except for the odd trim of spent flowers or untidy growth. Replace the plants every 3 to 4 years. Sage does well in large pots, but make sure that these too are well drained.

CULINARY

Sage Flowers and Bacon Crisp, p. 117
Sage and Pumpkin Soup, p. 103
Sage Flower Eggnog, p. 144

SNAPDRAGON

Antirrhinum majus

The snapdragon is indigenous to Europe and has been a much loved garden plant since before the Middle Ages, when it was considered an antidote against witchcraft. In Russia from the fifteenth century it was cultivated for the oil found in the seeds, which is said to be as pure and as healthy as virgin olive oil. Much folklore surrounds the flowers, which open obligingly when lightly squeezed to look just like a dragon's mouth. This little mouth acts as an insect trap, which closes once the insect has entered, trapping it inside. For this reason snapdragons were often planted alongside grains and vegetables as a protection for the crop in days gone by.

MEDICINAL USES

A **cream** for rashes and sunburn is made by simmering 1 cup of chopped snapdragon leaves and flowers in 1 cup of good aqueous cream in a double boiler for 20 minutes. Strain and mix in 2 teaspoons of vitamin E oil and store in a sterilised jar. This will soothe hot, irritated areas. At the end of a hot spring day outdoors where sunburn and windburn have taken their toll, the following **soothing lotion** will quickly calm the skin. Boil up 3 cups of snapdragon flowers and leaves in 2 litres of water for 15 minutes. Strain and add this to a warm bath or dab onto the area.

Remarkably effective for all types of inflammation, crushed warmed flowers mixed into a little almond oil will soothe aching sprains, strains, throbbing haemorrhoids and skin rashes and redness. Warm cotton cloths by wrapping them around a hot water bottle, spread with the mixture and place over an aching back or stiff shoulder or neck. Place the hot water bottle against the area and relax for 15 minutes. This will bring quick relief and soothe away anxiety and discomfort.

A gargle for mouth ulcers was made of the flowers and a few leaves, and for concert and opera singers snapdragon tea was once considered to be the most effective remedy for an aching, tired, strained throat. Perhaps its chemical content of mucilage, pectin, gallic acid and resin would account for its soothing anti-inflammatory action. Make the **tea** by pouring 1 cup of boiling water over ¼ cup of fresh flowers and a few leaves, and leave to stand for 5 to 6 minutes. Strain, sweeten with a touch of honey and sip slowly, gargle a little, then swallow.

CULTIVATION

It is best to sow the seed in autumn for a spring and early summer show. Treat it as an annual and sow the seed each year in a different area. Plant out the thumb-length seedlings in well-composted soil in full sun 20 cm apart and keep them moist until they establish well. Each flowering spike reaches 50 cm in height and mass plantings give a magnificent show. Snapdragons do not like hot weather.

CULINARY

Spring Pasta with Snapdragons, p. 117
Pan Fried Pork with Snapdragons, p. 118
Mulberry and Snapdragon Dessert, p. 134

St John's wort

Hypericum perforatum

Much has been written about this ancient and much revered plant, and research is still being conducted into its remarkable medicinal properties. In ancient times it was believed to have magical properties, and it was universally known as 'The Grace of God'. The crusaders took it, along with yarrow and borage, on their crusades as a pain reliever and styptic, and modern research has found these ancient uses to be medically sound.

Medicinal uses

Hypericum perforatum is not to be confused with the other *Hypericums*, including our own indigenous *H. revolutum*, which are unsafe to use medicinally. Dubbed 'Nature's Prozac', owing to its anti-depressant properties, it has also been found to be beneficial for menopause symptoms, liver and gall bladder ailments, anxiety, back pain, cold sores, chicken pox, shingles, neuralgia, stiff, aching joints and muscles, lack of vitality, stress and insomnia. It has been found to be so extraordinarily valuable for

its antiviral properties that it is at present being researched as a possible treatment for Aids.

Both an external and internal application of St John's Wort is effective. A **tea** made of the flowering tops is the easiest way to take it. Pour 1 cup of boiling water over ¼ cup of fresh flowers and buds. Leave to stand for 5 minutes, then strain, sweeten with honey if desired, and add a squeeze of lemon juice. Use this tea for any of the ailments listed above and add 1 tablespoon of sage leaves and flowers for coughs, colds and menopausal symptoms.

An effective **massage cream** can be made for rashes, grazes, insect bites, cold sores, minor burns, cramp and neuralgia, aching muscles, sciatica and backache. Simmer 1 cup of flowering tops in 1 cup of aqueous cream in a double boiler for 20 minutes, then strain. Add 2 teaspoons of vitamin E oil, mix well and pour into sterilised jars with well-fitting lids. Store any excess cream in the fridge and rub frequently onto the affected area.

Caution: Taking St John's Wort for some time may cause dermatitis in people with sensitive skin once the skin is exposed to the sun.

Cultivation

Growing this unobtrusive, tiny-leafed perennial groundcover is not easy. Although it prefers the cool, damp meadows of its native Europe and Britain it will do fairly well even in poor, sandy soil to which a little compost has been added, with afternoon shade. Once it is established and with a twice weekly watering, it will send up 45 cm tall flowering heads of tiny, yellow flowers. It is these bright flowering heads that are used medicinally. Propagate St John's wort by digging off a small piece with a sharp spade and replanting it immediately in a well-dug and lightly composted spot in full sun. Keep it moist for a week or two until it is well established and then water twice weekly.

Culinary

Beetroot and St John's Wort Health Salad, p. 104
Potato and St John's Wort Bake, p. 104
Stuffed Avocados with St John's Wort, p. 104

STRAWBERRY FLOWERS

Fragaria vesca species

The strawberry is unlike any other fruit in that the seeds are on the outside, and the fleshy fruit is actually the receptacle or pod. It is indigenous to Europe and America, and cultivation began in the early fourteenth century, using *fraises du bois*, literally 'strawberries of the forest', as the mother stock. From these the largest fruiting plants were kept, selected on the basis of flavour and sweetness. There are now literally hundreds of varieties of strawberry, particular to each country, so there are species suitable for all climates. Modern strawberries are based on *Fragaria chiloensis* and *F. virginiana*, which is indigenous to America. The exquisite Pink Panda is a hybrid with bright pink flowers.

MEDICINAL USES

Strawberry flowers and fruits are used in the cosmetic industry as extracts in oils and creams, and a beautiful astringent **face mask** can be inexpensively made by crushing fruit and flowers together and applying them directly to the face after washing it well. Lie still for 15 minutes and let the fragrant pulp do its work, clearing oiliness and blackheads, healing pimples, closing and refining the pores, and soothing rashes. A **tea** of leaves and flowers can also be made to help clear the skin. Use the tea as a **lotion** to splash onto the face after the strawberry face mask has been rinsed off in tepid water, and make an extra cup to drink – it is pleasant and easily digested. The **standard brew** is 1 cup of boiling water poured over ¼ cup of fresh strawberry leaves and a few flowers, left to stand for 5 minutes, then strained and sipped slowly.

The fruit of the strawberry is exceptionally rich in vitamins A, C and K, folic acid, betacarotene and potassium, and to a certain extent so are the leaves, flowers and the root. It has been used medicinally since ancient times, particularly for treating diabetes, cancer and uricaemia, and modern science has found that all parts of the strawberry plant have antiviral and antibacterial properties. A tea of leaves and flowers is also considered to be beneficial to the liver, kidneys and bladder and in America it is often prescribed for cystitis, and for mouth ulcers and gingivitis. Fresh fruits rubbed onto the teeth are said to whiten them and at the same time will clear any gum infections. Strawberry leaves and flowers were once used as a tea for treating typhoid, and today this same standard brew tea is used to treat diarrhoea, gastric ailments and jaundice.

CULTIVATION

Growing strawberries is easy. All varieties require well-composted, rich soil, full sun, a deep watering twice weekly and a straw mulch once the fruits start to form. Pine needles and pine bark make a superb mulch, and the strong scent of the pine needles is also a natural insect repellent. Plant each plant 40 cm apart and replace the mother plant every alternate year with new young runners.

CULINARY

Strawberry Tonic Wine, p. 144
Pink Panda Pink Punch, p. 144
Pink Panda Pashka, p. 135

SUNFLOWER

Helianthus annuus

The stately sunflower has been a valuable crop since ancient times, cultivated first in South America, particularly Peru, some 3 000 years ago. It is native to South and North America and possibly Mexico, and in ancient Peru it was an emblem of the Inca sun god. In the sixteenth century the sunflower was introduced to Spain from North America by explorers.

Sunflowers are a quickly maturing crop and fields of sunflowers are a breathtaking sight in summer, all turning their magnificent, glorious heads to face the sun as it moves from east to west. Bees love sunflowers because of their nectar and pollen and the seeds are favoured by many seed-eating birds.

MEDICINAL USES

Sunflower oil is one of the most versatile of all cooking oils, and is mild, bland and rich in linoleic acid, oleic and palmitic acids, and is also high in vitamins E, A and D. Like all oils rich in linoleic acid, particularly borage and evening primrose oil, it inhibits the dangerous build up of cholesterol deposits.

The young flowering buds are highly nutritious and were a favourite food of the Incas. The buds, as well as the maturing flower petals, contain traces of zinc, betacarotene, vitamins E, B3, B6, B1, B2, magnesium and manganese and chromium. The seeds are a superb health food, containing the same vitamins as the buds and petals, as well as calcium, potassium, phosphorus and iron in abundance. Hulled sunflower seeds are said to be diuretic and expectorant. A handful can be eaten once or twice a day and they are delicious raw or roasted in home-made breakfast cereals such as muesli.

The unhulled seeds can also be boiled and taken as a **tea**. Add 2 tablespoons of unhulled seeds to 2 cups of water and simmer for 20 minutes. Cool and strain. Take ½ cup twice a day.

Sunflower oil, seeds and young flowers are also believed to help in the formation of healthy tissue, to boost the immune system and to keep the joints supple. Interestingly, all parts of the sunflower are being tested to aid the regeneration of tissue in the kidneys after infectious kidney diseases and kidney stones. The leaves are being tested for malaria and can be taken as a **tea**. Use ½ cup chopped fresh leaves in 2 cups boiling water and leave to draw for 5 minutes. Strain and sip warm or cold throughout the day.

CULTIVATION

Sunflowers are an easy to grow annual and growing them is very rewarding. In spring dig over a patch of soil in full sun, add plenty of compost and water it well. Press the large seeds singly into the moist soil 20-30 cm apart and about 3 cm deep. Keep the soil moist with a light mulch of dry leaves, and do not allow it to dry out.

CULINARY

Sunflower Buds with Mustard Sauce, p. 118
Marinated Sunflower Bud Parcels, p. 118
Beetroot and Sunflower Petal Salad, p. 104

THYME

Thymus vulgaris ● *Thymus citriodorus*

Thyme is one of the world's favourite culinary herbs and one so common that one hardly stops to think of its amazing medicinal properties. *Thymus vulgaris*, or common thyme, and *T. citriodorus*, lemon thyme, are cultivated varieties of the mother of thyme, *T. serpyllum*, which is native to southern Europe. Thyme is a member of the Labiatae family, which cross pollinates easily, so there are literally hundreds of varieties of thyme. All seem to have similar properties and have been used medicinally by many cultures through the centuries. The Egyptians used thyme oil for embalming, the ancient Greeks and Romans used it in their baths and as incense in their churches.

MEDICINAL USES

Thyme is a superb antiseptic and tonic and a pleasant-tasting infusion of lemon thyme with a slice of lemon and a teaspoon of honey is a comforting treatment for a sore throat, cough and chest cold. Added to your daily food, thyme acts as a good digestive, boosts the immune system to fight colds and flu and helps build up energy and vitality. In days gone by, savoury teas of thyme, red pepper and lemon juice were drunk to ward off colds and to keep warm and fit during the long cold winters. A few carrots, a stick of celery and chopped onions were added to make a nourishing soup to clear chest infections, backache, coughs and bronchitis, and thyme is still used in this way today.

All the thymes are superb for treating fungal infections, whooping cough, pneumonia, asthma and hayfever, especially in children, worms in children and animals, as an expectorant to clear mucous from the body and for soothing muscular aches and pains. A lotion made of the cooled tea will soothe insect bites and stings, hot, sore eczema areas, and will help ringworm, athlete's foot, thrush, scabies and lice infestation. It is rich in thymol, which is a most effective antifungal, and this together with several flavonoids will relieve rheumatism and muscle spasms like stiff neck and cramps. All the thymes taken as a tea will impart a feeling of vitality and energy and relieve muscular and mental tiredness. The **standard brew** is 1 cup of boiling water poured over ¼ cup of fresh thyme sprigs, flowering ones included, infused for 5 minutes, then strained. Sip slowly.

CULTIVATION

Generally all thymes are easy to grow. They all need full sun and are not fussy about soil type, but they flourish in well-drained, sandy soil with a good bit of compost dug into it. They love hot, dry conditions and demand little except a good weekly watering and the occasional cutting back. Propagation is by small, rooted sprigs taken from the mother plant every 2 or 3 years. These should be kept protected in moist, shaded, well-composted bags until they are strong enough to take full sun, and subsequently planted out in the garden.

CULINARY

Thyme Immune-boosting Soup, p. 104
Thyme Flower and Savoury Fish, p. 119
Thyme Salt, p. 148

TUBEROSE

Polianthes tuberosa

The tuberose is a fairly rarely grown, 'old world' bulbous plant with an exceptional fragrance. In the late seventeenth and early eighteenth century the first bulbs were taken from Central America to Morocco, then to Egypt and France, where they are still in cultivation for their glorious, rich and hugely expensive oil. Pure absolute extraction of tuberose is the most expensive natural flower oil in the world, literally worth its weight in gold, and is used for the most exquisite perfumes mainly from France. One flowering head of tall, creamy white, lily-like flowers will scent an entire room with its haunting fragrance for a week.

MEDICINAL USES

The tuberose was used centuries ago in China to calm stomach disorders caused by anxiety and around the twelfth century recipes included the flowers in soothing teas for over-excited children and for nausea, vomiting and fevers. In Egypt, boiling water poured over the flowers was used as a **lotion** for skin oiliness, acne and enlarged pores. The most effective ratio is 2 cups of boiling water poured over 1 cup of flowers and buds, left to stand until cool, then strained and used as a mist in a bottle with a spray mechanism, or as a lotion.

Tuberose oil has been used for the last few years with astonishing results as a treatment for stress, hypersensitivity, anger, hostility, resentment, disorientation, emotional conflict and confusion. Tuberose is becoming an important healing oil, offering stability and counteracting drug and alcohol addiction, calming anger and resentment, alleviating burnout, dissipating anxiety and lifting the spirits. It is being researched for treating the emotions in terminal illnesses, particularly Aids and cancer.

A single flower added to a cup of green tea immediately imparts its rich oils and fragrance and this calms and settles a wildly beating, anxious heart. Taken as an after dinner tea, it will ease digestion and make even the most stressful day dissolve into restful calm – an ancient Chinese secret!

An easy to make **cream** does wonders for dry, brittle nails. Simmer 1 cup of chopped flowers in 1 cup of good aqueous cream for 20 minutes, then strain and add 2 teaspoons of vitamin E oil. Mix well and store in a sterilised jar. Massage frequently into the nails and cuticles.

CULTIVATION

Growing tuberose is easy, as the bulb is perennial. It needs well-dug, well-composted soil in full sun and the bulbs should be spaced 20 cm apart. A single stem 40-50 cm tall rises through the slender tuft of pale green leaves, topped with a mass of buds and flowers. The buds are palest pink and the flowers creamy white. Divide the clump every 2 years once it has flowered and replant the little corms or bulbs in new ground. The cycle usually takes 2 years and the bulbs can be planted in succession.

CULINARY

Tuberose and Pineapple Cordial, p. 144
Tuberose Vegetable Soup, p. 104
Tuberose Fridge Cake, p. 135

TULIP

Tulipa species

The tulip is a popular cool weather bulb indigenous to Persia and the name derives from the Turkish word *tulipan* or *turband*, indicating its turban-shaped flower. Its Latin name is *Tulipa gesnerana*. The bulbs have been in cultivation for over a thousand years, and it has always been the symbol of perfect love. Tulips grew wild along the Bosphorus and young men supposedly gathered them to send as symbols of love to girls in the harems beyond the palace gates, and this is probably where its symbolism began. In 1556 tulip bulbs were taken to Vienna, and from there to France and finally Holland, with which tulips have become synonymous.

Cooking with tulips dates back to the end of the sixteenth century, when the unopened buds were cooked with peas or finely cut green beans. The petals were also sugared and eaten with syrup as a dessert. Owing to the increase in exotic vegetables on offer in the world's market places today, this charming practice has mainly died out.

MEDICINAL USES

There are only a few references to poultices of tulip petals in ancient herbals. Perhaps the flowers were so expensive even then that they were not crushed for medicine. However, for burns, skin rashes, insect bites and bee stings a soothing **poultice** of the petals was used. Warm 4 flowers in hot water and break off the petals. While still hot roll the petals in a warm, wet towel to soften them, unroll and place the crushed petals over the area. Hold in place with the hot towel for 10 minutes. Some recipes suggest smoothing on a little castor oil to the burn or insect bite first before placing the petals over the area.

In the seventeenth century young girls crushed red tulip petals and rubbed them into their cheeks so that the petals would impart their colour, and the juice would help to clear up any spots.

Given that tulip growers in Holland still use crushed petals and the juice from the base of the flower to soothe scratches and rough skin on work-worn hands, it seems surprising that a hand and nail cream containing tulip extracts has not yet been formulated by an enterprising grower.

CULTIVATION

Tulips can be used to great effect in the spring garden, particularly when massed in areas of a single colour. The bulbs should be planted in late autumn when the soil has cooled down, spaced 15 cm apart in full sun, in well-dug, richly composted soil with a cooling mulch of rotted leaves. Water deeply twice a week to ensure uniform growth. The bulbs will take about 9 to 10 weeks to flower. Modern bulbs are cold treated and seldom excel after their first year of blooming, which means that new bulbs should be planted every year. Some tulip experts shade their bulbs between 11 am and 3 pm in autumn to keep them cool.

CULINARY

Tulip Syrup, p. 135
Tulips Stuffed with Chicken Mayonnaise, p. 119
Three Bean Salad with Tulips, p. 105

VIOLET

Viola odorata

The sweet violet is an ancient plant that has been grown and loved all over the world for centuries. It is native to Britain and widespread throughout Europe and Asia, and records of sweet violet from the first century AD in Turkey, Syria and Persia suggest that it is native to these areas as well. The violet was a favourite flower in ancient Greece and became the symbol of Athens, the flower of Aphrodite, the goddess of love, and also the flower of her son Priapus, the god of gardens and the male procreative power. Homer relates how the Greeks drank violet tea to 'temper their anger', made crowns and garlands of violets to save them from drunkenness and added the flowers to wine to add an extra bouquet.

MEDICINAL USES

The violet was used medicinally by the ancient Greeks and Romans, and later in the fifteenth and sixteenth centuries violet syrup was prescribed for coughs, colds, pneumonia and bronchitis. A tea of violet flowers and leaves soothes a headache and helps one unwind after a heavy and demanding day, and was popular as an after dinner tea in the eighteenth and nineteenth centuries. Violets have a relaxing and calming effect on the nervous system and a tea made of violet leaves and flowers will expel mucous from the nose, chest and lungs, clear mouth and throat infections, open blocked sinuses and will alleviate whooping cough and postnasal drip. To make **violet tea** use ¼ cup flowers and leaves and pour over this 1 cup boiling water. Stand for 5 minutes, strain and sweeten with honey if liked. A strong tea can also be used as a wash for eczema and rashes.

The flowers and leaves can be chewed to relieve a headache – chew 5 at first and take another 3 an hour later. Violets also have a gentle laxative effect, and bruised violet leaves make a soothing poultice for skin infections and inflammations. In Africa violets are used as a cancer remedy and crushed leaves are used as a poultice for skin cancer and growths. This remedy has also been used in Europe since the twelfth century!

CULTIVATION

Growing violets is rewarding, as they demand little and give so much in return. They thrive in cool, partially shady positions in rich, well-composted, moist soil. The clump spreads by runners, which can be separated from the mother plant and planted elsewhere, 30 cm apart. Keep them moist and shaded until they establish. They reach a height of no more than 10 cm and so make a lovely border or groundcover. The flowers are at their best at the end of winter and early spring, and the more you pick the more they bloom. Water deeply twice a week and give them the occasional spade of compost.

CULINARY

Chocolate and Violet Cheese Cake, p. 135
Violet Liqueur, p. 144
Violet Syrup, p. 145

WATERBLOMMETJIE

Aponogeton distachyos ● Cape pond weed

The waterblommetjie, or Cape pond weed, is part of a small genus of monocotyledonous water plants and is one of South Africa's most famous edible plants. Its spectacular free-flowering, forked inflorescences in late winter through to midsummer look like masses of white blossoms scattered over the surface of the water, keeping bees and dragonflies busy. The entire plant is high in vitamins and minerals and the early Cape settlers were taught by the indigenous Khoikhoi to use the plant both medicinally and as a nutritious food. Thanks to enterprising Boland farmers fresh waterblommetjies are now available not only to other provinces, but all over the world. Because they are so tough and adaptable, they are hardy enough to grow in the warmer parts of Europe and the British Isles, where they are fast becoming a popular pond plant.

MEDICINAL USES

Medicinally the San, or Bushmen, used the high juice content of the stems to treat burns, sunburn and rashes. Children growing up in the Cape near dams filled with waterblommetjies used crushed stems and squeezed the juice onto minor cuts, grazes, insect stings, mosquito bites and itchy areas. Leaves were used as a **poultice**, first warmed and washed in hot water and then held in place with a crêpe bandage on sprains or strains, bruised or inflamed areas and rheumatic joints.

For burns and sunburn a **soothing gel** can be made by crushing and mashing the stems and leaves to a pulp and spreading it over the area to form a protective covering. This should be left on for as long as possible, and repeated frequently until the pain and redness subside. For grazes, sores and infected bites the same method can be used. For pimples and acne, crush the flower petals and apply to the spot with a little stem juice and let it dry on the area. Repeat whenever necessary.

CULTIVATION

The tuberous rootstock settles easily into mud or a large compost-filled tub. The slender, oval leaves are about 2 cm long and often mottled with dark speckles, and between them the long flowering stalk with its forked cluster of succulent scales and white petals emerges.

Propagation is by division of the root stock. Slice off a piece that has an eye on it and press it firmly into rich compost mixed with a little sand in a large plastic tub about 40 cm deep. Soak it well and when it has stood for an hour or two to settle, lower it slowly and gently into the pond, deep enough to cover it with about 30 cm of water. It is surprisingly tolerant, but it does need full sun and still water. There it can remain for 2 to 3 years, after which it needs to be lifted, the old soil and compost replaced and the waterblommetjie plants divided again.

CULINARY

Traditional Cape Waterblommetjie Bredie, p. 119
Waterblommetjie Soup, p. 105
Waterblommetjie Stir Fry, p. 119

WATER LILY

Nymphaea alba

The exquisite water lily, woven so often into legend and fairy tales, is an ancient healing plant. Although most herbals describe the white water lily (*Nymphaea alba*), the other colours – red, pink, yellow and the exquisite blue *Nymphaea caerula* from South Africa – are to a large extent also used medicinally and in cooking. The scientific name *Nymphaea* is believed to have derived from the virgins in Greek mythology, with whom the water lily was associated. It was a symbol of purity, chastity and coldness, and in ancient Greece was believed to have anti-aphrodisiac qualities. Modern research has actually proved the opposite to be true!

In the Middle Ages the water lily symbolised the priesthood and young virgins had a water lily painted on their doors. The lilies' manner of rising unblemished, pristine and beautiful from the mud and slime of lakes, still mountain pools and dry water courses after the first rains has symbolised regeneration since the earliest times, as well as immortality, resurrection and life after death.

MEDICINAL USES

The white water lily was used medicinally by monks in Britain from the twelfth century and in the seventeenth century the herbalist Culpeper described it as being 'good for agues', and recorded that a 'syrup of flowers produces rest and settles the brain of frantic persons, the juice from the crushed petals and leaves takes away sunburn and freckles, from the face'. He also noted that the 'oil from the flowers cools hot tumours, eases pains and helps sores'. Interestingly, the leaves and petals have been proved to do just that! The French used the rootstock of both the white and yellow water lily for beermaking in the sixteenth and seventeenth centuries and at about the same time the Irish and Scots used the rootstock to extract a navy blue dye for colouring wool.

Chemical compounds in the flower and rhizome have been found to have tranquillising properties and the stem, juice and leaves are excellent for treating burns, sunburn, eczema and rashes and even freckles, as Culpeper noted. Rhizomes are eaten for their starch content in many parts of the world and the flower graces many a salad in gourmet cuisine the world over.

CULTIVATION

Growing water lilies is very rewarding and can become an engrossing hobby. The rhizome should be firmly planted in a 30 to 40 cm plastic pot with a good mixture of compost and sand and covered with pebbles. Once it has soaked well, it can be lowered into a still water pond in full sun. Divide the clump every 3 years by neatly cutting off the new little rhizomes and replanting them in fresh soil and compost.

CULINARY

Water Lily Salad, p. 105
Water Lily and Apple Dessert, p. 135
Watermelon Balls with Ricotta and Water Lily, p. 105

WINTER SAVORY

Satureja montana

Winter savory is an exceptionally pretty little herb. It forms a bright green, perennial groundcover about 14 cm in height, with a charming cushion-like spread. It makes an ideal path edging, container plant and focal point for hanging baskets. In spring and early summer it is covered with sprays of tiny white flowers that set bees humming and butterflies into a frenzy. The warm sun releases its strong oils and should you step on it, you will instantly be refreshed by its pungent oils that contain precious components like thymol and linalool.

MEDICINAL USES

Native to southern Europe and north Africa, winter savory has been used since ancient times to aid and stimulate digestion and ease colic, flatulence and a feeling of fullness. Herbals from the Middle Ages through to the eighteenth century show that the monks used it with honey to make a strong syrup for digestive problems as well as coughs, colds and chest ailments, and kept it at hand to add to mead as a powerful remedy for these ailments. Modern science has proved those medieval herbalists to be absolutely correct and in recent years doctors at Montpellier Hospital in France ran a series of tests using winter savory and lucerne (alfalfa) as a treatment for coughs, bronchitis, pneumonia, chest infections, asthmatic wheezing and persistent sore throats, and found winter savory to be a superb antiseptic for clearing infection and a powerful antibacterial agent.

Modern research has also found that the essential oil extracted from winter savory is beneficial for *Candida* overgrowth, the fungus that causes thrush, as well as other fungal infections. A **tea** of winter savory drunk twice daily (not during pregnancy) also greatly relieves the condition: use ½ cup fresh flowering tops with 1 cup boiling water, leave to stand for 5 minutes, then strain, sweeten with honey and sip slowly.

For treating winter respiratory ailments, coughs, colds and flu, add ¼ cup of fresh lucerne leaves and flowers to the above tea, sweeten with honey and add a squeeze of lemon juice. During a cold or bronchitis you can drink this three times a day. It will also loosen a cough and clear the nose. Interestingly, the classical Greek physicians Galen and Dioscorides used winter savory with thyme and classified them as heating and drying medicines, prescribing them for clearing mucous from the chest and sinuses. They also considered winter savory to have aphrodisiac qualities, following on from the ancient Egyptians, who used winter savory in love potions.

CULTIVATION

Plant rooted cuttings 50 cm apart in full sun in well-composted, well-dug soil. Winter savory is a most successful companion plant to tomatoes and keeps aphids and whitefly at bay.

CULINARY

Butter Beans and Winter Savory, p. 120
Winter Savory and Vegetable Soup, p. 106
Winter Savory Sauce for Pasta, p. 106

WISTERIA

Wisteria sinensis

This elegant vine with its exquisite pendulous, fragrant flowers in spring has been a much loved garden subject in western countries for a few hundred years. It originates in China, but was named in 1818 after an American physician and philosopher, Casper Wistar, professor of anatomy at the University of Pennsylvania. It had been cultivated in Britain and then later in Switzerland for about 100 years before that. In America it was commonly known as the Carolina kidney bean. *Wisteria floribunda* is a smaller, less showy variety of wisteria from Japan, which is also edible, but it is *Wisteria sinensis* that is commonly found in gardens today.

To the Japanese and Chinese, wisteria is a symbol of friendship and unity within the family, and most Japanese homes have at least one plant in their gardens, however small. Japan's ancient emperors and their retinues took flowering wisteria bonsais on their travels to give to their hosts as a sign of good will and friendship.

MEDICINAL USES

Wisteria flowers contain a sweet, heady nectar, and bees make an extraordinary honey from wisteria, which was used in the sixteenth and seventeenth centuries in Europe to alleviate coughs and dry sore throats. The honey mixed with crushed wisteria blossoms in spring was considered to be an energising, resistance-building tonic. The flowers in spring were used medicinally in a poultice for bruises and throbbing varicose veins. Bottles of fresh flowers and their buds were topped up with wine vinegar, corked and stored in a dark place for use when fresh flowers were not available. Cloths soaked in the mixture could be applied to ease several conditions, including pimples and infected spots.

CULTIVATION

Wisteria is a vigorous deciduous climber, and the sprawling, twisting vine may be trained into a standard or espaliered across a wall, or allowed to sprawl with glorious abandonment over trellises, pergolas and down banks. It does need some restraining, however, as it becomes large and powerful as it ages, but its adaptability to extremes of temperature and its vigorous speed of growth has made it a favourite the world over.

To grow wisteria it is important to obtain a grafted specimen from a nursery, as roots and cuttings could result in pale or small flowers. The plant requires a large, deep, richly composted hole and a position in full sun. Train the tendrils onto supports or twist them around sticks that can be removed once the stems are thick and mature. The buds form in midwinter on the attractive bare, grey branches. Give the vine a good bucket or two of rich compost and a deep weekly watering, which will ensure a mass of blooms. The flowers are followed by compound leaves, which give deep, dense shade all through the summer.

CULINARY

Wisteria Fritters, p. 136
Wisteria and Watercress Spring Salad, p. 106
Wisteria Country Borscht, p. 106

YARROW

Achillea millefolium

Often known as soldier's wound wort, yarrow is a remarkable, ancient herb commonly found in waste areas. It originated in Europe and as its common name implies, has been used since the beginning of time to staunch bleeding. The ancient Greeks used it to heal wounds and during the Trojan War, Achilles is said to have healed the wounds of his warriors by applying crushed yarrow leaves, hence the genus name *Achillea*. On their crusades the crusaders took two herbs with them, borage to give them courage and yarrow to heal their wounds.

Yarrow has always been associated with magic. Yarrow stalks stripped of their leaves and small branches have been used since the time of the druids in the centuries pre-Christ to foretell the future and divine the weather.

MEDICINAL USES

There are many hybrids of yarrow which are also grown for their showiness in the garden, but these are neither edible nor do they have medicinal properties. *Achillea millefolium* is the only edible one, and should not be taken for long periods as the build up can cause irritation to the skin and headaches. It should not be taken by pregnant women.

Through the centuries yarrow has been used in cosmetics as it is an exceptional astringent. Yarrow and chamomile are the only two herbs that contain the rare and exquisite azulene. Yarrow's action is tonic, it brings down fever, promotes sweating, relaxes the peripheral blood vessels, eases premenstrual tension and eases bloated, painful menstruation, restoring it to normal. It is a good anti-inflammatory, anti-spasmodic and anti-allergenic.

In 1597 the herbalist John Gerard noted that chewing the fresh green leaves was a good remedy for toothache, and modern medical science continues to prove these ancient remedies substantially correct and effective. A crushed leaf in the nostril will stop a nose bleed and a poultice of leaves will stop a cut or wound from bleeding.

CULTIVATION

Growing yarrow is easy and it is often grown in the garden for its showy sprays of tiny pink and white flowers, which are long-lasting in the vase. Clumps should be planted 50 cm apart in a sunny spot and will thrive in any type of soil. With compost and a twice weekly watering, the flowering heads will reach 50 cm in height from its perennial clump of fine feathery leaves. It is an excellent plant doctor, and planted next to rare or ailing plants, will give them a health boost and keep aphids away. Just a handful of leaves will speed the decomposition of a barrow load of undecayed compost.

CULINARY

Yarrow Kedgeree, p. 120
Yarrow Stir Fry, p. 120
Yarrow and Pumpkin Bredie, p. 120

YUCCA

Yucca gloriosa

The strange yet appealing yucca is native to the United States, Mexico and the West Indies and is part of the Agavaceae family, many species of which have tough, sword-like leaves. The leaves of the yucca are spiky and stiff and often razor-sharp, rising from the ground or from short woody trunks. In midsummer, huge panicles of exquisite lily-like, white flowers appear, in complete contrast to the leaves, often up to a metre long. These are so long-lasting and so spectacular in appearance, rich and creamy in texture and heady in fragrance, that the yuccas have long been cultivated in gardens and parks across the world as a feature plant.

The yuccas have a remarkable method of pollination. About an hour after dark on a summer evening, they emit a beautiful fragrance that attracts the yucca moth. As the moth darts from flower to flower seeking the fragrance, it burrows against the crown of elongated stamens in the heart of the flower and so fertilises the flowers, which then produce round juicy seeds.

MEDICINAL USES

The seeds, trunk and roots of the yucca contain saponins and have been used for centuries as a wound wash and lotion for rashes, scrapes and burns by American Indians. The roots and fruits were also used for washing hair, treating scalp problems such as hair loss, and soothing insect bites and itchy, raw, sore skin. To make a **soothing lotion** gently boil 2 cups of the mature seeds in 3 litres of water for 20 minutes in a pot with the lid on. Stand aside to cool. Use to wash or dab over the affected area.

Crushed and pounded flower petals have been used to heal sore fingers and cracked skin in harsh, dry climates, and the petals provide relief when packed around cracked heels and over grazes and bruises. Stems and roots boiled in water make a good soapy brew, which was used to wash clothes and soften animal hides to be cut and woven into whips and shoes.

CULTIVATION

As bold garden sculptures yuccas are perfect for landscaping, not only because of their unusual appearance, but because they are so resilient to extremes of weather, including long periods of drought. There are several yucca species used in landscaping. Some are smaller in size but all are edible. *Yucca filamentosa*, or Adam's needle, is a virtually stemless variety with long, curly threads along the edges of the spiky leaves. The species most often planted is *Y. gloriosa*, or Spanish dagger.

Plant yuccas in full sun with two or three buckets of compost. They all quickly adapt to any condition and withstand even poor soil, but with compost and a deep weekly watering, they will produce several towering flowering heads during summer.

CULINARY

Yucca Flower Soup, p. 107
Stuffed Yucca Flowers, p. 121
Yucca and Apple Crumble, p. 136

One can easily become obsessed by flowers – poets, artists and writers all over the world will testify to this. Some of the poems especially are haunting. Many years ago I came across this little poem about the Robinia (see False Acacia, p. 32) by J.C. Squire who wrote it in 1948. I found it so charmingly describing this long forgotten tree that I share it here with you:

And over all this rough and writhing boughs and tiniest twigs
Will spread a pale green mist of feathery leaf,
More delicate, more touching than all the verdure
Of the younger, slenderer, gracefuller plants around.
And when the leaves have grown
Till the boughs can scarcely be seen through their crowded plumes
There will softly glimmer, scattered upon him blooms,
Ivory white in the green, weightlessly hanging.

I could have added one line:
'And scenting the air with an unforgettable and glorious fragrance.'

RECIPES

LIGHT MEALS

... soups, salads, side dishes and snacks

ANISE PASTA CONFETTI SALAD

Serves 4-6

I make this bright salad for summer picnics when the anise flowers are at their best. It keeps well in the fridge.

300 g pasta shells or any small pasta
2 carrots, peeled and finely grated
1 red pepper, finely chopped
2 sticks celery and their leaves, finely chopped
2 tablespoons parsley, finely chopped
6 radishes, finely chopped

Cook the pasta in rapidly boiling water until *al dente*. Drain and rinse in cold water and leave to cool. Mix everything together and refrigerate.

DRESSING

½ cup grape vinegar
¾ cup anise flowers stripped off their stems
½ cup water
½ cup honey
2 teaspoons mustard powder
3 tablespoons olive oil

Place all these ingredients in a screw-top bottle and shake well. Leave to stand and infuse. Just before serving, shake the dressing, pour over the pasta salad and mix well.

> **Cook's Note**
> FRESH ANISE LEAVES CAN BE CHOPPED INTO SALADS, SOUPS AND STEWS AND THEY WILL GIVE A REFRESHING TASTE TO THE MOST ORDINARY DISH. SPRINKLED ON TOP OF FRITTERS, FRESH CHOPPED LEAVES AND FLOWERS WILL HELP WITH DIGESTION.

ARTICHOKES WITH MINT AND YOGHURT

Serves 4

Delicious as a summer starter or even as a supper dish. The dressing is a healthy alternative to butter.

4 large, trimmed artichokes

DRESSING

1 cup plain yoghurt
2 tablespoons mint, finely chopped
4 spring onions, finely chopped
juice of 1 lemon
2 tablespoons olive oil
sea salt
black pepper

Boil the artichokes in water with a sprig of mint and salt for about 45 minutes until they are tender. Drain. Pull away the tough outer leaves and open out the centre. Pull away the tight tiny pale leaves and with a teaspoon scrape out the thistle-like fluff, the choke. Leave to cool.

Mix together the dressing ingredients and pour into the centre of each artichoke. Dip each scale into it.

ARTICHOKE DIP

Serves 6

This is the most delicious and nourishing dip I know. Serve it with biscuits, chips, celery and carrot sticks or use it as a baked potato filling. Use tinned hearts if it's not artichoke season.

250 g artichoke hearts, freshly cooked and finely chopped
2 tablespoons finely chopped parsley
1 medium onion, finely chopped
2 tablespoons parmesan cheese
½-¾ cup good mayonnaise
juice of 1 lemon
sea salt and black pepper to taste

Mix everything well. For a smoother dip, whirl everything together in a blender. I often ring the changes with ½ cup chopped green pepper, or ¾ cup chopped fresh brown mushrooms, or ¾ cup mashed avocado. Try spreading a little as a pizza topping.

HEARTY BORAGE WINTER HEALTH SOUP

Serves 6-8

Borage survives the coldest winds, so you'll always be able to find something fresh and green during the winter frosts. This is my winter standby and I make a big pot every few days as it keeps well in the fridge. Soak the pulses overnight beforehand.

1 cup butter beans, soaked overnight
1 cup pearl barley, soaked overnight
1 cup lentils, soaked overnight
1 cup split peas, soaked overnight
3 large onions, finely chopped
a little sunflower cooking oil
2 sweet potatoes, grated
6 celery stalks and leaves
6 carrots, finely grated
2 cups borage leaves, finely chopped
4 tomatoes, skinned and chopped
sea salt and cayenne pepper to taste

Leek, kale and coriander flower soup, p. 91

Sun-dried tomato and dahlia bread, p. 92

Calendula omelette, p. 90

2 tablespoons soy sauce
2 teaspoons Marmite
juice of 1 lemon
about 2 litres water or stock

Drain and rinse the soaked beans, barley, lentils and peas. Brown the onions in the oil. Add the sweet potato and celery and stir fry. Once they start to brown, add all the other ingredients. Mix well and simmer gently. Add more water if necessary. Keep covered and on low heat. Adjust flavouring. Cook for about 1 hour or until the beans are tender. Serve with fresh brown bread and butter.

> **Cook's Note**
>
> THIS SOUP IS RICH IN VITAMINS, FILLING AND SATISFYING. RING THE CHANGES WITH GREEN PEPPERS, MUSHROOMS, CABBAGE OR KALE FINELY SHREDDED, SPRING ONIONS, GRATED PUMPKIN OR BUTTERNUT, OR SQUASH. IT KEEPS WELL IN THE FRIDGE.

BORAGE FRITTERS

Serves 4-6

This is a most delicious snack served as an appetiser or as a side dish to stews or roasts.

about 12 borage leaves
sunflower cooking oil

BATTER

1 cup flour
1 cup milk
1 beaten egg
½ cup water
1 teaspoon grated nutmeg
1 teaspoon crushed coriander
sea salt and black pepper to taste

Mix together all the batter ingredients until a runny batter is achieved. Heat the oil in a frying pan. Dip each leaf into the batter and lay it carefully in the hot oil, turning when necessary. Once it is golden brown, remove the leaves from the oil with tongs and drain on crumpled paper towels. Serve hot.

BUCKWHEAT FLOWER SALAD

Serves 6

This is a pretty, salt-free salad that is so loaded with nutrients it should be served daily! Onion or garlic can also be added.

2 cups buckwheat flowers
2 cups buckwheat leaves
2 cups thinly sliced cucumber
1 butter lettuce
2 cups chopped celery
1 cup thinly sliced radishes
2 cups carrot parings (pare with a potato peeler)
2 cups diced avocado

1 cup chopped green and red sweet peppers
½ cup chopped parsley
1 cup chopped fresh pineapple

Mix all the salad ingredients together and add the dressing while mixing. Serve immediately in a pretty glass bowl, decorated lavishly with more buckwheat flowers.

DRESSING

juice of 1 lemon
½ cup sesame seeds
½ cup olive oil
½ cup honey
½ cup grated ginger root

Mix together in a screw-top jar and shake well.

> **Cook's Note**
>
> YOU CAN BUY HULLED BUCKWHEAT AS FLOUR OR GROATS FROM YOUR LOCAL HEALTH SHOP, WHICH IS COOKED AS YOU WOULD COOK RICE, OR SIMPLY EAT THE LEAVES AND FLOWERS TO GIVE YOU A HEALTH BOOST. ROASTED BUCKWHEAT, OR KASHA, IS A FAVOURITE ASIAN DISH AND THE AMERICANS LOVE BUCKWHEAT CAKES AND PANCAKES, WHICH ARE EASY TO MAKE (SEE RECIPE ON P. 123).

BURDOCK FLOWER CLEANSING SOUP

Serves 4-6

This is a most unusual soup, very fresh and very green. It is so vitamin and mineral rich that I try to make it every few weeks, especially if I've been eating out a lot. It is a superb detoxifier, of particular importance after an anaesthetic or after a lot of X-rays, or if you've been plagued by boils or bad skin conditions and feel overloaded and burnt out. It will get rid of all sorts of toxins and acidity.

1 butter lettuce, roughly chopped
3 cups celery stems and leaves, chopped
1 cup chopped fresh parsley
1 cup torn up burdock leaves and stems
1 cup trimmed young burdock buds
2 onions thinly sliced, green tops too
2 cups fresh lucerne leaves stripped off their stems
1 cup pearl barley, soaked overnight
3 grated carrots
about 2 litres water
juice of 1 lemon
a little sea salt to taste

Bring everything to the boil in a heavy bottomed pot. Then turn down the heat and simmer gently with the lid on until the barley is soft – usually about 40 minutes. Top up with water if necessary. For a smooth soup liquidise everything and serve piping hot.

CALENDULA OMELETTE

Serves 1

A quick and easy supper dish and full of goodness.
Make individual omelettes and serve immediately.

2 eggs
2 tablespoons water
a pinch of salt
black pepper
½-¾ cup grated cheddar cheese
¼ cup parsley
½ cup fresh calendula petals

Mix together the grated cheese, parsley and
calendula petals and set aside. Whisk the eggs well
with the water and seasoning. Heat a little olive oil
in a frying pan and pour in the egg mixture. Allow
to set for about 3 minutes, tipping the pan to ensure
that the omelette cooks evenly. Spread the cheese
mixture over one half of the omelette and allow to
settle for a minute or two. As soon as the omelette is
cooked, flip over the one side to cover the cheese
mixture and slide it onto a hot plate. Decorate with
triangles of buttered toast and sprinkle with more
calendula petals. Serve immediately.

NEW POTATO SALAD WITH CALIFORNIAN POPPIES

Serves 4

750 g scrubbed tiny new potatoes

DRESSING

1 tablespoon balsamic vinegar
2 tablespoons olive oil
2 tablespoons good mayonnaise
2 tablespoons plain Bulgarian or Greek yoghurt
sea salt and black pepper to taste
1 cup lightly packed Californian poppy petals

Boil the unpeeled new potatoes in salted water until
tender. Leave them to cool with their skins on.
Meanwhile mix together all the dressing
ingredients, keeping aside a few petals for
garnishing. Turn the potatoes in the dressing and
serve with a sprinkling of chopped parsley in a glass
salad bowl. Keep in the fridge until ready and
decorate with the Californian poppy petals.

CALIFORNIAN POPPY AND AUBERGINE STIR FRY

Serves 4

This tasty salsa-like dish is delicious served with hot
crusty bread as a starter or with a salad as a lunch
dish.

3 medium-sized aubergines
¾ cup parmesan cheese
sea salt and black pepper to taste

juice of 1 lemon
½ cup chopped pecan nuts
½ cup sesame seeds
½ cup Californian poppy petals

Peel and slice the aubergines and soak in salted
water for 10 minutes, then drain. Sauté in the olive
oil until tender. Add all the other ingredients except
the cheese. Mash and mix well, stir frying all the
time. Spoon into a serving dish and sprinkle with
the cheese. Decorate with chopped parsley and a few
of the Californian poppy petals.

CARAWAY EGG AND POTATO SALAD

Serves 4-6

This popular salad can be served with cold meats or
cheese or simply with crusty bread.

about 8 medium-sized potatoes
1 butter lettuce
a few fresh spinach leaves
6 hard-boiled eggs
1 green pepper, thinly sliced
1 cup caraway flowers, broken up and stalks removed
juice of 1 lemon
sea salt and black pepper to taste

Boil the potatoes, peel off the skins and dice. Tear up
the lettuce and spinach leaves. Quarter the eggs.
Carefully mix everything together.

DRESSING

2 teaspoons crushed caraway seeds
4 tablespoons olive oil
2 teaspoons dry mustard powder
2 tablespoons balsamic vinegar

Place all the ingredients in a screw-top jar, seal well
and shake well. Pour over the salad and serve
immediately.

> **Cook's Note**
>
> THE BEAUTIFUL BLUE CHICORY FLOWERS CAN BE ADDED
> TO SOUPS, STEWS AND STIR FRIES AND SALADS. YOUNG
> PLANTS CAN BE STEAMED AND EATEN AS A VEGETABLE,
> OR COLD IN A SALAD. CHICORY HAS A SLIGHTLY BITTER
> TASTE.

CHICORY AND TUNA SALAD

Serves 4

For the greens use mustard greens, spinach, rocket,
butter lettuce or any other green leaves of your choice.

1 tin tuna in brine
2 cups green beans
1 sweet pepper, thinly sliced
2 cups greens
sea salt and black pepper to taste
juice of 1 lemon
1 cup good mayonnaise

1 teaspoon mustard powder
1 cup chicory flowers
½ cup finely chopped spring onions

Break up the tuna. Lightly cook the beans and refresh in cold water, then cut up. Shred the greens into small pieces. Mix everything together and serve decorated with chicory flowers with crusty bread as a lunch dish.

CHIVE AND GARLIC CHIVE HEALTH SALAD

Serves 4-6

This tasty salad will boost the immune system and is satisfying enough to have as a lunch dish served simply with brown bread and butter.

about 3 cups thinly sliced English cucumber
1 whole head celery, thinly chopped
2 ripe avocados, cut into squares
½ cup chopped parsley
½ cup stoned olives
2 cups watercress or land cress, lightly chopped
2 cups finely grated carrots
1 cup chive flowers
1½ cups chopped onion mixed with chopped garlic chives
1 cup mozzarella cheese, cut into small squares or coarsely grated

Mix all the ingredients together lightly.

DRESSING

½ cup lemon juice
½ cup olive oil
2 teaspoons mustard powder
½ cup honey
cayenne pepper
small pinch sea salt

Place all the dressing ingredients together in a screw-top jar and shake. Pour over the salad and decorate with garlic chive flowers.

LEEK, KALE AND CORIANDER FLOWER SOUP

Serves 4-6

Made at the end of autumn with the last of the coriander flowers, this warming soup is a marvellous immune system booster, keeping coughs and colds at bay.

1 large onion, finely chopped
2 tablespoons olive oil
4 thinly sliced leeks
4 cups finely chopped kale or cabbage
4 large potatoes, peeled and grated coarsely
1½ litres good chicken stock
½ cup coriander flowers, without stems
juice of 1 lemon
sea salt and black pepper to taste
125 ml thick cream

Lightly brown the onions in the olive oil. Add the leeks and stir fry until they become soft and lightly browned too. Then add the kale, particularly the green outer leaves, and the potatoes. Stir fry briefly. Add all the other ingredients and stir well. Cover and simmer for 15 minutes, stirring every now and then. Serve piping hot with a sprinkling of parsley and more coriander flowers.

GREEN BEAN AND POTATO SALAD WITH CORIANDER FLOWERS

Serves 4-6

I serve this quick and easy salad on summer picnics with cold chicken and everyone loves it.

4 cups young green beans
4 cups tiny new potatoes
1 medium sized onion, finely chopped

DRESSING

3 tablespoons brown grape vinegar
2 tablespoons olive oil
2 tablespoons coriander flowers stripped off their stems
1 teaspoon crushed coriander seed
1 tablespoon chopped parsley
2 teaspoons mustard powder
½ teaspoon cayenne pepper
1 tablespoon brown sugar

Cut the beans into 1 cm pieces and lightly cook. Quarter the potatoes and steam until tender. Mix both together with the finely chopped raw onion. Place all the dressing ingredients in a screw-top jar and shake up well until everything is well mixed and the sugar dissolved. Add a little sea salt to taste. Pour over the vegetables. Decorate with coriander flowers. Keep refrigerated before serving.

CORNFLOWER PASTA SALAD

Serves 4

Delicious hot or cold, this is an easy lunch dish that everyone enjoys, and it brightens up any meal.

2 cups farfalle (pasta bows)
4 medium-sized ripe tomatoes, thinly sliced
2 ripe avocados, sliced
8-10 slices mozzarella cheese
½ cup cornflower petals, pulled out of their calyx
½ cup chopped parsley
¾ cup chopped basil

DRESSING

3 tablespoons olive oil
3 tablespoons balsamic vinegar
2 teaspoons wholegrain mustard
2 tablespoons honey
½ cup sunflower seeds
½ cup sesame seeds

Cook the pasta in salted water until *al dente*, then drain, rinse and cool. Place in the centre of a flat dish and arrange the tomato, avocado and mozzarella slices all around it. Place the olive oil, vinegar, mustard and honey in a blender and blend. Add the sunflower and sesame seeds and whirl for another 2 minutes. Pour the dressing over the pasta and sprinkle with the cornflowers, basil and parsley. To serve it hot, add a little grated mozzarella cheese and push it under the grill until it sizzles, then finally sprinkle with the basil, cornflowers and parsley.

CREAM CHEESE AND DAHLIA DIP

This Mexican spread is delicious on toast and also makes a party dip for crudités, Melba toast and French fries. The Mexicans use chilli salsa instead of Worcestershire sauce.

250 g carton smooth cream cheese
1 cup finely grated mozzarella cheese
1 teaspoon mustard powder
1 tablespoon Worcestershire sauce or chilli salsa
2 tablespoons honey
1 teaspoon finely ground coriander seed
a little milk
½–¾ cup dahlia petals

Mix everything together well and add a little milk if it is too stiff. Spoon into a glass bowl and sprinkle with dahlia petals.

SUN-DRIED TOMATO AND DAHLIA BREAD

Serves 4-6

This is a delicious Mexican-type breads that is so quick and easy you'll make it often.

375 g white bread flour
1 teaspoon salt
3 teaspoons instant dried yeast
50 g sun-dried tomatoes drained from their oil and chopped
¾ cup multi-coloured dahlia petals
¾ cup luke-warm water
5 tablespoons luke-warm olive oil

Heat the oven to 220 °C. Sift the flour and salt into a large mixing bowl. Stir in the dried yeast, sun-dried tomatoes and dahlia petals. Warm the olive oil in a double boiler. Make a well in the centre of the flour and pour in the warm water and oil and mix well. It will form a soft dough. Turn out the

dough onto a floured board and knead it gently for about 7 minutes, turning it over and over. Grease a baking sheet and press it fairly flat into an oval loaf shape. Brush with olive oil and bake for about 30 minutes. It should sound hollow when you knock it and be lightly golden brown on top. Serve hot with butter.

> **Cook's Note**
>
> DANDELION WINE FEATURES IN ANCIENT RECIPES, AND IS STILL POPULAR. THE LONG TAP ROOT CAN BE DRIED, ROASTED AND GROUND TO MAKE A PLEASANT, HEALTHY VERSION OF COFFEE. YOUNG LEAVES AND FLOWERS ARE SUPERB IN SALADS AND CAN ALSO BE ADDED TO SOUPS, STEWS AND SAUCES.

DANDELION AND BACON SALAD

Serves 4

This one is the best known of all dandelion dishes.

about 4 cups fresh young dandelion leaves
2 cups dandelion flowers, calyxes removed
250 g streaky bacon
4 tablespoons olive oil
5 slices bread, cubed
sea salt and black pepper
2 tablespoons balsamic vinegar

Tear up the dandelion leaves and mix with the flowers. Chop up the bacon and fry until crisp. Drain and add the olive oil to the bacon fat in the pan. Fry the bread cubes in the fat and oil until golden. Drain. Mix the croutons and the bacon into the dandelion leaves and flowers. Serve in a glass bowl, and sprinkle the balsamic vinegar over it just before serving. Decorate with dandelion flowers.

DANDELION FLOWER OMELETTE

Serves 1

about 6 dandelion flower buds
butter
2 eggs
3 cups water
¾ cup grated cheddar cheese
3 cups parsley
sea salt and pepper

Pick flowers that are just about to open. Quickly sauté them in a little butter and set aside. Whisk the eggs with the water. Heat a little sunflower oil in a pan and pour in the egg and water mixture. Mix the sautéed dandelion flower buds with the parsley and cheese and as the omelette sets, sprinkle this on one half of it. Add sea salt and pepper, flip over the other side and let it settle for 1 minute. Slide the omelette out of the pan onto a hot plate. Serve immediately with hot buttered toast.

Dandelion and Beetroot Salad

Serves 4

Served either hot or cold, this is a delicious healthy salad that everyone loves. Serve it with chicken or fish.

2 cups dandelion leaves, roughly torn
2 cups dandelion flowers
about 6 cooked beetroots, peeled and thinly sliced
1 cup chopped celery

Dressing

1 cup brown grape vinegar
1 cup brown sugar
2 teaspoons mustard powder
1 teaspoon powdered coriander
½ teaspoon powdered cloves

Mix the dandelion leaves and flowers with the celery and beetroot slices. Heat the vinegar, sugar and mustard and stir until the sugar dissolves. Add the coriander and cloves. Pour the hot dressing over them and either serve hot sprinkled with dandelion flowers and parsley or leave it until it is cold.

Golden Day Lily and Yellow Peach Salad

Serves 4-6

This is a golden feast for both eye and palate and my favourite summer salad. I add dandelion petals, pumpkin flowers and yellow nasturtiums for festive occasions. It is spectacular!

6 large, firm yellow peaches, coarsely grated or thinly chopped
2 cups celery, thinly chopped
2-3 yellow sweet peppers, thinly sliced
about 12 yellow and orange day lilies and buds
6 raw baby marrows, thinly sliced
or ½ a peeled raw butternut squash, grated
4 hard-boiled eggs, chopped
1 cup grated cheddar cheese
about 1 cup good mayonnaise
black pepper and sea salt to taste

Mix everything together gently and spoon into a pretty glass salad bowl. Sprinkle with a little freshly grated ginger and decorate with yellow day lilies all around the bowl.

> **Cook's Note**
>
> ECHINACEA PETALS ARE FRESH-TASTING AND TENDER AND I ONLY RECENTLY STARTED USING THEM IN COOKING, AFTER A VISIT TO THE HERBAL CENTRE BY AN AMERICAN INDIAN WHO DESCRIBED TO ME HOW THEY FRIED THE PETALS WITH WATERCRESS, ONION AND MUSTARD LEAVES AND SPREAD IT OVER SWEET POTATOES. I FOUND THIS TO BE SO INTERESTING AND DELICIOUS, IT SPURRED ME ON TO START EXPERIMENTING WITH THIS WONDERFUL PLANT.

American Indian Savoury Echinacea Spread

Serves 4

This makes an excellent lunch dish. Baked potatoes or even pasta can be substituted for the sweet potatoes.

4-6 large sweet potatoes
3 medium onions, chopped
little olive or sunflower oil
1 cup celery stalks and leaves, finely chopped
2 cups mustard greens, roughly torn
2 cups watercress sprigs or land cress leaves
1 cup echinacea petals
sea salt and black pepper to taste
2 tablespoons honey

Boil the sweet potatoes in their skins in salted water with a cinnamon stick until cooked. Meanwhile fry the onion in the oil until it starts to brown, then add the celery stalks and leaves. Stir well. Add the mustard greens, then the watercress and echinacea petals. Stir well for about 1 minute and add the sea salt, pepper and finally the honey. Split open the hot sweet potatoes and pile the echinacea spread on top. Decorate with fresh echinacea petals and a wedge of lemon.

Echinacea Pane Bagno

Serves 4

Pane bagno literally means 'bathed bread' and it is a most delicious salad roll that is perfect as a lunch time snack or for a picnic.

4-6 large, freshly baked rolls or 1 French loaf
4 ripe tomatoes, thinly sliced
2 onions, thinly sliced
2 green peppers, thinly sliced
1 can tuna fish
sea salt and black pepper
fresh lemon juice
1 cup echinacea petals
1 cup stoned olives, chopped

Dressing

½ cup olive oil
½ cup white grape vinegar
2 teaspoons mustard powder
½ cup runny honey
pinch sea salt and black pepper

Split the rolls or French loaf horizontally along one side without cutting all the way through the crust. Lightly butter both sides. Mix all the dressing ingredients together in a screw-top jar and shake well. Open the bread so it lies flat and gently dribble a little dressing along both sides. Drain the can of tuna fish and mash with a little sea salt, pepper and a squeeze of fresh lemon juice. Arrange the sliced tomatoes, onions and green peppers on the rolls, and top with the mashed tuna. Finally sprinkle with the echinacea petals and olives. Close up the rolls or French loaf and wrap in cling wrap. Put a weight on them and leave for an hour to allow the dressing to soak in well. Just before serving, slice the rolls or loaf into manageable portions.

EVENING PRIMROSE STUFFED EGGS

Serves 6

Collect the evening primrose flowers in the early morning before they fade and refrigerate them. This is a favourite for summer picnics, and I make it often as a lunch time snack.

1 dozen eggs
1-2 tablespoons horseradish sauce
about ½ cup good mayonnaise
½ cup chopped parsley
½ cup finely chopped celery
1 tablespoon Worcestershire sauce
½ cup finely grated strong cheddar cheese
a little sea salt and freshly ground black pepper
1 cup roughly chopped evening primrose flowers

Hard boil the eggs and when they are cooked, throw off the boiling water and submerge them immediately in cold water. Peel the eggs, cut them in half and remove the yolks. Mash the yolks with the rest of the ingredients. Fill the hollows in the egg whites with the mixture and arrange the stuffed eggs on a flat dish on a bed of lettuce and watercress. Decorate each half egg with a petal of evening primrose and serve chilled.

EVENING PRIMROSE AND ONION SCONES

Serves 6

These tasty scones are much nicer than bread rolls as an accompaniment for supper, and are quick and easy to make.

1½ cups butter, coarsely grated
2 cups cake flour
1 tablespoon baking powder
1 teaspoon salt
3 spring onions, finely chopped
1 cup chopped evening primrose flowers
about ¾ cup buttermilk

Rub the butter into the flour. Add the baking powder, salt and pepper to taste, then the spring onions and chopped evening primrose flowers. Slowly add the buttermilk and mix it into a dough, adding more if it is too stiff. Turn out onto a floured board and knead briefly into a good ball. Pat out into an oblong about 2 cm thick and cut into neat squares about 5 cm in size. Lay these on a floured baking sheet. Brush the tops with buttermilk. Bake at 180 °C for about 10 minutes, or until they start to turn golden brown on top. Serve hot with butter.

BUTTERED BANANA AND FEIJOA BREAKFAST DISH

Serves 4

This is a delicious dish for a festive brunch, or even a Sunday family breakfast.

4 thick slices tomato
4 large black mushrooms
4 thick slices wholewheat toast, crusts removed
about 2 tablespoons butter
6 bananas, peeled and cut in half lengthways
1 cup feijoa flowers, calyxes removed
a little cooking oil
2 tablespoons chopped parsley
sea salt and black pepper to taste

In a large pan, fry the tomatoes and the black mushrooms in a little oil. Sprinkle a little salt and pepper on them and a little sugar on the tomatoes. Cook until tender. Butter the toast, place on individual heated plates, and top with the tomato and then the mushroom. Keep warm. Wipe the pan out and heat the butter. Add the bananas and the feijoa flowers and gently cook them in the butter for about 2 minutes. Arrange them around the tomato and mushroom toast and sprinkle with parsley. Serve immediately while hot, decorated with a few fresh feijoa flowers.

FENNEL FLOWER SLIMMER'S SALAD

Serves 4

This is my favourite salad and all of us, even those not anxious to slim, should have it once a week or once a fortnight to keep the body clear of toxins. Should you be coming down with flu or a cold, add extra lemon juice and sprinkle with cayenne pepper. This often stops the infection in its tracks.

1 butter lettuce, roughly torn
1½ cups chopped celery, leaves included
1½ cups alfalfa sprouts or fresh young lucerne leaves
1½ cups fennel leaves and flowers roughly chopped
1½ cups peeled chopped cucumber
1½ cups finely grated carrot
½ cup chopped parsley
juice of 1 lemon

Mix everything together in a large bowl and pour over the lemon juice. Decorate with fennel flowers. Do not add salt or pepper.

Fennel Flower Soup

Serves 4-6

Another superb detoxifying dish, this soup is so full of goodness you will make it often. It is a good anti-inflammatory as well as being rich in vitamins and minerals. It is excellent for bringing down high blood pressure.

3 cups leeks, finely chopped
about 1 tablespoon sunflower oil
2 cups chopped fennel stalks, leaves and flowers
1 cup pearl barley, soaked overnight
2 cups finely chopped celery
1½ cups finely grated turnip
1½ cups finely grated carrot
1 cup split peas
½ cup grated fresh ginger
juice of 1 lemon
sea salt to taste
a little cayenne pepper
about 1½ litres water or vegetable stock

Lightly brown the leeks in the sunflower oil. Add everything else and simmer for about 1 hour. Add a little extra water if necessary.

> **Cook's Note**
>
> THE LEEKS BROWNED IN THE OIL GIVE A GOOD FLAVOUR TO THE FENNEL FLOWER SOUP. FOR THOSE ON A FAT FREE DIET, OMIT THE OIL. FINELY CHOPPED FENNEL LEAVES ARE DELICIOUS IN FISH DISHES AND ON GREEN BEANS.

Baby Carrots with Fruit Sage and Honey

Serves 4-6

You can also use large carrots for this delicious dish but cut them thinly into rounds. Serve as a vegetable dish with roast meat or roast chicken.

about 36 baby carrots, well washed
4-5 tablespoons butter
¾ cup honey
1 teaspoon salt
½ cup sesame seeds
1 tablespoon freshly grated ginger root
juice of 1 lemon
2 tablespoons chopped fruit sage flowers, calyx removed

Boil the carrots in enough water to cover them until tender. Melt the butter and add all the other ingredients. Sauté while stir frying all the time. Keep turning the seeds and the fruit sage in the butter. Then drain the carrots in a sieve until they are dry and gently add them to the butter mixture. Turn them in the butter and honey until they are well coated and just starting to brown. Pour into a serving dish with the butter and honey mixture remains spooned over the top. Serve hot.

Fuchsia and Potato Mash

Serves 4

That familiar comfort food, the mashed potato, can become a party dish with a few brightly coloured fuchsia petals and a sprinkling of spices.

6 large or 8 medium potatoes
1 tablespoon butter
¾ cup hot milk
sea salt and black pepper
2 teaspoons crushed coriander
1 teaspoon powdered nutmeg
1 teaspoon powdered allspice (pimento berries)
about ¾ cup fuchsia petals
parmesan cheese
parsley
fuchsia flowers

Peel the potatoes and boil until soft. Drain off the water and immediately mash. Add the butter cut into small pieces, hot milk, sea salt and black pepper to taste. Mash until light and fluffy, adding more hot milk if necessary. Fork in the coriander, nutmeg and allspice. Lastly add the fuchsia petals. Pile into a glass serving dish. Keep hot, and just before serving top with a light sprinkling of parmesan cheese and decorate with chopped parsley and fuchsia flowers.

Cold Chicken and Fuchsia Salad

Serves 4

This is a superb lunch dish or picnic dish, and it can be varied with salads in season, such as avocados and winter lettuces.

about 1½ cups good mayonnaise
4 cups diced cooked cold potato
1 butter lettuce
1 cooked cold chicken cut into slices and bite-sized pieces
1 pineapple, peeled and cut into small wedges
about 3 cups torn fresh spinach leaves
2 cups chopped celery
juice of 1 lemon
1 cup fuchsia flowers
about 2 spring onions
4 hard-boiled eggs, shelled and quartered
sea salt and black pepper to taste

Mix the mayonnaise into the potatoes and season. Mix in the other ingredients, except for the fuchsia flowers, spring onions and hard-boiled eggs. Line a bowl with the lettuce leaves and pile the mixture into the lettuce-lined bowl and decorate with the eggs, spring onions and fuchsia flowers. Serve chilled with crusty brown bread.

GARLAND CHRYSANTHEMUM CROUTONS

Serves 4

Serve sprinkled over a light vegetable soup or as a snack with drinks, or mix it all into rice and serve with soy sauce.

sea salt and pepper to taste
2 teaspoons mustard powder
4 thick slices brown bread
¾ cup sunflower oil
2 cups garland chrysanthemum flowers cut into quarters
1 large onion cut into rings

Sprinkle salt, pepper and mustard powder over the bread and cut it into small squares. Heat the oil in a pan, and gently fry the bread with the onion rings and garland chrysanthemum until they all start to turn golden, turning often. It is easiest if you do small batches rather than all at one go. When the croutons start to crisp, lift out and drain on crumpled paper.

STUFFED GLADIOLUS FLOWERS

Serves 8

For a summer starter, this is real party fare. Choose fully open flowers and remove the sheath of the calyx.

2-4 flowers per guest
2 cups mashed, drained tuna
¾ cup good mayonnaise
⅓ cup sesame seeds
½ cup finely chopped celery
½ cup finely chopped green pepper
juice of 1 lemon
sea salt and black pepper to taste

Mix the tuna, mayonnaise and the rest of the ingredients well. Spoon teaspoonfuls into each open flower and pat into shape. Arrange the flowers in a circle on a bed of lettuce on a serving platter. Serve chilled with lemon wedges.

GLADIOLUS AND AVOCADO OPEN SANDWICH

Serves 4-6

This is so quick and easy, and always popular. Open sandwiches can be varied according to ingredients, but this combination remains a favourite and is spectacularly beautiful.

8 slices dark rye or pumpernickel bread
horseradish sauce
8 thin slices ham
cucumber slices
8-10 gladioli flowers, calyxes removed
and petals separated
2 avocados, mashed with salt, pepper and lemon juice
1 cup grated mozzarella cheese

1 butter lettuce
cherry tomatoes
chopped parsley

Spread the bread with butter, followed by a thin layer of horseradish sauce. Lay the ham over it, on top of the ham lay cucumber slices, on top of that lay gladiolus petals so that the petals form a frill around the edge of the bread, pile on the mashed avocado and top with the mozzarella cheese. Arrange on lettuce leaves on individual plates with cherry tomatoes. Sprinkle with parsley.

GOLDEN ROD SOUP

Serves 6-8

This is an old American Indian recipe and I find it so delicious and so health building that I make it every autumn when the golden rod is flowering.

2 cups chopped onion
little olive oil
2 cups chopped celery
3 cups green mealies, cut off the cob
2 cups grated sweet potato, skin left on
2 cups grated butternut or pumpkin
2 cups chopped green pepper
2 cups peeled, chopped tomato
2 cups golden rod flowers pulled off their stems
juice of 2 lemons
sea salt and cayenne pepper to taste
about 2½ litres of water

Lightly brown the onion in a little bit of olive oil, then add the celery. Stir fry briefly, then add all the other ingredients, stirring well. Cover and simmer until tender. For a change you can add 2 cups mushrooms or 2 cups leeks, or replace the water with chicken stock. It keeps well in the fridge. Serve it hot with crusty brown bread.

HOLLYHOCK AND GREEN BEAN SALAD

Serves 4-6

The hollyhock is supposed to enable one to see fairies, so this delicious salad should do the trick!

about 4 cups young green beans
1 large onion

DRESSING

1 cup plain Bulgarian yoghurt
½ cup fresh lemon juice
½ cup honey
½ cup chopped spring onions
2 teaspoons mustard

Top and tail the beans and simmer in salted water until tender. Strain and cool. Slice an extra large onion into fairly thick rings. Place a handful of beans through each onion ring and place on individual plates. The bean bundles look as though they are neatly tied by the onion. To make the dressing, whirl the ingredients in a liquidiser and pour over the beans. Place two hollyhock flowers over each end of the beans. Sprinkle with parsley and serve chilled with cold chicken or cold meat.

Hyssop Green Salad

Serves 4

Served to clean the palate, this salad is so refreshing I serve it with any rich meat dish.

3 cups torn or thinly shredded lettuce
2 cups watercress
2 cups chopped celery
1 cup thinly sliced cucumber
½ cup hyssop flowers pulled off their calyxes
juice of 1 lemon
parsley, chopped

Mix everything together, tossing lightly. Sprinkle the lemon juice over everything and add a little chopped parsley.

Lavender Cheese Squares

Serves 4

This is one of my favourite recipes for a teatime snack, a lunch dish with soup or a supper dish served with avocado salad. To ring the changes, try sliced tomatoes under the cheese or gherkins on slices of onion, or asparagus spears.

6 slices brown bread
butter
½-¾ cup mayonnaise or chutney
2 teaspoons lavender flowers stripped
off their stems and calyxes
1½ cup grated mozzarella cheese
a little chopped parsley
cayenne pepper

Toast the bread and butter while hot. Mix the lavender into the mayonnaise or chutney and spread onto the toast. Sprinkle the mozzarella cheese liberally over the slice, sprinkle with parsley and dust with cayenne pepper. Place under the grill for about 4 minutes, or until the cheese starts to bubble. Cut into squares and serve hot.

> **Cook's Note**
>
> FEW PEOPLE HAVE EVER THOUGHT OF COOKING WITH LAVENDER, BUT JUST A LITTLE GIVES A WONDERFULLY FRESH TASTE AND ENHANCES OTHER FLAVOURS SO REMARKABLY THAT INVENTING OTHER DISHES WITH LAVENDER CAN BECOME AN ENGROSSING HOBBY. LAVENDER FLOWERS CAN BE SPRINKLED OVER A FRUIT SALAD WHILE THE LEAVES CAN BE ADDED TO STEWS AND BRAISED MEAT DISHES. LAVENDER IS ALSO AN EXCELLENT ADDITION TO MARINADES FOR GAME.

Cajun Potatoes with Lavender

I serve this with crusty brown bread and feta cheese. It is satisfying, filling and healthy.

Serves 4

about ½ cup olive oil
2 large onions, peeled and thinly sliced
6 medium potatoes, peeled and thinly sliced
about ½ cup water
juice of 2 lemons
1½ cups tomato puree
black pepper to taste
sea salt to taste
2 tablespoons lavender flowers
2 tablespoons chopped parsley

Heat the olive oil in a large pan and fry the onion until lightly golden. Add the potatoes and stir fry. Add the water and all the other ingredients except the parsley. Cover and simmer gently for a few minutes, checking every now and then to see if the potatoes are tender. Stir gently. Serve piping hot with chicken or fish, sprinkled liberally with parsley.

Flax Flower and Potato Soup

Serves 4-6

Filling and sustaining, this is an exceptional soup for a supper when you are overtired. It keeps well in the fridge. Try it warmed or chilled.

1 medium onion, finely chopped
a little olive oil
500 g leeks, sliced and trimmed
1 green pepper, finely chopped
500 g potatoes, peeled and roughly diced
1 litre chicken stock
sea salt and black pepper to taste
1 teaspoon freshly grated nutmeg
1 teaspoon paprika
500 ml milk
150 ml thin cream (optional)
½ cup flax flowers, calyxes removed

Brown the onion in the olive oil, add the leeks and green pepper and cook for 5 minutes, stirring frequently. Add the potatoes and stock. Bring to the boil and simmer for 10 minutes or until the vegetables are cooked. Allow to cool a little. Pour into a liquidiser and blend. Return to the pan, add the sea salt, pepper, nutmeg, paprika and milk and heat thoroughly. Finally, stir in the cream if you are serving the soup hot or chill the soup before adding the cream and stir in the cream just before serving. Pour into individual soup dishes and decorate with floating flax flowers and chopped parsley.

ICED AVOCADO AND LUCERNE SOUP

Serves 4

A delicious lunch time dish, this is a quick energiser and easy to make. Prepare it no more than 1 hour before serving as the avocados will discolour.

2 ripe avocados
juice of 1 lemon
2 sticks celery, finely chopped, leaves included
2 cups plain Bulgarian yoghurt
½ cup lucerne flowers and a few leaves, finely chopped
1½ cups good chicken stock
sea salt and black pepper to taste
½ teaspoon cayenne pepper
1 tablespoon parsley, finely chopped

Peel and cut up the avocados, add sea salt and pepper and mash finely. Add the celery, then all the rest of the ingredients, whipping smoothly until they are well blended. Chill in the refrigerator, resting the bowl on a bed of ice. Serve chilled in individual dishes, sprinkled with parsley and decorated with lucerne flowers.

LUCERNE FLOWERS AND VEGETABLE TEMPURA

Serves 4

These Japanese-inspired fritters make an unusual snack and are easily and quickly made.

2 carrots, peeled and cut into strips
1 large onion, sliced and rings separated
1 cup mangetout peas, topped and tailed
2 cups lucerne flowers, stems still attached
2 cups sliced button mushrooms

BATTER

1 extra large egg
1 cup flour
1 teaspoon salt
½ teaspoon cayenne pepper
½-⅓ cup warm water

Mix the salt and cayenne pepper into the flour and break the egg into it. Add the warm water and mix to a light batter, adding a little extra water if necessary. Have a large flat pan ready with hot sunflower oil. Dip each piece of vegetable and the flowers individually into the batter and then into the pan. Do 4 or 5 pieces at a time. Fry until crisp and golden, remove with a slotted spoon and drain on crumpled paper towels. Serve hot with sweet ginger sauce as a dip.

SWEET GINGER SAUCE

2 tablespoons clear honey
1 tablespoon hot water
¼ cup finely grated fresh ginger
3 tablespoons soy sauce
2 tablespoons red wine

Dissolve the honey in the hot water. Place all the ingredients in a screw-top jar and shake well. Pour into a bowl and serve as a dip with the tempura.

MORINGA HEALTH SALAD

Serves 4

This basic salad can be varied with vegetables in season. The mung beans and alfalfa sprouts are an excellent addition.

2 cups moringa leaves and flowers, stripped off their stems
1 cup chopped celery
1 cup chopped green pepper
1 cup chopped, peeled cucumber
2 cups watercress leaves
1 cup cooked fresh asparagus spears
2 cups diced pineapple
1 cup diced mangetout or sugar snap peas
2 cups butter lettuce or kale leaves
mung beans (optional)
alfalfa sprouts (optional)

Mix everything together lightly. Dress only with lemon juice and sprinkle with finely chopped parsley. Do not use salt and pepper. Decorate with moringa flowers.

MYRTLE AND CHEESE SPREAD

Serves 6

Use this tasty spread as a sandwich filling or on toast as a supper dish, or serve on biscuits as a snack.

2 cups finely grated cheddar cheese
1 cup smooth cottage cheese
2 teaspoons mustard powder
1 cup mayonnaise
½ cup myrtle flowers, calyxes removed
1 teaspoon freshly ground black pepper
1 tablespoon finely chopped capers or nasturtium seeds
1 teaspoon celery seed
1 tablespoon finely chopped tarragon
juice of 1 lemon

Mix everything together well, making sure that it is thoroughly blended. Spread onto toast, top with tomato slices and place under the grill until it bubbles.

Nasturtium Cheese Dip

Serves 6

This is a lovely spread or dip served with crudités, biscuits, toasted bread or crisps, and turns cold meat and chicken into party fare.

1 cup finely grated Gouda cheese
1 cup cream cheese
½ cup white wine
½ cup finely chopped celery
1 tablespoon Worcestershire sauce
½ cup finely chopped green pepper
about ¾ cup finely chopped nasturtium
flowers and leaves
juice of 1 lemon

Mix everything together and pile into a bowl. Stand the bowl on a large glass plate and surround with biscuits, toast or crackers and decorate with nasturtium flowers.

> **Cook's Note**
>
> RIPE NASTURTIUM SEEDS PACKED INTO SMALL BOTTLES OF VINEGAR MAKE SUPERB SUBSTITUTES FOR CAPERS, AND THINLY SLICED IN STIR FRIES THEY GIVE A DELICIOUS BITE. NOTE THAT CAPERS ARE NOT NASTURTIUM SEEDS BUT AN UNRELATED SHRUB, *CAPPARIS SPINOSA*, WHICH GROWS IN THE MEDITERRANEAN REGION.

Grilled Aubergine Salad with Egg and Nasturtium Flowers

Serves 6

This is a deliciously sustaining Greek-style lunch or supper dish, and makes an easy party dish served simply with baked or boiled potatoes or some crusty bread.

2 medium-sized aubergines, stalks removed
and sliced thinly lengthways
about ½ cup olive oil
2 green peppers, thinly sliced lengthways
6 hard-boiled eggs, peeled
sea salt and black pepper
8 anchovy fillets, chopped
1 large avocado, peeled and diced
about 1 cup nasturtium flowers
about 8 spring onions, split in half lengthways
olive oil
balsamic vinegar
½ cup finely chopped parsley

Brush the aubergines with a little olive oil and place them under the grill for about 6 to 10 minutes. Add the green peppers and dry grill them, turning them until they are charred all over. Slice the peeled hard-boiled eggs in half and sprinkle them with crushed sea salt and black pepper and the chopped anchovy fillets. Place the peppers in a plastic bag to sweat and when cool, remove the skins. Squeeze a little lemon juice over the avocado to prevent it from turning brown. Arrange all the ingredients on a large platter and tuck in the nasturtium flowers and spring onions. Drizzle with a little olive oil and balsamic vinegar. Sprinkle with chopped parsley.

An alternative dressing is:

juice of 1 lemon
2 tablespoons honey
1 tablespoon chopped, pickled nasturtium seeds
2 tablespoons olive oil

Place all the ingredients in a screw-top jar and shake well. Pour over the salad just before serving.

Pansy and Asparagus Cheese Bake

Serves 6-8

I make this every spring when both fresh asparagus and pansies are at their best.

750 g fresh green asparagus spears
2 cups milk
2 eggs, well beaten
2 tablespoons flour
1 cup grated gouda cheese
sea salt and black pepper to taste
1 medium onion, finely chopped
1 cup brown breadcrumbs
1 tablespoon mealie meal
2 tablespoons finely grated parmesan cheese
1 tablespoon butter
about 10 heartsease or other violas

Cut the asparagus into 2 cm lengths and cook in boiling salted water. When just tender, drain and arrange in a glass baking dish. Whisk the milk into the eggs with the flour, then the gouda cheese, salt and pepper. Finally whisk in the chopped onion. Mix together the brown breadcrumbs, mealie meal and parmesan cheese. Pour the egg mixture over the asparagus and top with the cheese and breadcrumb mixture. Dot with butter and bake at 180 °C for about 20 minutes or until the egg mixture is set and the cheese topping starts to brown. Decorate with violas just before serving.

> **Cook's Note**
>
> USE PANSIES TO DECORATE BOTH SWEET AND SAVOURY DISHES. THEIR COLOURFUL FACES AND TENDER, PLEASANT TASTE WILL TRANSFORM AN ORDINARY DISH INTO SOMETHING MOST UNUSUAL AND EYE-CATCHING.

PINEAPPLE SAGE AND GRAPEFRUIT HEALTH BREAKFAST DISH

Serves 1

1 large ruby grapefruit
1 tablespoon sesame seeds
2 teaspoons grated fresh ginger root
2 tablespoons soft brown caramel sugar
½ teaspoon freshly grated nutmeg
1 tablespoon pineapple sage flowers

Carefully cut and scoop segments out of the grapefruit, place in a bowl and add the sesame seeds, ginger root, sugar and nutmeg. Mix everything together well and add the flowers at the end. Mix lightly. Spoon into a glass bowl and serve chilled, decorated with a few fresh flowers.

> **Cook's Note**
>
> BECAUSE OF THEIR DISTINCTIVE PINEAPPLE TASTE, PINEAPPLE SAGE FLOWERS CAN BE ADDED TO DRINKS, FRUIT SALADS AND DESSERTS, AND THEIR BRIGHT RED COLOUR LENDS AN EXOTIC LOOK TO ANY DISH. A QUICK AND EASY DESSERT FOR A HOT SUMMER SUNDAY LUNCH IS TO SCOOP BALLS OF VANILLA ICE CREAM INTO A DISH AND COVER WITH FINELY CHOPPED FRESH PINEAPPLE THAT HAS BEEN SPRINKLED WITH LOTS OF PINEAPPLE SAGE FLOWERS.

COUSCOUS AND PINEAPPLE SAGE

Serves 4

Couscous is an ancient grain devised by the Berbers of North Africa from millet and then later from wheat. The national dish of Morocco, it is full of vitamins and minerals. Couscous is available in most supermarkets and, like rice, is superb with meat, stews and spicy relishes.

2 cups couscous, the instant, commercial kind
½ cup pineapple sage flowers
1 cup finely chopped or grated fresh pineapple
½ cup finely chopped parsley
juice of 1 lemon
½ tablespoon finely crushed coriander seeds

Simply cook the couscous according to the directions on the box. I usually soak the grains for 5 minutes in warm water and then I steam them in a steamer, separating the grains with a fork. When fluffy and tender, serve on a flat warm dish and, at the last minute, sprinkle with the flowers, pineapple, parsley, lemon juice and coriander seeds. Serve hot with a rich meat or chicken stew.

PLUMBAGO AND BEETROOT SALAD

Serves 6-8

This is a traditional salad with a difference. It keeps beautifully bottled or in the fridge for up to 2 months and goes particularly well with a braai or barbecue.

10-12 well-scrubbed, medium-sized beetroots, unpeeled
1 tablespoon coriander seeds
1 teaspoon whole cloves
2 bay leaves
½ tablespoon allspice berries
1 crushed nutmeg
1 cup brown grape vinegar
1 cup brown sugar
½ cup water
½ cup plumbago flowers pulled out of their sticky calyxes

Boil the beetroots until they are tender. Meanwhile, tie all the spices in a square of muslin and boil with the vinegar, sugar and water with the lid on for 10 minutes. Slide the skins off the beetroot and coarsely grate them. Spoon into jars or a bowl. Sprinkle with the plumbago flowers. Remove the spices and pour the hot vinegar mixture over it. Serve either hot or cold as a salad or relish. Decorate with more fresh plumbago flowers.

PLUM BLOSSOM AND CELERY CHEESE PLATTER

Serves 4

This is delicious as a light lunch or served in the traditional way as the ending to a meal. You can combine any of your favourite cheeses, moistened if necessary with a little cream or milk to obtain a smooth consistency.

6 long celery sticks, washed and cut into 10 cm lengths
½ cup mashed feta cheese
½ cup cream cheese
½ cup soft goat milk cheese
paprika and sea salt to taste
½ cup plum blossoms

Mix the cheeses together in a food processor to form a smooth paste. Mound up the cheese neatly in the hollow of each stick of celery. Sprinkle with sea salt and paprika and plum blossoms. Serve on a bed of lettuce with savoury biscuits.

RED SALAD WITH POPPY SEED VINAIGRETTE

Serves 6

A spectacular red salad, this is unusual and very festive.

4 large tomatoes, sliced
2 sweet red peppers, diced
2 cups sliced strawberries
2 cups thinly sliced radishes
1 cup poppy petals

Arrange all the ingredients on a flat glass dish. Pour the poppy seed vinaigrette over it just before serving.

Poppy seed vinaigrette

3 tablespoons chopped fresh chives
¾ cup olive oil
½ cup brown grape vinegar
2 teaspoons mustard powder
½ cup brown sugar
2 tablespoons poppy seed
sea salt and black pepper to taste
2 tablespoons orange juice

Place all the ingredients in a glass screw-top bottle, seal well and shake.

Poppy Petal Muffins

Makes 12 large muffins
Quick and easy and simply delicious, these muffins are a treat for Sunday breakfast or a teatime snack.

½ cup sugar
zest of 1 lemon
2 tablespoons water
2 cups cake flour
3 teaspoons baking powder
5 tablespoons butter
2 eggs
¾ cup milk
¾ cup plain yoghurt
2 tablespoons poppy seed
½ cup chopped fresh poppy petals

Pre-heat the oven to 180 °C. In a small saucepan simmer the sugar, butter, lemon zest and water for 2 minutes, stirring until the sugar dissolves. Mix together the flour and baking powder. In a separate bowl, whisk together the eggs, milk and yoghurt until creamy. Add the lemon zest and sugar and whisk well. Add the flour mixture, poppy seed and the poppy petals. Stir well. Spoon into well-greased muffin pans, but do not fill quite to the top as the muffins will rise. Bake for 15 minutes or until a skewer inserted into the middle of the muffin comes out clean. Remove from the pan and split open while still slightly warm, spread with butter and strawberry jam and top with a little whipped cream and a poppy petal. Serve immediately.

Prickly Pear Salad

Serves 4-6

1 butter lettuce
1 cup good mayonnaise
8 prickly pears, peeled and sliced into
1 cm thick rounds
1 small pineapple, peeled and thinly sliced
2 cups green melon, scooped into balls
1 cup celery, chopped
½ cup chopped basil
½ cup chopped parsley
sea salt, paprika and black pepper to taste

On a flat glass dish place the butter lettuce leaves neatly, starting at the edge. With a spoon, spread a little mayonnaise on each leaf. Arrange the prickly pear slices and the pineapple slices over the lettuce. Add the melon balls and the celery pieces and spread evenly. Finally sprinkle the chopped basil and parsley, sea salt, paprika and black pepper over everything. Serve chilled.

Prickly Pear Breakfast Dish

Serves 1
Much loved by children, this cool refreshing breakfast dish gives energy, vitality and much enjoyment! To ring the changes, slice in ½ a banana or a whole one if you're hungry!

2-3 prickly pears, peeled and sliced
1 cup plain yoghurt
2 tablespoons sultanas, soaked in hot water
for 1 hour beforehand
1 tablespoon chopped pecan nuts
⅔ cup cornflakes
honey to sweeten

Place the prickly pear slices in a porridge bowl. Add the yoghurt and sprinkle with the sultanas, pecan nuts and cornflakes to add crunch. Dribble with honey and stir carefully. Immediately go outside and eat it in the garden.

Pumpkin Flower Soup

Serves 4-6
This treasured standby provides a boost of energy and a storehouse of health.

2 cups chopped onion
a little olive oil
2 cups chopped celery
6 cups peeled, diced pumpkin
6-10 pumpkin flowers, roughly chopped
½ cup honey
sea salt and cayenne pepper to taste
juice of 1 lemon
2 cups lucerne leaves and flowers (optional)
about 1 litre chicken or vegetable stock or water
½ cup parsley

In a large, heavy-bottomed pot, sauté the onion in the oil until transparent. Add the celery and stir fry for a minute or two. Add the pumpkin, stir fry for a minute or two and then add all the other ingredients except for the parsley. (If you are living on a farm and have them available, the lucerne leaves and flowers may be added for extra energy.) Add the chicken or vegetable stock or water. Stir well. Cover and simmer for about 20 minutes or until the pumpkin and celery are tender. Blend in a liquidiser if you prefer, or serve as it is with a sprinkling of parsley and hot crusty bread.

STUFFED SQUASH FLOWER SALAD

Serves 4-6

This is a most acceptable salad for a summer lunch and so quick to prepare. Use any variety of squash or pumpkin flower.

12-14 squash or pumpkin flowers

STUFFING

1 tin tuna, drained and mashed
½ cup good quality mayonnaise
juice of 1 lemon
¼ cup finely chopped chives
¼ cup finely chopped parsley
1 tablespoon Worcestershire sauce
½ cup smooth cream cheese
½ cup finely chopped green pepper
sea salt and black pepper to taste

Mash and mix the stuffing ingredients together well. Spoon the mixture carefully into the squash or pumpkin flowers. Arrange the stuffed flowers carefully on a bed of butter lettuce on a large platter, stalk sides facing inwards. Place slices of avocado (drizzled with lemon juice to prevent it from turning brown) and whole radishes between the flowers. Serve with brown bread and butter.

POTATO AND HAM FRITTATA WITH ROCKET

Serves 6

Potato and ham has to be one of the most delicious combinations there is. Every Christmas I cook a leg of pickled pork, which my family finds more delicious than ham, and make this light, old-fashioned dish with the leftovers.

6 large potatoes, peeled
3 tablespoons olive oil
1½ cups chopped onions
300 g thinly sliced cooked ham, cut into neat squares
3 tablespoons chopped parsley
½ cup milk
salt and pepper
small knob butter
3 eggs, beaten
½ cup grated gouda cheese
½ cup rocket flowers

Boil the potatoes in salted water until tender. Heat the oil in a frying pan and sauté the onions until lightly browned. Add the ham and parsley and stir fry briefly. Set aside. Mash the potatoes with the milk, a little salt and pepper and a small knob of butter. Lay the onions and ham in a baking dish. Spread the potatoes on top of them and pour over the egg and parsley mixture, making holes in the potato so that it can penetrate. Sprinkle with cheese and bake at 180 °C for about 10 minutes or until the eggs are set. Sprinkle over the rocket flowers just before serving. Serve with a green salad.

MUSHROOM AND ROCKET SOUP

Serves 6

Rich and tasty, this is a wonderfully sustaining soup that is a meal in itself.

1 medium onion, finely chopped
2 tablespoons sunflower oil
250 g large brown mushrooms, chopped
2 teaspoons fresh thyme
1 cup finely chopped fresh celery
1½ litres good beef or chicken stock
sea salt and black pepper to taste
1 litre milk
½ cup finely chopped fresh parsley
1 cup rocket flowers

Sauté the onion in the oil until it just starts to brown. Add the mushrooms, thyme and celery and stir-fry for a few minutes. Add the stock and seasoning. Simmer for about 6 minutes. Add the milk and simmer gently for about another 6 minutes. Serve in big bowls with croutons and sprinkle with parsley and rocket flowers. Add a squeeze of fresh lemon juice if desired, and place a lemon wedge on the edge of each soup bowl.

ROCKET AND CHICKEN LIVER PÂTÉ

Serves 4-6

Served on buttered toast, this delicious Mediterranean dish is one of the best pâtés I know and it is easy to make.

1 cup finely chopped onion
2 tablespoons butter
350 g chicken livers
sea salt and black pepper to taste
juice of 1 lemon
2 teaspoons fresh thyme
2 tablespoons medium dry sherry
½-¾ cup thinly sliced, stoned olives
½ cup rocket flowers

In a large frying pan, fry the onions in the butter until they just start to brown. Trim the chicken livers and chop them up. Add to the onion and butter and fry gently. Add the sea salt, black pepper and lemon juice and stir well. Finally add the thyme, olives and sherry and stir well until everything is thoroughly mixed. Spoon into a glass dish and sprinkle the rocket flowers over the top. Chill and serve with toast or biscuits.

ROSELLE SALAD

Serves 4-6

Roselle's high vitamin C, iron, calcium and potassium content make this salad a superb health builder. It may be served as an accompaniment to a meal or as a substantial meal in itself, with brown bread.

4 cups watercress
1 cup roselle leaves, torn into small pieces
2 cups roselle flowers and calyxes broken
off their seed capsules
2 cups finely chopped sweet peppers
2 cups chopped celery leaves and stalks
1 cup chopped button mushrooms
2 cups cooked chick peas
½ cup finely chopped parsley
1 cup chopped onions (optional)
juice of 1 lemon
½ cup olive oil

Mix everything together and add in the oil and lemon juice.

ROSE-SCENTED GERANIUM MASHED POTATOES

Serves 4

Delicate, tasty and so unusual, serve this delicious side dish with chicken breasts and new peas.

6 large potatoes, peeled and boiled until soft
1 tablespoon butter
sea salt and black pepper to taste
about ½ cup milk
1 teaspoon cinnamon
squeeze lemon juice
½ cup rose-scented geranium flowers

Mash the potatoes with the butter, salt and pepper. Add a little milk to keep it all light and fluffy. Add the cinnamon and a squeeze of lemon juice and a little more milk if necessary. Finally add the rose-scented geranium flowers. Spoon into neat little heaps. Keep hot until ready to serve and decorate each heap with a scented geranium flower.

SAGE AND PUMPKIN SOUP

Serves 6-8

This is real comfort food for a cold winter's night and a health booster.

8 cups peeled and diced pumpkin
3 onions, finely chopped
2 tablespoons grated ginger root
sea salt to taste
1 small chilli, finely chopped
or 2 teaspoons cayenne pepper
½ cup parsley
¼-½ cup chopped sage leaves and flowers
about 2 tablespoons olive oil
½ cup brown sugar
about 2½ litres chicken stock

Sauté the onions in the oil until they start to brown, then add all the other ingredients except for the parsley. Simmer gently and add more water if necessary. Test if the pumpkin is tender after 20 minutes. Pour into a liquidiser and whirl until smooth. Reheat if necessary. Serve in hot soup bowls with brown crusty bread and sprinkle the parsley over the top. Decorate with a few sage flowers.

YELLOW SORREL SALAD

Serves 4-6

This is the first spring salad and all of these are spring ingredients – its sharp piquant taste makes it a firm favourite with everyone. Serve with sorrel mayonnaise (see recipe below).

1 butter lettuce
2 papinos or 1 medium pawpaw, peeled and diced
2 oranges, peeled and sliced
2 cups celery, sliced
2 cups watercress
2 cups finely grated carrots
2 avocados, peeled and diced
1 cup grated fresh peeled butternut
4 hard-boiled eggs, peeled and sliced
black pepper
1 cup Cape sorrel flowers

Line a dish with butter lettuce leaves. Lightly mix everything except the sorrel flowers and the eggs. Spoon onto the bed of lettuce leaves, place the sliced egg over the top. Grind some black pepper over it all and sprinkle with sorrel flowers.

SORREL SALAD DRESSING

Makes 1 small bottle

This is a type of quick mayonnaise that is made so easily that I always have the ingredients in the fridge, and it is far healthier than the stabilised and preserved commercial mayonnaises.

½ cup thick cream
½ cup plain yoghurt
½ cup runny honey
½ cup apple juice
2 teaspoons mustard powder
1 tablespoon finely chopped parsley
1 tablespoon finely chopped chives
sea salt and black pepper to taste
½ cup fresh Cape sorrel flowers

Whisk the cream lightly until it holds its shape. Add the yoghurt and whisk lightly. Mix the honey and apple juice and mustard powder together and add to the cream and yoghurt mixture. Add the parsley, chives, sea salt and black pepper to taste, and finally stir in the Cape sorrel flowers. Pour into a small jug to serve, and serve with the yellow sorrel salad or with fish or chicken dishes.

Beetroot and St John's Wort Health Salad

Serves 4

This is a real health booster salad. The yellow petals brighten up this dish – and our mood as well!

4 well washed fresh beetroots
2 peeled apples
juice of 1 lemon
black pepper and coriander seeds in a pepper grinder
½ cup finely chopped parsley
½ cup St John's wort flowers

Grate the beetroots and apples. Mix well and spoon into a bowl. Pour over the lemon juice. Grind the pepper and coriander seeds over it and sprinkle with parsley and the St John's wort flowers.

Potato and St John's Wort Bake

Serves 4

About 8 medium potatoes peeled and sliced very thinly
4 tablespoons butter softened to room temperature
sea salt and black pepper to taste
2 cloves garlic finely chopped (optional)
2-4 teaspoons freshly grated nutmeg
200 ml cream
200 ml milk
1 cup St John's wort flowers,
petals pulled out of their calyxes

Grease a baking dish well. Scatter the garlic over the base of the dish. Layer the potatoes overlapping them slightly, and season with the sea salt, nutmeg, black pepper and a light sprinkling of the St John's wort petals. Dot with butter. Whisk the milk and cream together. Pour over the cream mixture and bake uncovered at 180°C until the potatoes are tender and the top layer is golden and crisp – about 1½ hours.

Stuffed Avocados with St John's Wort

Serves 4

This makes an excellent starter.

2 large avocados, cut in half and the stone removed
lemon juice
1 tin sardines, drained and mashed
1 small onion, finely chopped
1 cup St John's wort flowers, calyxes removed
sea salt and black pepper

Scoop out the flesh of the avocados carefully so as not to damage the skins, and mash. Sprinkle with lemon juice to prevent it from turning brown. Mix in the sardines, onion, St John's wort flowers and the salt and pepper. Spoon into the empty skins, sprinkle with more lemon juice and serve on a bed of lettuce. Sprinkle with St John's wort flowers.

Beetroot and Sunflower Petal Salad

Serves 6

The sunflower petals turn an old favourite into a striking summer salad.

3 medium-sized onions, thinly sliced
about 3 tablespoons olive oil
12 small young beetroot, peeled and thinly sliced
1 cup water
1 tablespoon flour
2 tablespoons honey
2 tablespoons lemon juice
sea salt and black pepper to taste
1 cup sunflower petals

Sauté the onion rings in the oil, then add the beetroot. Stir fry briefly and add ½ cup water. Mix the flour with the honey, lemon juice, salt and pepper and stir into the onions and beetroot. Add another ½ cup water and the sunflower petals. Turn down the heat and cover the pot. Simmer gently for about 15 minutes, then remove from the heat and allow to cool. Sprinkle with a little chopped parsley. Serve as a salad with cold chicken.

Thyme Immune Boosting Soup

Serves 6-8

This is our grandmother's recipe. A true comfort soup that no one ever tires of.

a little olive oil
3 cups onions, roughly chopped
2 cups potatoes, finely grated
1½ litres good chicken stock
1 cup pearl barley, soaked overnight
2 cups carrots, finely grated
2 cups celery, finely chopped, leaves included
1 small red chilli, finely chopped, seeds removed
or 1 teaspoon cayenne pepper
juice of 2 lemons
2 teaspoons finely grated lemon zest
½ cup fresh thyme leaves and flowers
sea salt to taste

Fry the onions in the oil until they start to brown, add the grated potatoes and stir fry until they start to colour. Then add all the other ingredients and simmer with the lid on until everything is tender and the soup is tasty. Serve steaming hot with crusty brown bread.

Tuberose Vegetable Soup

Serves 6

This is adapted from the old Chinese recipe. It is light and refreshing, perfect as a starter to be followed by a rich meal.

Dandelion and bacon salad, p. 92

Yarrow kedgeree, p. 120

2 tablespoons olive oil
2 cups finely chopped onions
2 cups thinly sliced mushrooms
2 cups chopped green peppers
4 cups diced celery stalks
2 litres chicken stock
1 cup cooked brown rice
2 tablespoons pure soy sauce with no MSG added
3 tablespoons fresh lemon juice
sea salt and black pepper to taste
1 cup tuberose flowers lightly sliced
nutmeg

Fry the onions in the olive oil, add the mushrooms and brown lightly. Add the green peppers and celery and stir fry for 3 minutes. Add all the other ingredients and simmer gently for about 15 minutes. Serve hot in bowls with a fresh tuberose flower floating on top. Dust with nutmeg.

THREE BEAN SALAD WITH TULIPS

Serves 6
Perfect for a vegetarian meal, this salad keeps well in the fridge.

1 cup large white butter beans
1 cup haricot beans
2 cups green beans, finely sliced lengthways
petals of 3-4 tulips, thinly sliced
plus 3-4 unsliced tulips

DRESSING

½ cup runny honey
½ cup good olive oil
½ cup fresh lemon juice
2 tablespoons balsamic vinegar
3 teaspoons mustard powder
½ cup finely chopped onions
a little garlic (optional)
about 2 teaspoons sea salt
1 tablespoon crushed coriander seed
1 tablespoon crushed sesame seed

Soak the white butter and haricot beans overnight. The next day, boil them until they are tender. Boil the green beans until they are tender but still fairly crisp. Allow all the beans to cool.

Mix together the dressing ingredients, pour into a jar with a tight-fitting lid and shake vigorously. Pour over the salad and fold in well. Place the petals of 3 or 4 tulips around the dish, filling with a little of the bean salad, and grind black pepper over everything. Serve with crusty bread.

WATER LILY SALAD

Serves 4
Multicoloured water lily petals look festive in a salad and have a crisp texture.

1 pineapple, thinly sliced
1 small cucumber, thinly sliced
1 apple, peeled and finely grated
1 medium-sized raw beetroot, finely grated
1 green pepper, diced
petals from 2 or 3 water lilies, pulled from their calyxes
juice of 2 oranges
2 tablespoons honey
2 tablespoons chopped pecan nuts
2 teaspoons crushed coriander seed
sea salt and paprika to taste

Arrange the pineapple and cucumber in a flat glass dish. Mix together the apple and beetroot and pile the mixture in the centre. Sprinkle with green pepper. Arrange the water lily petals around the beetroot and apple to create a circle like a flower. Mix the orange juice with the honey and pour over everything. Sprinkle with the pecan nuts, coriander, salt and paprika. Serve chilled.

WATERMELON BALLS WITH RICOTTA AND WATER LILY

Serves 6-8
This is such a pretty starter for a Christmas dinner, your guests cannot fail to be impressed.

half a watermelon
250 g ricotta cheese
4 tablespoons finely chopped fresh mint
about 1½ cups fresh multicoloured water lily petals
1½ cups litchi juice
about 2 teaspoons ground ginger or
2 tablespoons grated fresh ginger

Scoop out neat balls from the watermelon half and arrange them in individual glass dishes. Using a teaspoon, scoop out small amounts of ricotta cheese and drop them over the watermelon. Sprinkle with chopped mint. Tuck the water lily petals all around the edges, drizzle with a little litchi juice and finally sprinkle with ginger. Serve chilled.

WATERBLOMMETJIE SOUP

Serves 6-8
This soup varies from area to area of the Cape and all sorts of vegetables can be added.

2 large onions, finely chopped
3 tablespoons olive oil
2 cups finely chopped celery
2 cups finely grated carrots
6 cups waterblommetjies, well washed
3 cups peeled and diced tomatoes
4 potatoes, peeled and finely grated
½ cup honey
1 litre chicken stock
juice of 1 lemon
sea salt and black pepper to taste
1 litre milk

Sauté the onion in the oil. Add the celery and carrots and stir fry until the onions are golden and the carrots and celery start to turn light brown. Add all the ingredients except for the milk. Simmer until tender, adding a little extra chicken stock if necessary. Stir every now and then. Add the milk just before serving. Serve piping hot with crusty brown bread.

Winter Savory and Cabbage Mealie Soup

Serves 6-8

Hearty, warming and delicious. Use fresh mealies in season and 'samp' in winter.

4 onions finely chopped
2 cups chopped brown mushrooms
2 cups celery, finely chopped
4 cups green outer cabbage leaves, finely shredded
2 tablespoons winter savory flowering sprigs
2 cups 'samp' or 'stampmielies', soaked for
at least 3 hours in warm water
or 4 cups green mealies cooked and cut off their cobs
about ½ cup olive oil
juice of 2 lemons
2 teaspoons crushed coriander seed
2 tablespoons chopped parsley
2 litres good strong chicken stock
sea salt and black pepper to taste

In a large heavy pot fry the onions in the oil until golden brown. Add the mushrooms and fry until golden, then add the celery and finally the cabbage with the winter savory sprigs. Stir fry well. Add all the other ingredients and simmer gently for about 40 minutes. Serve the soup in individual bowls and sprinkle some chopped parsley and lots of little winter savory flowers pulled from their calyxes over the top. Serve with brown bread rolls.

Winter Savory Sauce for Pasta

Serves 4-6

This simple cheese sauce is easily and quickly made and can top toast, pasta, cauliflower and cabbage.

1 litre milk
3 tablespoons flour whisked into 2 eggs
sea salt, black pepper and paprika to taste
3 teaspoons mustard powder
2 cups finely grated cheddar cheese
1 cup ricotta or smooth cream cheese
1 tablespoon winter savory flowers and a few tiny leaves

In a heavy saucepan simmer the milk, then add the flour and egg mixture, whisking all the time. Add the sea salt, black pepper, paprika and mustard powder and the winter savory. As it starts to thicken, turn down the heat and briskly stir in the cheddar cheese and the ricotta or cream cheese. If it gets too thick, add a little milk and stir to a smooth paste-like consistency. Pour immediately over the hot pasta and dust with more paprika or serve over hot buttered toast.

Wisteria and Watercress Spring Salad

Serves 4

As one emerges from winter into spring, a fresh salad seems very appealing and this one is particularly so. Fresh watercress with its wonderful tonic effects make this an excellent health salad.

4 cups watercress sprigs
2 cups thinly sliced cucumber
2 large, sweet oranges
2 cups nasturtium flowers and a few leaves
1 cup diced feta cheese
½ cup chopped parsley
½ cup chopped celery leaves
1 cup wisteria flowers, pulled off their stems

Dressing

½ cup balsamic vinegar
2 teaspoons crushed coriander
2 tablespoons honey
1 teaspoon mustard powder

Arrange the watercress and cucumber in a salad bowl. Peel each orange segment and place on top of the watercress and cucumber, along with the nasturtiums, feta, parsley and celery. Sprinkle with wisteria flowers. Put the dressing ingredients into a jar, seal and shake. Pour the dressing over the whole salad just before serving.

Wisteria Country Borscht

Serves 6

This rich red, refreshing beetroot soup is perfect for a warm spring luncheon and with the sweetness of the wisteria, makes a party meal. You can serve it hot without the yoghurt and with a spoon of sour cream instead, but traditionally borscht is served chilled.

1 large onion, finely chopped
1 large leek, thinly sliced
a little olive oil
1 large carrot, finely grated
2 sticks celery, finely chopped
about 6 medium-sized raw beetroot, peeled and grated
2 litres good stock
sea salt and coarsely ground black pepper
juice of 2 lemons
about ½ cup good red wine
1 tablespoon honey
1 cup wisteria flowers, stems removed
250 ml plain Bulgarian yoghurt
½ cup finely chopped parsley

Sauté the onion and the leek in the oil. Add the carrot and the celery and stir fry until they start to brown lightly. Add all the other ingredients except the wisteria flowers, yoghurt and parsley. Simmer for about 40 minutes with the lid on until all the vegetables are tender. At this point you can strain and discard the vegetables and serve a clear soup, or put everything through a liquidiser. Chill if desired and serve with a spoon or two of yoghurt in each bowl, a grinding of black pepper and sprinkled with parsley and wisteria flowers.

Yucca Flower Soup

Serves 4

This can be served as a soup dusted with paprika, or poured over a bowl of rice and eaten as a main course like the Mexicans do, with garlic and chillis added.

1 cup split peas
2 cups chopped onions
½ cup olive oil
3 cups yucca petals
1 cup chopped green pepper
4-6 large tomatoes, skinned and chopped
3 tablespoons brown sugar
sea salt and black pepper to taste
juice of 1 lemon
paprika to taste
2 litres good stock

Soak the split peas in boiling water for 1 hour. In a heavy bottomed pot, fry the onions in the olive oil until golden. Add the yucca petals and green pepper. Stir fry until they start to brown. Add all the remaining ingredients, including the peas, and simmer gently for about 5 minutes.

MAIN MEALS

... casseroles, stews, stir fries and vegetarian dishes

ANISE HYSSOP AND MUSHROOM STIR FRY

Serves 4

The typically liquorice-like taste of the anise hyssop makes it a marvellous addition to celery and mushrooms, and this vegetarian dish is so quick and easy to prepare that I always keep a pack of mushrooms in my fridge and celery and anise hyssop growing close to the kitchen door.

2 finely chopped onions
3-5 thinly sliced leeks
about 3 tablespoons olive oil
1 cup anise hyssop flowers lightly broken up
1 packet mushrooms, thinly sliced
1 head of celery, about 6 stalks
sea salt and cayenne pepper to taste
juice of 1 lemon
about 1 cup water
dash Worcestershire sauce
1 cup grated mozzarella cheese

Brown the onions and leeks in the olive oil with the anise hyssop flowers. Add the mushrooms and lightly brown them, then the celery and lemon juice and salt and pepper. Stir fry gently. Add the water and let it sizzle quickly, stir frying all the time (this makes a superb sauce). Lastly add the dash of Worcestershire sauce and the mozzarella cheese. Serve hot with brown bread and butter or mashed potatoes or brown rice, and a green salad.

PORK POT ROAST WITH ANISE HYSSOP

Serves 6

This makes an interesting change for Sunday lunch. It needs to be slowly and succulently cooked in one of those heavy cast iron pots with a good lid.

about 10-12 thin slices of very lean pork
sunflower oil
4 large onions, thinly sliced
3 large red or green sweet peppers, thinly sliced
sea salt and black pepper to taste
juice of 2 lemons
6 large potatoes, peeled and cut in half
6 large carrots, peeled and cut into strips
1 cup anise hyssop flowers, stripped of their stalks
a few anise hyssop leaves
¾ cup sultanas

2 cups chopped celery
½ cup chopped parsley
about 1 litre water
4 cups fresh garden peas

Brown the meat on both sides in a little sunflower oil. Add the onions and brown. Gradually add all the other ingredients except the parsley and peas. Adjust the seasoning, cover and turn down the heat to simmer. Add water as needed and taste every now and then. I often add another dash of lemon juice or more salt and pepper. Simmer gently, stirring every now and then until the meat is tender and the vegetables cooked. Boil the peas separately with a sprig of mint. Serve the meat in its big cast iron pot with the peas and parsley sprinkled over it, with brown rice.

> **Cook's Note**
>
> IN SRI LANKA BANANA BUDS ARE A WELL-LOVED VEGETABLE BOILED AND SERVED WITH LEMON JUICE, SALT AND FISH, AND IN CHINA THEY ARE PICKLED. ALWAYS PREPARE THE FLOWERS WITH SALT AND LEMON JUICE BEFORE COOKING WITH THEM, AS DESCRIBED IN THE RECIPE BELOW.

BANANA BLOSSOM PAELLA

Serves 4-6

This is an easy to prepare Mauritian recipe that varies from village to village as the ingredients become available through the season.

Note: To prepare banana flowers for cooking, remove the tough, sheath-like covering from the flower. Slice the flower thinly crosswise, sprinkle with salt and let it stand for an hour. Squeeze it with the salt, add lemon juice and squeeze again, then rinse. This removes any milky sap and astringency and makes the flower more tender.

4 medium onions, chopped
4 cups white fish, skinned deboned and cubed
a few shrimps or langoustines, shelled and deveined
¼-½ cup olive oil
2 cups banana flowers, shredded and rinsed
2 green or red sweet peppers, cut into strips
½ cup desiccated coconut
½ cup sesame seeds
juice of 1 lemon
sea salt and cayenne pepper to taste
½ cup chopped mint

108

In a large wok brown the onions and fish in the oil. Add the banana flowers and stir fry for about 10 minutes. Then add the green or red peppers and stir fry, turning frequently. Add all the other ingredients except the mint and keep stir frying. Finally add the mint. Serve immediately, on a bed of rice. Add a little water to the juices in the pan and pour over everything.

Banana Flower Kari-Kari

Serves 4

This quick and delicious dish was probably first enjoyed in the Philippines. It has many variants, but this is the plainest.

> 2 cups thinly shredded banana flowers, turned in salt and lemon juice
> 4 cups slivered topside beef
> sunflower oil
> 3 garlic cloves, thinly slivered
> 2 medium onions, thinly sliced
> 2 cups green spring onions, chopped
> 1-2 tablespoons grated ginger root
> 2 tablespoons soy sauce
> about 1 cup water
> salt and pepper to taste

Prepare the banana flowers with salt and lemon juice as described in the recipe above. Meanwhile gently sauté the beef in the oil until brown, then add the garlic and onion. When soft, add the banana flowers that have been drenched in fresh lemon juice. Add the spring onions and grated ginger root, soy sauce and water, and salt and pepper to taste. Simmer gently for about 10 minutes, adding more water if necessary. Serve with rice or pasta.

Banana Flower and Mushroom Sauce

Serves 4

This is rich and satisfying. Dip fresh bread in it for a summer supper. Soak the raisins overnight beforehand and prepare the flowers as described above.

> 2 medium minced onions
> ½-¾ cup olive oil
> 3 cups finely chopped brown mushrooms
> 2 cups banana flowers, thinly sliced and prepared as described on p. 108
> 2 tablespoons lemon juice
> sea salt and cayenne pepper to taste
> 1-2 tablespoons rich soy sauce
> ½ tablespoon Worcestershire sauce

> 1 cup seedless raisins, soaked overnight and then finely chopped
> 1 cup minced celery
> about 2 cups water

Brown the onions in the olive oil, then add the mushrooms and then the banana flowers. Stir fry for 5 minutes, then add the soy sauce, Worcestershire sauce, raisins and celery. Stir fry briskly, then add the lemon juice, salt and pepper. Adjust water and simmer gently for 5 minutes or until everything is tender. Add a little more water. Serve as a dip with chips or pour over baked potatoes or pasta or rice.

Roasted Okra with Bergamot Flowers

Serves 4

This is an extraordinary lunch dish that I have grown very fond of ever since I grew a magnificent crop of okra in my kitchen garden. The secret is to use very young and tender pods. Serve it with roast chicken and roast potatoes.

> about very young 20 okra pods
> olive oil
> salt and black pepper
> ½ cup chopped bergamot petals
> juice of 1 lemon
> parmesan cheese
> Tabasco sauce

Trim the stalks off the pods. Dip each pod into olive oil and lay them on a baking sheet. Sprinkle with salt, black pepper, chopped bergamot petals and lemon juice. Roast for 20 minutes or until the pods start to crisp. Sprinkle with parmesan cheese and a few drops of Tabasco, and serve hot.

Buckwheat Flower Stir Fry

Serves 2-4

I love stir fries and make them often, especially after a hard day when there is little energy left to make a big meal. Use whatever ingredients you have for variety. Serve it with buckwheat groats (cook them as you would cook rice) or brown rice or even just brown bread and butter. It is nourishing and filling and very healthy.

> 1 medium-sized aubergine
> 1 large onion, finely chopped
> 2-4 tablespoons olive oil
> 2 cups chopped buckwheat flowers
> 2 cups peeled grated potato
> 2 cups thinly sliced mushrooms
> 2 cups grated or thinly sliced courgettes
> 1 tablespoon fresh thyme
> 1 tablespoon chopped mint
> sea salt and black pepper to taste
> juice of 1 lemon

Peel and slice the aubergine thinly and soak in cold, salted water while you prepare the rest. Fry the onion in the olive oil until it starts to brown. Add the buckwheat flowers and stir fry, then add the potato. Add a little more oil if necessary and once the potato starts to brown, add the aubergine slices. (Pat the aubergines dry before adding to the stir fry.) Stir fry well. Add all the other ingredients, shaking the pan and stirring all the time. Serve hot on rice with a green salad and squeeze more lemon juice over it.

CALENDULA CURRY

Serves 6-8

Nourishing and warming on a winter's night, this is a hearty standby dish that freezes well and keeps well in the fridge. Omit the meat if you are vegetarian and substitute with mushrooms.

500 g diced lean beef (topside or rump)
2 cups chopped onions
½ cup sunflower cooking oil
2 cups diced carrots
2 cups chopped celery
3 cups chopped tomatoes
2 cups chopped green peppers
3 cups peeled, diced potatoes
1-2 cups calendula petals
½ cup honey
½-¾ cup fruit chutney
2 tablespoons curry powder mixed with a little milk
about 1 litre water
salt and cayenne pepper to taste

In a heavy bottomed pot, brown the meat and onions in the oil. Add all the other ingredients. Simmer gently, stirring every now and then. Adjust the flavour if necessary and add more water if it boils away. Simmer until the meat is tender. Serve piping hot, sprinkled with more calendula petals, with brown rice and peas.

> **Cook's Note**
>
> CALENDULA IS USED AS A NATURAL YELLOW FOOD COLOURING IN THE FOOD INDUSTRY. THE BRIGHT ORANGE PETALS CAN BE ADDED TO EVERYTHING FROM DRINKS TO JAMS, CURRIES TO DESSERTS, RICE DISHES TO PANCAKES. I SPRINKLE THE FRESH PETALS ON EVERY DISH ALL THROUGH THE WINTER (NEVER USE THE GREEN PARTS – IT IS ONLY THE PETALS THAT HAVE MEDICINAL PROPERTIES).

CARAWAY FISH CURRY

Serves 4

Nourishing, delicious and easy, this dish is good as it is, or it can be spiced up with aubergines, mushrooms, mango slices or pawpaw slices for example.

4-6 deboned hake fillets
sunflower cooking oil
juice of 1 lemon
sea salt and cayenne pepper to taste
1 tablespoon finely grated ginger
2 teaspoons crushed caraway seeds
4 large tomatoes, peeled and chopped
4 medium onions, finely chopped
a few fresh green curry tree leaves
2 tablespoons honey
1 teaspoon ground coriander seed
1-2 teaspoons turmeric
1-2 teaspoons good curry powder
1 cup caraway flowers

Gently fry the fish in a little sunflower cooking oil with lemon juice, sea salt and cayenne pepper, ginger and caraway seeds. Meanwhile soak the tomatoes in boiling water to facilitate peeling, then peel and chop. Add to the fish and gently simmer. In another pan, fry the chopped onion in a little oil until it browns. Add the curry leaves (if you have them), honey, spices and caraway flowers and cook for a few minutes. Then mix it all into the fish and tomato mixture. Add a little water if necessary and simmer for 4 minutes. Serve with rice and decorate with caraway flowers.

CHICORY STIR FRY

Serves 4

The apple is an excellent complement to the chicory in this thoroughly tasty and nutritious stir fry. It must be served immediately.

olive oil
2 medium-sized onions, chopped
2 cups thinly sliced leeks
2 cups thinly sliced brown mushrooms
2 apples, peeled and coarsely grated
½ cup parsley
2 sticks celery, chopped (leaves included)
1 cup chicory flowers
1 cup peeled and coarsely grated sweet potato
sea salt and cayenne pepper to taste
juice of 1 lemon
½ cup sesame seeds
1 dessertspoon Worcestershire sauce

Start off by stir frying the onions and leeks in the olive oil, browning them well. Then add the mushrooms and stir fry briskly. Add the apples, parsley, celery, chicory flowers and sweet potato and season with salt and cayenne pepper. Finally add the lemon juice, sesame seeds and lastly add the Worcestershire sauce. Stir fry until tender and serve piping hot with brown rice.

> **Cook's Note**
>
> REMEMBER, CHICORY IS A BITTER HERB AND THE APLLE TAKES SOME OF THE BITTERNESS OUT. BUT, LIKE DANDELION, IT IS SO GOOD FOR YOU IT IS WORTH USING OFTEN.

CREAMED SPINACH AND CHIVE FLOWER SUPPER DISH

Serves 4

A nourishing and delicious vegetarian dish that everyone enjoys and it helps keep colds and flu at bay.

large bunch chopped spinach
(to make 4 cups cooked)
2 cups chopped onion
1 cup chive flowers
2 tablespoons butter
3-4 tablespoons cornflour
500 ml milk
1 cup plain Bulgarian yoghurt
sea salt and black pepper to taste
2 teaspoons mustard powder
1 cup grated cheddar cheese

Cook the spinach, onion and chive flowers in a little salted water for about 6 minutes. Strain well. In another pan, melt the butter, mix in the cornflour and add the milk and yoghurt slowly, whisking all the time. Lastly, as it thickens, add the seasoning and mustard powder and the cheese. Mix the white sauce into the spinach and onions, spoon into a baking dish, top with more grated cheese and quickly brown the cheese under the grill for a few moments. Serve hot, decorated with chive flowers, with crusty brown bread.

CAULIFLOWER AND CLOVER CHEESE

Serves 4

This is a nourishing supper dish. The clover lends its delicious honey-like taste to the cheese sauce.

1 large or 2 small cauliflowers
500 ml milk
1 cup clover flowers
2 eggs, well beaten
2 tablespoons flour
sea salt and cayenne pepper to taste
½ cup cold milk
1 cup grated strong cheddar cheese

Break the cauliflowers into florets and boil in salted water for 20 minutes. Heat the 500 ml milk with the clover flowers to boiling point and turn down the heat. Whisk the eggs with the flour, salt and pepper and add about ½ cup of cold milk. Gradually add this to the hot milk and clover and stir briskly while it thickens, being careful not to let it burn. Finally add the cheese, keeping some aside for the top.

Drain the cauliflower well and place in an ovenproof dish. Pour the cheese sauce over it and sprinkle with more cheese. Place it under the grill to melt the cheese and serve piping hot, decorated with clover flowers.

LENTIL AND CLOVER RISOTTO

Serves 4

This quick and easy vegetarian dish is full of healthy goodness.

1 large onion, finely chopped
2 tablespoons olive oil
1 cup finely chopped green pepper
2 cups cooked lentils
1 cup cooked brown rice
1 cup mung bean sprouts
1 cup clover flowers
1 tablespoon finely chopped parsley
juice of 1 lemon
sea salt and black pepper to taste

Fry the onions in the oil until golden brown. Add the green pepper and stir fry well. Then add everything else and stir fry. Add a little water and quickly cook through with the lid on for 6 minutes. Serve piping hot, decorated with clover flowers, with a salad.

AUBERGINE AND CORIANDER FLOWER LUNCH DISH

Serves 4

This superb way of serving aubergine was given to me by an Indian chef.

4 medium-sized aubergines
2 large onions, thinly sliced
2 tablespoons olive oil
3 large tomatoes, skinned and chopped
juice of 1 lemon
2 tablespoons freshly grated ginger root
1 tablespoon coriander flowers, without stems
1 teaspoon crushed coriander seed
1 large green pepper, thinly sliced
sea salt and pepper to taste
2 tablespoons honey

Peel and slice the aubergines, sprinkle well with salt, and cover with a heavy weight to allow them to exude their bitter juices for about 20 minutes. Sauté the onions in the oil until lightly brown. Rinse the aubergines and add to the onion along with the tomatoes. Stir fry well. Then add all the other ingredients and stir well. Cover with a well-fitting lid and turn down the heat. Simmer gently for about 7 minutes. Serve with brown rice and decorate with coriander flowers.

MEXICAN MEALIE AND CHILLI DISH WITH DAHLIA FLOWERS

Serves 4-6

Exotically different, this bright, spicy and delicious country dish varies from village to village in its native Mexico. Serve it in the green mealie husks for a braai or a picnic.

6 mealies
1 cup onion, finely chopped
about ½ cup olive oil
½-1 hot fresh chilli, finely chopped
2 green peppers, finely chopped
2 cups chopped spring onions
sea salt and black pepper to taste
juice of 1 lemon
about ¾ cup mixed dahlia petals

Boil the mealies until tender, then cool slightly and cut off the cobs. Brown the onion in the oil, add the chilli and green pepper, then stir in the mealies and spring onions. Add the sea salt, black pepper and the lemon juice. Lastly add the dahlia petals. Serve hot in a wooden bowl and decorate with dahlia petals.

Day Lily Stir Fry

Serves 4

This is a tasty, quick and easy supper dish that can be served in minutes and can be varied according to the ingredients you have at the time.

a little olive oil
2 onions, thinly sliced
1 packet large brown mushrooms, roughly sliced
2 green peppers, thinly sliced
8 baby marrows, cut into thin strips
about 10 day lily flowers and buds, thinly sliced
juice of 1 lemon
sea salt and black pepper to taste
about ½ cup chopped parsley

In a large wok or pan heat the olive oil and add the onions. Let them lightly brown and then add the mushrooms, green peppers and baby marrows and stir fry well, turning constantly. Add the day lilies, lemon juice, sea salt and pepper and stir well. Finally add the parsley and serve piping hot with brown rice.

> **Cook's Note**
>
> COOKING WITH DAY LILIES IS AN ONGOING PLEASURE. THEIR CRISP, GREEN BEAN-LIKE TASTE ENHANCES SALADS AND STIR FRIES. BUDS AND FLOWERS CAN BE STEAMED OR FRIED AND THEY COMPLEMENT JUST ABOUT ANY DISH.

Steamed Day Lilies and Asparagus

Serves 4

In spring when the first asparagus comes into the market, the first day lilies start to flower. Pick the buds just as they start to colour and steam them with the asparagus for a deliciously healthy spring treat.

2-3 packets asparagus
4 cups day lily buds

Sauce

2 eggs, beaten
2 cups full cream milk
2 teaspoons mustard powder
1 tablespoon butter
2 tablespoons cornflour
1 teaspoon salt
black pepper to taste
1 cup grated cheddar cheese

Place the flower buds and asparagus in a steamer and cook until they are tender. For the sauce, whisk the eggs into the milk and mustard powder. Heat the butter and the cornflour, stirring well. Add the egg and milk mixture and stir well until it thickens. Add the salt, pepper and cheese, stirring all the time until it reaches the correct consistency. Remove from heat. Place the asparagus spears neatly on individual plates, surrounded by the day lily buds. Pour over the sauce and decorate with day lily petals. Serve hot as a nourishing lunch dish.

Roast Pork and Fruit Sage

Serves 6

Superb for a Sunday dinner and it is equally delicious cold.

2½-3 kg leg of pork
sea salt and black pepper to taste
2 onions, peeled and sliced thinly
2 apples, peeled and sliced thinly
½ cup fruit sage flowers chopped, calyx removed
1 cup chopped celery stalks and leaves
½ cup honey mixed with
2 teaspoons mustard powder
1 large sheet of tin foil

Preheat the oven to 180 °C. Trim the pork of excess fat and place on a double layer of tin foil. Spread the honey and mustard all over the pork. Sprinkle with salt and pepper, then lay the celery and fruit sage over the surface and cover with the onion rings and apples and sprinkle with a little more salt and pepper. Wrap up the tin foil tightly so that all the juices are retained. Place in a large baking tray and roast until tender, about 1 hour and 10 minutes. Serve with roast potatoes and roast onions and vegetables and decorate with fruit sage flowers. The flowers give an exotic taste to the pork!

Garland Chrysanthemum Stir Fry

Serves 4

The spicy taste of these easy to grow flowers gives this basic stir fry a different taste. Add seasonal ingredients to ring the changes.

sunflower cooking oil
1 cup finely chopped onions
1 cup thinly shredded carrots
3 cups thinly shredded cabbage
½ cup thinly shredded ginger root
1 cup garland chrysanthemum petals
1 cup garland chrysanthemum leaves
juice of 1 lemon
sea salt and black pepper to taste
dash of soy sauce

Fry the onions in a little oil until they start to brown. Then add the carrots and the cabbage and stir fry briskly. Add all the other ingredients and keep moving in the pan until the vegetables are tender but still crisp. Do not overcook. Serve piping hot with rice.

GLADIOLUS AND BEAN STEW

Serves 6-8

I first tasted this tasty stew in the Eastern Cape over 30 years ago. The elderly farm worker who gave me the recipe said his grandmother cultivated wild gladiolus around their grass hut especially for this. Use any organically grown gladiolus flower. The beans have to be soaked overnight beforehand.

500 g haricot beans
500 g large butter beans
4 large onions, finely chopped
a little sunflower oil
6 large tomatoes, skinned and chopped
1 finely chopped chilli, seeds removed
1 tablespoon crushed coriander seeds
1 cup brown sugar
1 cup brown grape vinegar
1 litre hot water
3-4 cups gladiolus flowers, roughly chopped
1 cup celery leaves
a little parsley

Soak the haricot beans and butter beans overnight. Next morning sauté the onions in the oil, then add the tomatoes, chilli, coriander seeds, sugar, vinegar and water. Rinse and drain the beans, and add them. Simmer gently with the lid on, adding more water from time to time and stirring well frequently. When the beans are tender, add the gladiolus flowers, celery leaves and parsley. Simmer only 5 minutes more. Serve piping hot with 'stywe pap', polenta or brown rice.

CHICKEN AND HAWTHORN FLOWER STIR FRY

Serves 4

This is a delicious supper dish that takes so little time and effort, I make it when the spring blossom is at its best. The chicken breasts are easiest to slice when semi-frozen. You can substitute thin slices of beef or mutton for the chicken.

3 skinless chicken breast fillets, thinly sliced
2 leeks, thinly sliced
2 cups thinly sliced button mushrooms
1 cup thinly sliced celery
1 peeled, grated apple
1 cup hawthorn buds and flowers stripped off their stalks
a little olive oil
sea salt and black pepper
fresh lemon juice to taste

First brown the chicken and the leeks, then add everything else, stirring all the time. Once the chicken is done, spoon out onto a bed of brown rice, decorate the plate with fresh hawthorn blossoms all around, and serve hot.

HYSSOP MEAL-IN-ONE CHICKEN DISH

Serves 4-6

This is a popular, easy to make chicken dish that I do on top of the stove in a large cast iron pot. It keeps well and reheats well. The hyssop imparts a delicious, fresh flavour that combines well with all the vegetables. For a change add sliced mushrooms, sliced aubergine and sliced tomatoes.

1 large chicken, cut into pieces or 1 pack chicken pieces
2 large onions, peeled and sliced
olive oil
2 green peppers, sliced
3 green mealies, cut off the cob
4 large potatoes, peeled and cubed
2 cups peeled, diced carrots
½ cup hyssop flowers
about 1 litre chicken stock
salt and pepper to taste
juice of 1 lemon

Brown the chicken pieces and the onion in the oil. Add all the other ingredients and stir, adding the chicken stock last. Simmer with the lid on for about 30 to 40 minutes, stirring every now and then, or until the chicken is tender. Just before serving, thicken the sauce with a little cornflour mixed with water if desired. Serve with brown rice or with crusty bread.

JUDAS TREE STIR FRY

Serves 4

For a quick supper dish, this is delicious. Vegetables in season can be added for a change.

2 onions, thinly sliced
4 potatoes, peeled and thinly sliced
2 cups thinly sliced mushrooms
2 cups Judas tree flowers
juice of 1 lemon
a little olive oil
½ cup chopped chives or spring onions
sea salt and black pepper to taste
½ cup parsley

Heat the oil in a frying pan or wok and lightly brown the onions. Add all the other ingredients except for the parsley. Stir fry quickly. Serve piping hot sprinkled with parsley and decorated with Judas tree flowers.

SPAGHETTI AND TOMATO WITH LINSEED

Serves 4-6

A quick and easy supper dish, which is dead simple.

500 g spaghetti
1 large onion, peeled and chopped
1 clove garlic, finely chopped (optional)
4 large tomatoes, skinned and chopped
2 tablespoons brown sugar
sea salt and freshly ground black pepper
½ cup linseed
6 finely chopped sweet basil leaves
freshly grated parmesan cheese
½ cup flax flowers
a little olive oil

Bring 4 litres of salted water to the boil, add the spaghetti and boil rapidly until *al dente* or just tender. Meanwhile fry the onion and garlic, if desired, in a little olive oil, add the tomatoes and stir fry. Add the sugar, sea salt and pepper and the linseed, and stir well until the tomatoes have softened. Remove from the stove and keep hot. Strain the pasta, return it to the pan with 1 tablespoon of olive oil in it. Add a little sea salt and black pepper and stir well until the pasta is well coated. Add the tomato sauce, mix in the chopped basil leaves and pour into a deep bowl. Sprinkle with the parmesan cheese and dot with the flax flowers. Serve immediately.

MINT AND MUSHROOM SUPPER DISH

Serves 4

A satisfying vegetarian dish that is easy to make.

4 cups button mushrooms
4 medium onions, peeled and sliced
4 large tomatoes, peeled and sliced
sea salt and black pepper to taste
½ cup finely broken up mint flowers
and chopped leaves
1 cup good vegetable stock
2 cups fresh wholewheat breadcrumbs
1 cup grated mozzarella cheese
mint flowers for decoration

Arrange the mushrooms in an ovenproof baking dish, cutting the larger ones in half if they are too big. Top with onion rings and tomatoes, sprinkle with salt and pepper and the mint flowers and leaves. Add the stock. Mix together the breadcrumbs

and mozzarella cheese and sprinkle over the dish. Bake at 180 °C for about 20 minutes or until the onions and mushrooms are tender and the topping lightly browned. Decorate with mint flowers and serve piping hot with brown rice.

CHICK PEA AND MORINGA FLOWER SUPPER DISH

Serves 4

This traditional moringa recipe was given to me by an Indian homeopathic doctor who believes we should be enjoying this magical tree in some form or other at least twice a week.

2 cups chick peas
2 bay leaves
1 large onion, finely chopped
a little olive oil.
2 tomatoes, skinned and chopped
2 cups moringa flowers and leaves
2 teaspoons fresh origanum
1-2 tablespoons freshly grated ginger
2 tablespoons soy sauce
2 tablespoons runny honey
2 tablespoons lemon juice
2 tablespoons good fruit chutney

Soak the chick peas overnight. Next morning place them in fresh water with the bay leaves and boil until tender. Discard the bay leaves and drain. Meanwhile, fry the onion in a little olive oil. Add the tomatoes and stir fry quickly. Add the moringa flowers and leaves, origanum and freshly grated ginger. Mix together the soy sauce, runny honey, lemon juice and chutney and as the tomato mixture simmers, stir this in. Finally add the chick peas and stir well so that they are well coated with the fragrant mixture. Serve hot with crusty brown bread and decorate with fresh moringa flowers.

MULLEIN AND CARROT LUNCH DISH

Serves 4

I make this recipe every summer and it always draws compliments.

8-10 carrots, peeled and thinly
sliced lengthways
1 large onion, finely chopped
a little olive oil
2 cups thinly sliced mushrooms
1 cup milk
2 cups cooked butter beans
½ cup brown sugar
½ cup honey
sea salt and black pepper to taste
1 cup mullein flowers
½ cup parsley

CROUTONS

4 slices wholewheat bread
½ cup butter or sunflower oil

Cook the carrots in salted water until tender, then drain. Meanwhile fry the onion in a little olive oil, add the mushrooms and the milk and simmer gently. Add the butter beans, sugar and honey and stir in the drained carrots. Add salt and pepper and stir gently so as not to break up the carrots. Finally add the mullein flowers and spoon into a serving dish.

Make the croutons by cutting the wholewheat bread into small squares and frying them in a little butter or sunflower cooking oil in a flat pan, turning them frequently. Drain them on absorbent paper. Add the hot croutons to the carrot dish and sprinkle with parsley. Serve with a green salad.

STUFFED MARROW WITH MULLEIN FLOWERS

Serves 4-6

1 large green marrow
6 potatoes, peeled and halved
3 onions, peeled and halved

STUFFING

2 onions, chopped
450 g topside mince
1 cup breadcrumbs
2 tomatoes, peeled and chopped
2 carrots, finely grated
1 tablespoon fresh thyme
1 cup mullein flowers
½ cup raisins
sea salt and black pepper to taste
1 green pepper, finely chopped
½ cup parsley
a little sunflower cooking oil

Peel the marrow with a potato peeler if the skin is tough. Cut off the ends and remove the seeds. Sauté the onion, add the mince and brown lightly. Add the breadcrumbs and the rest of the ingredients. Add a little water and simmer until done. Spoon the mixture into the marrow and use toothpicks to hold the ends in place. Place on a baking tray. Tuck the potatoes and onions around it. Dribble with a little oil and bake at 200 °C for about 30 minutes or until the vegetables are cooked. Serve with brown rice and peas and decorate with fresh mullein flowers.

MUSTARD FLOWER VEGETABLE CURRY

Serves 6

This is a warming, substantial dish that can easily be varied according to what's in season.

2 cups sliced onions
½ cup olive oil
2 cups peeled, diced potato
1½ cups peeled, sliced carrots
2 cups chopped tomatoes
2 cups cauliflower florets
2 cups sliced green beans
½ cup grated fresh ginger
1 cup mustard flowers
½ cup desiccated coconut
2 teaspoons ground coriander seeds
1 teaspoon cayenne pepper
1 teaspoon turmeric
½ cup honey
sea salt to taste
1 litre good vegetable stock
½ cup seedless raisins
½ cup pecan nuts

Brown the onions in the oil in a large pot. Add all the vegetables and stir fry briefly. Mix the spices with a little water. Add the stock and simmer. Then add the spice mixture, the nuts and raisins and all the other ingredients. Simmer with the lid on until the vegetables are tender. Serve decorated with fresh mustard flowers and brown rice.

GRILLED MUSHROOMS WITH PEACH BLOSSOM

Serves 4

This is a quick and easy supper dish. Ring the changes with different sauces such as fresh tomato sauce, green pepper and onion sauce or cheese sauce. The peach blossom gives a light and delicate taste to the otherwise fairly strong flavours.

8 large brown mushrooms
butter
juice of 1 lemon
1 large onion, peeled and finely chopped
olive oil
2 cups peeled, diced tomatoes
2 tablespoons honey
2 teaspoons chopped fresh origanum
1 cup chopped celery
sea salt and pepper to taste
¾ cup peach blossom petals
chopped parsley

Place the mushrooms stalk side up on a flat baking dish and dot with butter. Squeeze over the lemon juice. Place under the grill for about 10 minutes. Meanwhile, make the sauce.

Brown the onion in a little olive oil. Add the tomatoes and simmer until tender. Stir in the honey. Add the origanum, celery and seasoning. Stir for a minute or two. Pour over the mushrooms and finally sprinkle with the peach blossom petals and a little chopped parsley. Serve with brown rice.

LAMB AND POTATO POT ROAST WITH PLUMBAGO

Serves 4-6

8 lamb loin chops, trimmed of excess fat
½ cup sunflower cooking oil
2 large onions, peeled and sliced
6 potatoes, peeled and quartered
1 cup plumbago flowers pulled out of their sticky calyxes
sea salt and black pepper to taste
juice of 1 lemon

In a heavy cast iron pot heat the oil and brown the chops. Add the onion and potato and stir fry until they start to brown. When they are well browned, add the plumbago flowers and just enough water to make a gravy. Season with salt and pepper and add the lemon juice. Stir frequently to prevent sticking and add a little more water when necessary. Turn down the heat, cover and simmer until the potatoes are tender. Serve piping hot with brown rice and vegetables, decorated with plumbago flowers.

PLUM BLOSSOM AND PUMPKIN SUPPER DISH

Serves 4

In the old days on the farm, the last of the winter stored pumpkins would have been used in the early spring when the nights were still chilly to make this deliciously sustaining dish with the first spring plum blossom.

4 cups peeled, diced pumpkin
1 tablespoon butter
½ cup brown sugar
2 teaspoons cinnamon
1 cup chopped onion
1 cup chopped celery
2 tablespoons sunflower oil
½-¾ cup plum blossom
½ cup seedless raisins or sultanas, soaked
for 20 minutes in hot water
½ cup sesame seeds
½ cup sunflower seeds
1 teaspoon mustard powder
salt and pepper to taste
1 cup grated cheddar cheese

Cook the pumpkin in salted water until tender. Drain and mash in the butter, sugar and cinnamon. Stir fry the onion and celery in the oil until they just start to brown. Add the plum blossom, drained raisins and sesame and sunflower seeds. Season with mustard powder, salt and pepper. Finally add the pumpkin and stir fry until everything is thoroughly mixed. Spoon into a serving dish, sprinkle with the grated cheese and place briefly under the grill to melt the cheese. Serve piping hot.

BAKED PUMPKIN WITH STUFFED PUMPKIN FLOWERS

Serves 4-6

This hearty vegetarian dish is deliciously sustaining when one is overtired.

a little olive oil
12 pumpkin flowers
1 cup finely mashed feta cheese
1 cup finely grated cheddar cheese
sea salt and black pepper
1 tablespoon fresh thyme
1 tablespoon fresh tarragon
a little yoghurt
2 large onions, thinly sliced into rings
2 cups sliced mushrooms
6-8 peeled, thin slices pumpkin
a little brown sugar
butter
2 cups chicken stock

Stuff the pumpkin flowers with the feta cheese, cheddar cheese, sea salt, black pepper, thyme and tarragon, moistened with a little yoghurt. Pour the olive oil into a large baking pan. Place the stuffed pumpkin flowers in the pan. On top of the pumpkin flowers lay the onion rings, mushrooms and pumpkin pieces. Sprinkle with a little brown sugar and dot with butter. Pour the chicken stock down the side of the pan and roast gently for about 30 minutes at 180 °C until the pumpkin is tender and starting to brown. Check that it does not dry out, and add more water if necessary. Serve at the table directly from the pan. The juices will have mingled deliciously with the pumpkin flowers under all the vegetables. Serve with brown rice.

> **Cook's Note**
> ROSEMARY IS SUPERB HERB IN COOKING, PARTICULARLY IN LAMB AND PORK DISHES, AS IT HELPS TO BREAK DOWN FATS. THE FLOWERS, TOO, ADD A SUBTLE TASTE TO SWEET OR SAVOURY DISHES. ROSEMARY HAS A STRONG FLAVOUR AND SHOULD BE USED SPARINGLY.

LAMB CHOPS WITH ROSEMARY

Serves 4

This is my favourite meat dish. The chops must be well browned and slightly crisp.

8 lamb loin chops
sunflower oil
2 large onions, sliced into rings
6 large potatoes, peeled and sliced
sea salt and black pepper to taste
juice of 1 lemon
2 thumb-length sprigs fresh rosemary
1 tablespoon rosemary flowers

In a cast iron pot brown the chops in a little oil until they are almost cooked through, moving them frequently. Add the onions and potatoes, salt and pepper and stir fry until they start to brown. Add the lemon juice, rosemary and a little water to make a rich gravy. Simmer with the lid on for about 25 minutes, until the potatoes are cooked. Taste and adjust the seasoning if necessary. Serve in the cast iron pot, sprinkled with rosemary flowers, with brown rice and vegetables.

GRILLED ROSEMARY SOSATIES

Serves 4-6

The home-made rosemary skewers impart their delicious fragrance and flavour to the sosaties. The fruit can be varied according to what's in season.

12 rosemary branches, about 25 cm long, leaves
stripped and sharpened at one end
24 pickling onions, peeled
24 chunks aubergine
24 thick wedges green pepper
24 wedges yellow peaches, mangoes or apples
24 blocks mozzarella cheese
24 wedges tomato
24 button mushrooms

MARINADE

2 cups good tomato sauce
½ cup vinegar
½ cup rosemary flowers
½ cup honey
1 tablespoon wholegrain mustard
2 tablespoons Worcestershire sauce
sea salt and black pepper to taste

Thread each rosemary skewer with alternating chunks of vegetable, fruit and cheese. For example, start off with an onion, follow with aubergine, green pepper, peach, cheese, tomato, mushroom, then repeat until the skewer is full.

Whisk together the marinade ingredients well and lay the sosaties in the marinade, turning them to coat them evenly. Place the sosaties on a hot grill and turn to cook them evenly. Sprinkle with more rosemary flowers and serve with baked potatoes.

SAGE FLOWERS AND BACON CRISP

Serves 4

A quick and easy way to turn scrambled or poached eggs into party fare. It can also be eaten on toast and is good in a cheese sandwich.

500 g rindless lean bacon
1 cup sage leaves and flowers
coarsely ground black pepper
1 tablespoon parsley

Chop the bacon roughly into 2 cm pieces. In a large frying pan fry the bacon in its own fat, turning frequently. Add the whole sage leaves and flowers. Stir fry briskly until the bacon browns. Season with pepper, then lift the crisply fried leaves and flowers and drain on crumpled paper for a few seconds. Place in a bowl. Mix with the parsley and sprinkle over scrambled or poached eggs. Decorate with fresh sage flowers.

> **Cook's Note**
>
> COOKING WITH SAGE IS A REAL ART. AS IT IS SO PUNGENT, THE LEAVES CAN BE USED WITH THE FLOWERS, BUT REMEMBER A LITTLE GOES A LONG WAY. SAGE IS A TRADITIONAL HERB TO ADD TO POULTRY STUFFING AS IT HELPS TO BREAK DOWN FAT AND GIVES A FRESH TASTE TO THE DISH. IT IS EXCELLENT WITH EGGS, CHEESE AND VEGETABLES. THE FLOWERS ARE PERHAPS BEST IN COOKING, AS THEY ARE NOT SO PUNGENT. STRIP THE FLOWERS FROM THEIR CALYXES AND EAT ONLY THE TENDER PETALS.

SPRING PASTA WITH SNAPDRAGONS

Serves 4

Their bland taste makes snapdragons perfect for both sweet and savoury dishes, and combined with spring and early summer ingredients they make for an unforgettable experience.

250 g angel hair pasta or spaghetti
3 cups mangetout peas
½ cup olive oil
2 cups finely chopped onions
2 cups thinly sliced brown mushrooms
1 cup finely chopped celery
1 cup mixed colours snapdragon flowers,
removed from their calyxes
sea salt and black pepper to taste
2 tablespoons balsamic vinegar
¾ cup parmesan cheese
½ cup chopped parsley

Cook the pasta in boiling salted water until tender. Drop in the peas and cook 1 minute. Drain. Fry the onions in the olive oil until they are transparent. Add the mushrooms, celery, snapdragons and the seasoning. Stir fry briefly until they are just tender. Add to the drained peas and pasta and pour over the balsamic vinegar. Spoon into a serving dish, sprinkle with the finely grated parmesan cheese and the chopped parsley. Decorate with a few fresh snapdragon flowers and serve hot.

Pan Fried Pork and Snapdragons

Serves 4

Hearty and appetising, this unusual pork dish is always a winner.

3 tablespoons sunflower cooking oil
4 lean pork loin chops, about 200 g each
2 onions cut into thin rings
1 tablespoon green peppercorns,
soaked for about 1 hour in
1 tablespoon white grape vinegar
salt and freshly ground black pepper
juice of 1 lemon and a little grated lemon zest
1 litre strong chicken stock
6-8 early peaches, peeled and stoned
1 cup snapdragon flowers, calyxes removed

Fry the chops in the oil until brown. Add the onions and fry until they start to brown. Add the peppercorns and vinegar, sea salt, pepper, the lemon juice and zest, peaches and the stock. Gently simmer with the lid on for 10 minutes or until the meat is tender. Finally add the snapdragon flowers and mix in well. Serve with brown rice and salad, decorated with snapdragon flowers.

Cape Sorrel and Pickled Fish

Serves 8-10

This is a traditional Cape dish that is not only enjoyed by South Africans but visitors from overseas always ask for the recipe. Serve it cold with salads.

2,5 kg any firm white fish – Cape salmon,
kingklip or kabeljou are best!
4 onions, neatly sliced
4 teaspoons salt
2 teaspoons cayenne pepper
¾ cup sugar – brown treacle is best
1 tablespoon turmeric
750 ml brown grape vinegar
125 ml water
About ½ cup thinly sliced fresh ginger
20 coriander seeds
¾ cup sultanas
4 fresh lemon leaves

Cut the fish into neat small portions. Mix all the ingredients and simmer in a heavy bottomed pot for 15-20 minutes. Stir well, then add the fish pieces, carefully so as not to break them. Simmer for another 20 minutes with the lid on. Carefully lift the fish out of the sauce and place in a glass or stainless steel dish. Pour the sauce over it, removing the lemon leaves. Leave to cool. Finally, just before serving, sprinkle with 1 cup fresh sorrel flowers. This keeps well in the fridge.

Sunflower Buds with Mustard Sauce

Serves 4-6

Served with a salad and cold meats, this is an unusual and delicious party dish.

12-14 small flower buds, about 6 cm in diameter
2 teaspoons salt

In a pot, cover the flower buds with water, add the salt and bring to the boil. Simmer for about 6 minutes. Strain through a colander and repeat the process with fresh water. Boil for a further 6-7 minutes or until tender. Strain, arrange in a glass dish and keep warm while you prepare the mustard sauce.

Mustard Sauce

3 eggs, well beaten
1 tablespoon cornflour
1 teaspoon sea salt
2 teaspoons mustard powder
½ cup brown sugar
½ cup brown grape vinegar
1 cup milk

Mix together the cornflour, salt, mustard powder and sugar and add to the beaten eggs. Whisk until creamy. Add the vinegar gradually. Warm gently on the stove on a low heat. Gradually add the milk, beating constantly, whisking while it thickens. Remove the sauce from the stove as soon as it bubbles and pour it over the cooked sunflower buds. Serve piping hot with rice.

Marinated Sunflower Bud Parcels

Serves 4-6

These sunflower parcels can be grilled on the coals of a fire or under the oven grill, and served directly from the foil.

10-12 sunflower buds about 6 cm in diameter
mild fruit chutney
fresh lemon juice
2 medium onions, thinly sliced
salt and pepper
olive oil
feta cheese, cubed

Parboil the buds for about 10 minutes in salted water. Remove from the water and rinse under a cold tap. Lay them face down in a dish and spoon over the chutney. Leave them to marinate for about 2 hours, turning them over from time to time. Place each head separately on squares of aluminium foil, squeeze over some lemon juice, place 3 or 4 thin onion slices around it, sprinkle with salt and pepper, add a dash of olive oil and a few cubes of feta cheese and carefully dot with the chutney marinade. Wrap the parcels neatly and place on the coals of the fire or under the oven grill for 20 minutes. Serve in the foil parcel.

THYME FLOWER AND SAVORY FISH

Serves 4

The most delicious thyme for this recipe is lemon thyme.

4-6 deboned skinned fish fillets
olive oil and butter – about 3 tablespoons each
2 beaten eggs
2 teaspoons paprika
1 cup flour seasoned with salt and black pepper
juice of 1 lemon
2 tablespoons fresh thyme flowers and
leaves, stripped off their stalks
lemon wedges for serving

Whisk the egg with the paprika until frothy. Pour into a flat dish and lay the fish in it spooning over the rest. Spread the seasoned flour in a flat dish and roll the egg-basted fish in the flour, coating it evenly. Meanwhile heat the oil and the butter together in a large frying pan and place the fish gently in the pan. Fry until golden, using a spatula to carefully turn the fish over and fry on the other side. Drain on crumpled kitchen paper and place on a serving dish. Keep warm until ready to serve. Sprinkle with lemon juice and thyme flowers. Serve with mashed potato or baked potato and extra lemon wedges.

TULIPS STUFFED WITH CHICKEN MAYONNAISE

Serves 4-6

For those first warm days of spring this is the perfect recipe for a luncheon party to celebrate the season!

1 medium-sized cold roast chicken
2 tablespoons chopped fresh parsley
¾ cup finely chopped celery
½ cup finely chopped green pepper
½ cup finely chopped spring onion
sea salt and black pepper to taste
1 cup good mayonnaise
about 12 tulips

Finely slice and chop the chicken from the bone. Mix together all the ingredients, except for the tulips. Remove the stamens and pistils from the tulips, leaving a little bit of stalk attached. Stuff the flowers with the chicken mayonnaise mixture. Arrange the flowers neatly in a circle on a bed of butter lettuce and pile any leftover chicken mayonnaise in the centre. Dust with black pepper and serve chilled.

TRADITIONAL CAPE WATERBLOMMETJIE BREDIE

Serves 6-8

This is the recipe I was taught by a Cape farmer's wife when I was 22 years old. I have loved it ever since!

1 kg waterblommetjies
1-2 kg lamb loin chops, rib or leg trimmed of fat
about ¾ cup runny honey
3 large onions, chopped
2-4 tablespoons fat or cooking oil
2-3 cups water
1 cup white wine
1-2 cups fresh sorrel leaves or Cape sorrel
(*Oxalis pes-caprae*)
sea salt and black pepper to taste
4 large potatoes, peeled and diced
4 carrots, peeled and diced (optional)
1 cup chopped celery stalks (optional)

Soak the waterblommetjies in water to release any grit that may have lodged between the petals and scales of the flower. Brush the lamb with honey. In a heavy-based saucepan brown first the onions and then the lamb in the oil or fat, turning often. Add all the other ingredients, turn down the heat, cover and simmer gently until the meat is tender. Stir every now and then, taking care not to break up the potatoes. Add more water if necessary, and add the wine last. Serve piping hot on a bed of rice.

WATERBLOMMETJIE STIR FRY

Serves 4

Quick and easy, this is an ideal supper dish.

2 cups chopped onion
½ cup extra virgin olive oil
2 cups finely chopped lean bacon
2 cups thinly sliced brown mushrooms
2 cups grated potato
2 cups waterblommetjies, well washed
juice of 1 lemon
½ cup parsley
sea salt and black pepper to taste
1-3 teaspoons grated fresh ginger root
2 teaspoons fresh marjoram
dash balsamic vinegar

Soak the waterblommetjies to release any grit. Sauté the onions in the oil until they become transparent, then add the bacon and mushrooms. As they start to brown, add the potato, then the waterblommetjies and lemon juice. Add the parsley, seasoning, ginger, marjoram and lastly the balsamic vinegar. Serve piping hot with crusty brown bread or brown rice and a salad.

Butter Beans and Winter Savory

Serves 6

This is the best bean dish I make – it keeps beautifully in the fridge, is tasty and is so rich in protein and fibre it should be included in our weekly menus far more than it is. Cooked with winter savory it greatly reduces indigestion and flatulence.

400 g large white butter beans
2 sprigs winter savory
½ cup good olive oil
2 cups chopped onions
2 cups chopped celery
1 cup honey
½ cup winter savory flowering sprigs,
stripped off their stalks
sea salt and black pepper to taste
juice of 2 lemons
½ cup balsamic vinegar
1 cup tomato paste
parsley

Soak the beans with 2 sprigs winter savory in warm water overnight. Next morning discard the water and rinse the beans. Bring to the boil with enough cold water to cover them and tuck in 2 to 3 sprigs winter savory. When the beans are tender, drain, discard the sprigs and return to the pot to keep warm. In a large pan fry the onions in the olive oil until they brown, add the celery and then stir fry all the other ingredients, including the beans. Add a little water to stop burning, stir frequently and simmer for 10 minutes. Serve piping hot sprinkled with parsley and a few winter savory flowers pulled from their calyxes. With brown bread and a green salad this is a sustaining meal.

> **Cook's Note**
>
> YARROW HAS LONG BEEN USED BY BOTH THE CHINESE AND EUROPEANS IN COOKING. VERY YOUNG YARROW FLOWERS, BUDS AND LEAVES HAVE A PUNGENT TASTE THAT IS PARTICULARLY GOOD WITH CURRIES AND STIR FRIES.

Yarrow Kedgeree

Serves 4-6

Tasty and unusual, this dish will become a family favourite.

675 g hake fillets
sea salt and black pepper
a few lemon slices
bay leaf
2 onions, thinly sliced
2 tablespoons butter
3-4 teaspoons young yarrow flowers and buds
stripped off their stems
2 teaspoons mild curry powder
2 teaspoons turmeric

2 cups cooked brown rice
1½ cups good strong vegetable stock
½ cup sultanas soaked in hot water for 2 hours
juice of 1 lemon
½ cup chopped almonds
finely chopped parsley

Boil the brown rice for about 40 minutes until cooked. Poach the fish in water with salt and pepper, the lemon slices and bay leaf for about 10-15 minutes or until cooked. Drain well and flake the fish. Fry the onions in the butter until they start to brown, add the yarrow flowers and stir fry. Add the curry powder, then the turmeric, cooked rice, stock, sultanas and lemon juice. Add the flaked fish and fork lightly until it is well mixed. Taste for seasoning. Turn into a serving dish and sprinkle with the chopped almonds and finely chopped parsley. Serve hot.

Yarrow Stir Fry

Serves 4

This is a quick and easy supper dish.

olive oil
about 2½ cups very thinly sliced lean beef
2 onions, peeled and chopped
2 potatoes, peeled and coarsely grated
½ cup young yarrow flowers and buds,
stripped off their stems
1 green pepper, chopped
2 large tomatoes, peeled and sliced
2 tablespoons honey
sea salt and coarsely ground black pepper
juice of 1 lemon
1 teaspoon good curry powder

In a large wok or pan, heat the olive oil and lightly brown the thin strips of meat. Add the onions and stir fry until golden. Add the potatoes and stir fry until they are cooked and browned. Add the yarrow flowers, stir fry for a few seconds, then add the rest of the ingredients. Serve piping hot with a salad.

Yarrow and Pumpkin Bredie

Serves 6

This old-fashioned, hearty pumpkin stew needs a long cooking time for the flavours to combine.

1 kg lean stewing lamb
2-3 tablespoons sunflower cooking oil
2 large onions, sliced
2 teaspoons curry powder
2 tablespoons grated fresh ginger
2-3 tablespoons young yarrow flowers and buds
stripped off their stems
3 cups good vegetable stock or water
500 g potatoes, peeled and sliced
1½ kg pumpkin, peeled and diced
2 teaspoons nutmeg
sea salt and black pepper to taste
juice of 1 lemon

Lavender biscuits, p. 130

Orange blossom sago pudding, p. 132

Buckwheat cake, p. 123

In a heavy-based cast iron pot, brown the lamb in the oil. Add the onions and sauté until golden. Add the curry, ginger and yarrow flowers and stir fry until golden. Add all the remaining ingredients and cover the pot. Simmer gently for about 1½ hours or until very tender and full of flavour. Add more stock or water if necessary during the cooking time and give it a good stir every now and then to prevent sticking and burning. Serve with rice or couscous.

STUFFED YUCCA FLOWERS

Serves 6

Fish or chicken can be used instead of the mince in this exotic party dish.

24 fully open yucca flowers
4 cups cooked rice
2 cups chopped onions
½ cup olive oil
500 g lean topside mince
1 cup grated carrots
2 cups skinned, chopped tomatoes
2 teaspoons spicy curry powder
sea salt and black pepper to taste
juice of 1 lemon
1 teaspoon red hot chilli (optional)
1 teaspoon chopped garlic (optional)
1 tablespoon brown sugar
½ cup good fruit chutney

Cook the rice. Sauté the onions in the olive oil until golden. Add the minced meat and fry until brown. Add the carrots, 1 cup of tomatoes, curry powder, salt, pepper and lemon juice, and the chilli and garlic if desired. Add a little water and cook until full of flavour and well done. Drain the meat mixture over a pot and catch all the juices. Spoon the meat into the yucca flowers and place them on a bed of cooked rice on a serving dish. Add the extra cup of tomatoes to the meat juices in the pan, add the brown sugar and chutney and cook for about 5 minutes, stirring constantly. Adjust the seasoning and pour the piping hot sauce over the stuffed flowers. Serve hot with a salad.

> **Cook's Note**
>
> THE YUCCA IS SO EASILY GROWN AND OFFERS SUCH BEAUTY AND ABUNDANCE IN ITS FLOWERING SPIKE, WE SHOULD LEARN FROM THE WEST INDIANS HOW TO USE IT IN COOKING AS THEY DO. IT IS SUPERB CHOPPED INTO STIR FRIES, CASSEROLES, SOUPS AND PICKLES.

DESSERTS

... cakes, biscuits, puddings and sweets

ALMOND BLOSSOM AND STRAWBERRY ICE-CREAM

Serves 6-8

As the first strawberries are in the shops and in the garden at the same time as the almond blossom, I always make this special ice-cream in spring and after the winter it is a much appreciated treat. It is one of the prettiest desserts, perfect for a spring birthday party or a wedding.

4-5 cups hulled and sliced strawberries
juice of 1 lemon
1 tin sweetened condensed milk
3 cups heavy cream
3 tablespoons white sugar
1 cup almond blossom petals

Liquidise the strawberries and the sugar. Add the lemon juice. Pour into a bowl and whisk in the condensed milk until it starts to thicken. In another bowl whisk the cream until it doubles in bulk, then add to the strawberry and condensed milk mixture. Fold in the almond blossom petals. Pour into two shallow ice-cream trays and freeze.

Stir every now and then to break up the ice crystals. Serve sprinkled with more almond blossom petals and fresh strawberries in pretty glass bowls.

ALMOND BLOSSOM CHOCOLATE CAKE

Serves 6-8

This is real angel food, wickedly rich, but so superb you'll want to make it often for special occasions. Take care not to overcook it or it will dry out. I leave it slightly underdone and moist in the centre. Since it contains no flour it can't upset the digestion. It is best made a day ahead as it matures beautifully. It can also be served as a dessert.

175 g milk or dark chocolate
broken into pieces
4 tablespoons butter
4 tablespoons castor sugar
3 large eggs, separated
6 tablespoons ground almonds
1 cup fresh fine brown breadcrumbs
175 ml thick cream

about ¾ cup icing sugar
2-4 tablespoons dark rum
1 cup almond blossom petals
stripped off their calyxes

Preheat the oven to 190 °C. Warm the chocolate in a double boiler with the butter until both are melted and well mixed. Whisk the sugar and egg yolks together and add this to the chocolate and butter mixture. Stir in 4 tablespoons of the ground almonds, keeping the other 2 tablespoons aside, and the breadcrumbs. Beat the egg whites and fold into the mixture very gently and evenly.

Butter a spring form cake tin (20 cm in diameter) with a good layer of butter and sprinkle in the remaining ground almonds. Spoon in the cake mixture and bake in the centre of the oven for 25 minutes until almost done. Allow to cool in the tin on a wire rack. It will deflate slightly.

For the icing, gently remove the cake from the spring form tin and place on a plate. Whip the cream, sweeten to taste with the icing sugar and add the rum, and fold in about 2 tablespoons of the almond blossom petals. Pipe the cream or spread it decoratively over the cake and sprinkle the remaining almond blossom petals over it.

ANISE APPLE DESSERT

Serves 6

Quick, easy and delicious either hot with cream and custard or cold with ice-cream.

6 Golden Delicious apples
a few thin strips fresh ginger
sultanas
½ cup honey
1 cup sunflower seeds
1 cup anise flowers
½ cup soft butter

Place the apples in a steamer, unpeeled but cored. Into the cores press the ginger and some sultanas. Steam for 15 minutes. Mix the honey with the sunflower seeds, anise flowers stripped off their stems, and the butter. Spoon over the apples and cover and steam for a further 15 minutes. Serve either hot or cold with the fragrant sauce poured over.

Bergamot and Peach Jelly

Serves 4-6

This was one of my children's favourite puddings, which I made often during summer with a basket of ripening peaches that needed to be used and a whole row of bright bergamot in flower. It's pretty enough to be a party treat as well.

10 peaches
3 tablespoons gelatine
1 cup warm water
1 litre unsweetened peach and orange
or peach and mango juice
1 cup bergamot flowers, stripped
off their calyxes
honey if desired

Peel and slice the peaches. Mix the gelatine with warm water until dissolved. Stir the gelatine into the fruit juice and add a little honey if it is not sweet enough. Add the peaches and finally toss the bergamot flowers stripped off their calyxes into the mixture. Pour into a glass bowl and set in the fridge. Once set, serve with whipped bergamot cream or custard decorated with bergamot flowers.

Bergamot Cream

250 ml heavy cream
1-2 tablespoons icing sugar
½ cup bergamot petals

Whip the cream with the icing sugar. Lightly fold in the bergamot petals. Spoon into a pretty glass bowl and decorate with bergamot flowers.

Buckwheat Cake

Serves 6

This cake keeps well and is the ideal lunchbox treat.

1 cup sunflower oil
4 eggs
1 cup runny honey
1½ cups buckwheat flour
½ cup buckwheat flowers broken to small pieces
2 teaspoons powdered cinnamon
2 teaspoons powdered allspice
4 teaspoons baking powder

Preheat the oven to 180 °C. Line a cake tin with oiled grease-proof paper. Whisk the oil, eggs and honey together until creamy. In another bowl, mix the buckwheat flour with the flowers, cinnamon, allspice and baking powder. Add the egg, oil and honey mixture. Lightly beat until well blended. Pour into the prepared cake tin and bake on the middle shelf for 30-35 minutes or until lightly browned. Serve with tea or coffee or as a dessert with apple purée or sliced peaches and cream.

Calamint or Emperor's Mint Conserve

Pick about 10 flowering sprigs and crush them lightly with a rolling pin. Sprinkle layers of dark caramel sugar under and over the sprigs and seal in a wide-mouthed jar. After a week remove the sprigs and again seal the jar. Use this sugar to flavour puddings, herb teas and after dinner coffee.

Peach and Calamint Dessert

Serves 4-6

This light, fragrant dessert is perfect after a heavy meal.

12 large yellow peaches peeled and sliced
2 tablespoons thinly sliced fresh ginger root
1 cup sultanas
sugar to taste
½-¾ cup tiny calamint flowers,
pulled out of their calyxes
2 apples, peeled and roughly chopped
2 cups apple juice
a little water
2 sprigs fresh calamint leaves

Simmer everything together until the apples and the peaches are tender. Discard the calamint sprigs. Serve hot or cold with whipped cream sprinkled with more of the exquisite tiny mauve or white calamint flowers.

Calendula Custard

Serves 4

This was my children's favourite dessert served either hot or cold, on its own or with apple tart, stewed rhubarb or peaches.

1 cup calendula petals
1 litre hot milk
piece of vanilla pod
or 1 teaspoon vanilla essence
3 eggs
1 cup sugar
1 tablespoon cornflour
1 teaspoon cinnamon
1 teaspoon allspice

Bruise the petals well to release the bright yellow colouring. Heat the milk in a double boiler and add the petals, keeping it just under boiling point. Add the vanilla. Beat the eggs with the sugar and cornflour, cinnamon and allspice. Carefully whisking all the time, add this mixture to the simmering milk. Remove the vanilla pod. Whisk gently until it thickens. Serve with whipped cream and sprinkle with calendula petals.

CALIFORNIAN POPPY SPRING FRUIT SALAD

Serves 4-6

This is such a treat as the warmer days tumble together. Nicest of all are the early peaches, but make this with any fruit in season.

brown sugar to taste
2 cups well ripened mulberries, stalks removed
2 cups thinly sliced strawberries
4 pears, peeled and chopped
2 apples, peeled and grated
4-6 early peaches peeled and sliced
2 papinos or small pawpaws
juice of 1 orange
1 cup Californian poppy petals

Sprinkle the sugar over the mulberries and strawberries and let them stand at room temperature for at least 2 hours. Then mix everything together and save some of the Californian poppy petals to decorate. Serve in a pretty glass bowl with whipped cream.

CARAWAY FLOWERS AND PEACH PASHKA

Serves 4

This is a lighter version of the traditional Russian dessert. You can use strawberries and peaches, or apricots and mangoes, or any combination of your choice.

2 tablespoons thin clear honey
1 cup plain Bulgarian yoghurt
250 g smooth cottage cheese
4 cups mashed fruit, such as peaches and strawberries
2 cups caraway flowers, stripped off their stems

Mix the honey into the yoghurt and then mix in the cottage cheese. Add the mashed fruit and the caraway flowers. Spoon into a cheesecloth-lined wet, clean flower pot. Chill, leaving it to drain over a bowl. Take out of the mould after 2 hours and serve it on a glass plate decorated with fruit slices and umbrels of pretty caraway flowers. Serve with caraway tea or after dinner coffee.

CRYSTALLISED CARPET GERANIUM FLOWERS

My grandmother taught me the wonderful art of crystallising violets when I was about 5 years old, and I've since experimented with lots of other flowers. Carpet geranium is one of the best. The flowers should have a bit of stalk still attached.

about 5 carpet geranium flowers
2 egg whites, softly beaten but still fairly runny
castor sugar

Dip each flower into the egg white and paint inside and out with a paint brush, holding it by its little stalk handle. Have ready a baking tray lined with greaseproof paper and sprinkled with a little castor sugar. Dip the flower into the castor sugar and sprinkle some over it, so that all surfaces are coated. Arrange the flowers on the baking tray, place in the preheated warming drawer of the oven and turn off the heat. Leave the flowers there until they are dry. During winter or damp weather, switch the warming drawer on for about 10 minutes every now and then, and then off again. Store in a sealed container. Use to decorate cakes and desserts.

PEAR AND CARPET GERANIUM STIR FRY

Serves 4

This is a delicious, quick and easy dessert and everyone's favourite.

6 large ripe pears, peeled, cored and cut into pieces
about 2-3 tablespoons butter
about 3 tablespoons brown sugar
½-¾ cup chopped pecan nuts
½ cup carpet geranium flowers

In a wok or frying pan stir fry the pears in the butter, adding the sugar and the pecan nuts, for about 5 minutes. Just before serving, add the carpet geranium flowers and spoon into individual glass bowls. Serve warm with whipped cream, decorated with more fresh carpet geranium flowers.

CHAMOMILE FRUIT JELLY

Serves 4-6

This is a superb summertime supper dessert for the whole family and is especially good at the end of a hectic day when the children are stressed as well. Grape, apple, mango or litchi juice may be used instead of orange juice and pieces of fruit may be set into the jelly too.

juice of 6 oranges
½-¾ cup runny honey
1 litre chamomile tea
4 tablespoons gelatine

Make the chamomile tea by pouring 1 litre of boiling water over 3 tablespoons fresh chamomile flowers or 1½ tablespoons dried flowers, leave to draw for 10 minutes, then strain. Mix the honey into the warm chamomile tea and taste, adding a little more if necessary. Dissolve the gelatine in 1 cup of hot water and add to the tea, then add the orange juice. Stir well, pour into a pretty glass bowl and leave to set in the fridge. Serve with custard or cream.

CHICORY AND PEAR DESSERT

Serves 4

The end of the summer is the time to make this delicious dessert, when the chicory is in full bloom and the pears are ripening. You can also serve it with custard or ice-cream.

6-8 pears
1½ cups water
¾ cup soft brown sugar
3 cardamom pods, crushed
1 cup chicory flowers

Peel and core the pears and cut into small pieces. Bring the water to a brisk boil, add the pears, sugar, cardamom pods and chicory flowers and simmer gently for just 5 minutes. Remove from the stove and cool. Serve in individual glass dishes with whipped cream and decorate with fresh chicory flowers.

BUTTERSCOTCH AND CORNFLOWER SAUCE

Serves 4-6

Served over rice puddings, plain yoghurt, ice-cream or custard, this is the quickest and easiest sauce to prepare and makes a party dish out of everyday ingredients. Try it over baked apples or bread and butter pudding, or topping a plain vanilla cake.

250 ml cream
250 ml sugar
250 ml golden syrup
4 tablespoons butter
one stick cinnamon
½ cup cornflower petals

Pour the cream into the top of a double boiler and warm. Add the sugar and syrup, then the butter, cinnamon and cornflower petals pulled out of the calyx. Simmer gently on low heat, stirring every now and then, for 45 minutes. Once it starts to thicken, stir well and serve hot over any dessert.

STRAWBERRY AND BANANA DESSERT WITH CORNFLOWERS

Serves 4

This has to be the quickest dessert I know and much loved by my children. I make it in spring when strawberries and cornflowers are at their best.

4 cups hulled sliced strawberries
4 bananas, sliced thinly
½ cup cornflower petals
juice of 1 orange, mixed with a little honey
whipped cream
desiccated coconut

Sprinkle the strawberries with sugar, and in individual glass dishes place layers of bananas and strawberries, ending with strawberries on top. Pour over the orange juice. Top with a dollop of whipped cream and sprinkle coconut on top. If you are lucky enough to find a fresh coconut, drain off the milk by piercing the three soft holes, saw it in half and then grate the precious flesh and use it instead of desiccated coconut. It is superb! Finally decorate with the beautiful blue cornflowers.

CRAB APPLE BLOSSOM SPONGE FINGERS

Makes around 20 biscuits

This is an ancient spring recipe from Scotland. When the crab apples aren't in blossom I use peach blossom, wisteria and even borage flowers, depending on what's flowering. They are the easiest of all biscuits to make and keep well. I serve them with creamy desserts and ice creams, as well as for a teatime treat.

50 g castor sugar
2 eggs
1 teaspoon vanilla essence
1 teaspoon grated lemon rind
½ cup crab apple petals, stripped off their calyxes
50 g cake flour

Preheat the oven to 180 °C. Whisk the sugar, eggs and vanilla essence until light and creamy. Mix the lemon rind and the petals into the flour, then gently fold into the egg and sugar mixture with a metal spoon. Onto a well greased and floured baking tray, place elongated finger shapes a tablespoon at a time and spaced 3 or 4 cm apart. Sprinkle with a little castor sugar and bake for 7-8 minutes or until just browning at the edges. Remove carefully while hot with a spatula and allow to cool and firm on a wire rack. Store in an airtight tin.

DELICIOUS MONSTER AND LITCHI DESSERT

Serves 4

This is a truly amazing taste experience and ever since I first tasted it, I watch eagerly to see if my delicious monster flowers will ripen during litchi season.

2 tablespoons gelatine
1 cup warm water
1 litre litchi juice
4 cups litchis, peeled, stoned and sliced
1 ripe flowering delicious monster spadix, scales carefully removed and finely mashed
a little sugar

Dissolve the gelatine in the warm water and stir into the litchi juice. Taste for sweetness, adding a little sugar if necessary, and stir well. Add the litchis and finally the mashed spadix. Pour into a glass bowl and set in the fridge. Serve with whipped cream.

PARADISE ICE-CREAM

Serves 4

This unforgettable dessert is one of the quickest summer treats I know. Use either home-made or bought vanilla ice-cream.

vanilla ice-cream
pulp from 4 granadillas
about 1 cup finely crushed pineapple
one ripe delicious monster spadix, scales
removed and finely mashed
whipped cream

In individual glass bowls spoon in three or four ice-cream balls. Over them pour a little granadilla pulp and on top of that a spoonful or two of pineapple pulp mixed with the mashed delicious monster spadix. Top finally with a little whipped cream. This is what eating in paradise must be like!

ECHINACEA AND MELON FRUIT SALAD

Serves 4-6

This pretty and healthy dessert is cool and green on a hot summer's day.

1 ripe green melon
4 kiwi fruits, peeled and sliced
3 cups green grapes, cut in half and seeds removed
4 prickly pears, peeled and sliced
1 cup echinacea petals
½ cup honey mixed into ½ cup warm water

Remove the seeds from the melon and cut the flesh into squares. Mix everything together in a glass bowl and pour over the honey and warm water mixture. Stand in the fridge to chill. Decorate with more fresh echinacea petals and serve with whipped cream.

ELDER FLOWER FRITTERS

Serves 4

These fritters are the most beautiful dessert or tea party treat and are quickly made. Always make more than you think – they are so delectable!

12 large elder flower heads, fully open
sunflower oil

BATTER

3 eggs
3 tablespoons sugar
1 teaspoon cinnamon
1 cup cake flour
1 cup milk
½ cup water

To make the batter, beat the eggs well with the sugar and cinnamon and then whisk together with the flour, milk and water to a runny consistency. Heat a little sunflower oil in a large pan. Holding each elder flower by its stalk, dip the whole flower into the batter and then immediately transfer it to the pan of hot oil. Let it cook for about 2 minutes or until it is golden brown. Transfer it to a pile of crumpled paper kitchen towel and let it drain. Snip off the stems after placing the flowers on a plate and dredge with icing sugar. Serve warm with whipped cream and sprinkle with more tiny elder flowers, stripped off their stems.

ELDER FLOWER AND RHUBARB DESSERT

Serves 6

Elder flowers add a muscatel-like flavour to the tart rhubarb and lessen the need for so much sugar. Use this as a dessert or as a pie filling. Peaches, apples or pears can be added for a change of flavour.

12-20 long rhubarb stalks
about 4 cups sugar
4 cups elder flowers, stripped off their stalks
a little water

Strip the leaves off the rhubarb and cut the stems into 4 cm lengths. Place in a deep pot with the sugar, elder flowers and water and simmer gently, stirring every now and then until the rhubarb is tender and breaks up. Do not let it burn. Stand aside and cool. Serve on pancakes with whipped cream or ice-cream, and decorate with more elder flowers sprinkled over the top.

EVENING PRIMROSE AND PEAR DESSERT

Serves 4-6

This is an easy autumn dessert, which can be made with the abundance of evening primrose flowers that last longer than one night in the cooler days.

about 12 pears
1 litre water
1 cup sugar
1 cup lightly chopped evening primrose petals
½ cup evening primrose buds (optional)

Core and quarter the pears and lightly poach them in the water and sugar until tender, usually about 10 minutes. Remove from the stove and cool. Just before it is completely cool, stir in the lightly chopped evening primrose petals. Serve with whipped cream or custard, decorated with more evening primrose petals. For a slightly stronger flavour cook the pears with ½ cup of evening primrose buds. Add the flowers at the end.

FALSE ACACIA FLOWER FRITTERS

This makes a spectacular and unusual party dish.

1 cup flour
1 cup water
1 cup milk
2 eggs, well beaten
several sprigs false acacia flowers
sugar
brandy
sunflower oil

Make a thin batter by mixing together the flour, water, milk and well-beaten eggs. Pick fresh sprays of false acacia flowers, sprinkle them with sugar and let them lie in a little bowl of brandy while the batter rests for 30 minutes. Heat a frying pan with a little sunflower cooking oil, then dip the flowers into more sugar and into the batter. Fry gently in the hot oil, holding the flower spray by its stalk. Turn until golden on both sides, then drain on crumpled paper. Serve with whipped cream or ice-cream, and dust with icing sugar. Decorate the plate with fresh false acacia flowers.

BRAZILIAN FEIJOA CONSERVE

The succulent pink, curiously folded petals and red stamens of the feijoa flower have been used for centuries by the Brazilians as a conserve.

4 cups feijoa flowers, calyxes removed
3-4 cups sugar
3 cups chopped ripe apricots, peaches, nectarines or plums, or a mixture
1 stick cinnamon
½ cup water

Simmer everything together on low heat, stirring every now and then, until the fruit is tender, usually about 20 minutes. Stand aside and cool. Serve over ice-cream or with custard and cream or spoon over baked custard and rice pudding. It keeps well in the fridge. The Brazilians serve it over steamed couscous or polenta.

FEIJOA FRUIT SALAD

Serves 4-6

Any fruit in season can be used, but I prefer the exotic spring fruits for this light, refreshing dessert. It makes a pretty party dish.

3 cups strawberries, hulled and sliced
2 cups mulberries, stalks removed
1 cup feijoa flowers
3 cups early peaches, peeled and sliced
about 1 cup granadilla juice
3 bananas, thinly sliced
1 small pineapple, peeled and grated coarsely

Sprinkle the strawberries and mulberries with sugar and stand in a warm spot to absorb the sugar for about an hour. Then mix everything together and stand covered for an hour before serving to enable the juices to mingle. Dribble with a little honey and serve with whipped cream, decorated with feijoa flowers.

FRUIT SAGE DESSERT WHIP

Serves 4-6

2 large eggs, separated
300 ml thick cream
6 tablespoons white sugar
3 tablespoons gelatine
4 tablespoons hot water
300 ml plain yoghurt
pulp of 4 granadillas
½ cup fruit sage flowers calyxes removed

Whip the egg whites. Whip the cream. Whip the yolks with the sugar. In a small bowl dissolve the gelatine in the hot water and cool by standing the bowl in a large bowl of iced water. Now working quickly, add the cooled gelatine to the egg yolks and then add the yoghurt and the granadilla pulp, whisking evenly all the time. Now add the cream and fold in the egg whites. Pour into a pretty glass dish and carefully place the fruit sage flowers in a pretty pattern over the top of the dessert. Chill until set. Decorate with a little spray of fresh flowers as you take it to the table.

> **Cook's Note**
>
> FRUIT SAGE FLOWERS HAVE A FRUITY, SWEET TASTE. SPRINKLE THEM ONTO SALADS AND SCATTER THEM OVER DESSERTS AND INTO FRUIT DRINKS OR USE THEM AS AN ATTRACTIVE GARNISH. REMOVE THE CALYXES BEFORE SERVING.

FUCHSIA ICE-CREAM TOPPING

Serves 4-6

Use this as a topping for ice-cream, rice pudding, sago pudding, mashed bananas or even oats porridge. It is so pretty that served with cream it quickly makes a party piece. For the fresh fruit use peaches, nectarines, strawberries, mangoes, mulberries or a combination. Select small fuchsia flowers so that you can keep them whole.

3 cups fresh fruit, peeled and cut up
sugar to taste (about 1 cup)
little water – about ½ cup
½ cup desiccated coconut
1 cup small fuchsia flowers

Simmer the fruit, sugar, water and coconut gently in a double boiler, stirring often, until tender and syrupy. Cool. Add the fuchsia flowers and pour over the ice-cream or pudding. Decorate with more fresh fuchsia flowers. For a beautiful summertime party dish, layer ice-cream and the topping and fresh fuchsia flowers in individual tall glasses. Serve decorated with a mint leaf or two and a fresh exquisite fuchsia flower and eat with long spoons.

GARDENIA CHOCOLATE MOUSSE

Serves 6-8

This decadent mousse is food for the gods and so easy to make.

250 g dark Albany chocolate
4 eggs, separated
2 tablespoons soft butter (at room temperature)
4 tablespoons castor sugar
3 tablespoons dark rum
1 cup cream
4 tablespoons thinly sliced gardenia petals

Break the chocolate into pieces and melt in a double boiler. Whisk the egg whites until stiff. Whisk the butter and sugar together until creamy, then add the beaten egg yolks and rum. Whisk the cream until stiff. Gently combine all four together and finally add the gardenia petals. Pour into a pretty glass bowl and refrigerate. When you are ready to serve, decorate with a sprinkling of gardenia petals and a whole flower in the centre.

GARDENIA AND LITCHI FRUIT SALAD

Serves 6

This is one of the most exquisite desserts I've ever known, and perfect for a special occasion. The litchis are an essential ingredient, but the other fruits can be varied according to what's in season, such as mango slices, peaches, grapes, watermelon, kiwi fruit or green melons. Tinned litchis can be substituted for fresh ones.

4 cups peeled, stoned litchis
3 cups mango or peach slices, or other fruit
5-6 tablespoons grape juice
1 tablespoon grated ginger
2 tablespoons castor sugar
3 gardenia flowers, petals separated and calyxes discarded
1 cup whipped cream

Arrange the fruit in individual glass dishes with a dash of grape juice. Mix the ginger and castor sugar together and sprinkle a little over the fruit. Keep chilled. Just before serving, chop the gardenia petals, sprinkle over the fruit and top with the whipped cream.

GARLAND CHRYSANTHEMUM AND APPLE DESSERT

Serves 4

Delicious on a winter's night and so quick and easy to make. Serve with custard or cream for a party dish.

6 apples, peeled and cored
2 litres water
1 cup sugar

TOPPING

1 cup garland chrysanthemum flowers, quartered
½ cup butter
1 teaspoon cinnamon powder
1 teaspoon all spice powder
½ cup soft brown sugar
¾ cup pecan nuts, finely chopped
1 cup sunflower seeds

Cook the apples in the water with the sugar for 15 minutes. For the topping, gently fry the garland chrysanthemums in the butter, add the spices and stir fry well. Then add the sugar, pecan nuts and sunflower seeds and cook for 2 minutes. Spoon the cooked apples into a glass dish, sprinkle with the spicy topping and keep hot in the oven. Serve hot with whipped cream or custard, decorated with a sprinkling of garland chrysanthemum petals.

PASSION FLOWER CAKE TOPPING

Bake your favourite sponge cake in a large cake tin or pyrex dish and use this incredible topping instead of icing. The sides of the dish need to be high to hold the topping while it sets.

4 bananas, thinly sliced
1½ cups granadilla pulp
1 cup sugar
2 tablespoons gelatine
1 carton smooth cream cheese
1 cup granadilla flowers

Gently poach the bananas in the granadilla pulp with the sugar. Remove from heat and allow to cool. Mix the gelatine in a little warm water and add to the banana and granadilla mixture. Mix well. Fold in the cream cheese. Discard the calyxes from the flowers, strip off the petals, chop them up and mix in. Pour the topping over the cake and place in the fridge to set. It should take about an hour. Serve decorated with whipped cream and fresh granadilla flowers.

PASSION FLOWER TROPICAL FRUIT SALAD

Serves 6

Make this in midsummer with all those exotic fruits available. Change the fruits according to whatever is in season.

1-1½ cups granadilla pulp
1 cup granadilla flowers, cut into quarters,
calyxes discarded
2 cups papino, cut into cubes
2 cups peeled, cubed mango
2 cups peeled litchis, cut in half
1 cup kiwi fruit, peeled and sliced

Mix about half a cup of sugar into the granadilla pulp if it is too tart. Mix all the fruit together gently and place in a glass bowl. Pour over the granadilla pulp. Sprinkle with the granadilla flowers and place a whole flower in the centre. All around the sides of the bowl pipe rosettes of whipped cream. Serve with extra whipped cream or with ice-cream. Wait for the applause!

HAWTHORN PANCAKES WITH LEMON CURD

Serves 4-6

This is a delicious teatime treat and so quickly made in spring when the flowers are abundant.

sunflower cooking oil
about 1 cup milk
1 egg
2 cups cake flour
a little water
½ teaspoon sea salt
1 cup hawthorn buds and flowers,
pinched off their stems
lemon curd

In a large flat pan, heat a little oil. Whisk the egg into the milk. Whisk together the flour, milk and egg mixture and a little water to a runny consistency. Add the sea salt and the hawthorn buds and flowers. Drop a spoonful or two at a time into the pan and tilt it so that it is thinly spread. As soon as it bubbles, flip it over. When it is done, slide it onto a plate. Spread with lemon curd and roll it up. Keep it hot. Add a little cream when serving and decorate with fresh hawthorn flowers.

HOLLYHOCK SUMMER FRUIT SALAD PANCAKE

Serves 4-6

1 ripe melon spanspek or green melon, cut into cubes
1 pineapple, thinly sliced and then cut into cubes
2 cups grapes, seeded

2-3 cups mango, peeled and cubed
2 bananas, thinly sliced
juice and pulp of 6 granadillas
petals from about 6 hollyhock flowers, calyxes discarded

Mix all the fruits together. Then make 4-6 large, thin pancakes.

PANCAKE BATTER

2 cups flour
1 cup milk
1 cup water
2 beaten eggs
pinch salt

Whisk everything together well to make the batter. In a large, flat pan heat a little oil, pour in about ½ a cup of batter and tilt the pan to spread it thinly. Flip over to cook the other side. On pretty individual plates place the pancakes, top with spoonfuls of the fruit salad, decorate with whole hollyhock flowers and serve dusted with icing sugar and whipped cream.

HOLLYHOCK SCONES

Makes 10 scones

This is a quick and easy recipe, and a favourite Sunday afternoon treat. They are nicest eaten hot and fresh.

2 cups cake flour
pinch salt
1 tablespoon baking powder
5 tablespoons butter, grated coarsely
about 6 hollyhock flowers
2 eggs
½ cup milk
4 tablespoons sugar
½ cup granadilla pulp

Sift flour, salt and baking powder into a large bowl. Rub in the butter until it resembles fine bread crumbs. Dissolve the sugar in the milk. Whisk the eggs and the milk with the sugar until creamy, add the granadilla pulp and whisk well. Add to the flour mixture and lightly mix to form a ball. Turn out onto a floured board and pat out to 2 cm height. Cut out round shapes with a pasty cutter. Place on a floured baking sheet and bake at 180 °C for about 10 minutes or until they begin to turn golden. Cool slightly. Split, spread with butter and a hollyhock flower – remove the calyx – or a few petals. Dust with icing sugar and decorate the plate with hollyhock flowers. You can spread the scone with strawberry jam or honey before topping it with the hollyhock petals.

> **Cook's Note**
>
> HONEYSUCKLE FLOWERS ARE DELICIOUS ADDED TO GREEN SALADS AND FRUIT SALADS, WHISKED INTO DRINKS AND USED TO DECORATE PUDDINGS, AND COOKED IN SYRUP MAKE A DELICIOUS SAUCE OVER RICE AND SAGO PUDDING.

HONEYSUCKLE FRUIT SALAD

Serves 4-6

1 papaw peeled, seeded and diced
juice of 2 oranges
4 ripe guavas, peeled and grated
2 ripe bananas, peeled and diced
2 cups sultana grapes, seeds removed
2 Golden Delicious apples, peeled and grated
1 cup honeysuckle flowers

Mix everything together in a glass bowl. Dribble a little honey over it and sprinkle with honeysuckle flowers. Serve chilled with custard, whipped cream or ice-cream.

POACHED NECTARINES AND HYSSOP

Serves 4

This is a delicious dessert and very quick and easy to make.

1½ cups castor sugar
2½ cups water
½ cup hyssop flowers calyx removed
4 large or 8 small nectarines,
pricked all over with a fork

Choose a pot large enough to hold all the nectarines. Boil the sugar and water for 5 minutes before lowering in the nectarines and the hyssop flowers. Turn down the heat and cover the pot. Let the nectarines simmer for about 4 minutes. Remove from the stove. Cool. Carefully remove the nectarines and place them in a glass bowl. Pour a little of the syrup over them and decorate with fresh hyssop flowers. Serve with whipped cream, custard or vanilla ice-cream.

JASMINE AND STRAWBERRY DESSERT

Serves 4

This is the prettiest and most enchanting party dish I know. Serve it on hot summer nights under the stars with the scent of jasmine in the air, to a group of appreciative friends.

3-4 cups fresh strawberries
1 cup jasmine flowers pulled out of their calyxes
castor sugar
2 tablespoons Tia Maria or your favourite liqueur
about 4 cups soft vanilla ice-cream
1 cup whipped cream

Hull the strawberries and cut them into thin slices. Sprinkle them with castor sugar and leave to stand at room temperature for at least an hour before serving. Meanwhile, marinade the jasmine flowers in the liqueur. When ready to serve, spoon a layer of strawberries into individual glass bowls, followed by a layer of ice-cream and a layer of marinated jasmine flowers, then repeat the layers, finishing with a layer of flowers. Top with whipped cream and decorate with whole strawberries and fresh jasmine flowers.

JUDAS TREE FLOWER AND MULBERRY JELLY

Serves 4-6

Judas tree flowers and mulberries are ripe at the same time, so this is a delicious springtime dessert.

1 cup white sugar
2 cups mulberries, stalks removed
2 cups water
1½ tablespoons gelatine
mixed into ½ cup warm water
1 cup Judas tree flowers
1 cup cream

Put the sugar, mulberries and water together in a pot and bring to the boil. Simmer for 10 minutes. Allow to cool, then blend in the liquidiser. Add the dissolved gelatine. Pour into a bowl, add the Judas tree flowers and stir well. Refrigerate to set. Meanwhile, whisk the cream until it stands in peaks and refrigerate. Before serving, spread the cream over the surface of the jelly and decorate with a sprinkling of Judas tree flowers.

LAVENDER BISCUITS

Makes about 24

These are an excellent tuck box filler and keep well in a sealed tin.

4 tablespoons soft butter
4 tablespoons castor sugar
1 cup cake flour
2 teaspoons baking powder
1 beaten egg
2 tablespoons fresh lavender flowers,
stripped off their stalks

Cream the butter and the sugar together until light. Add the flour, baking powder and beaten egg and lastly the lavender flowers. Knead to a smooth consistency, adding a little extra flour if necessary. Pat out gently on a lightly floured board and cut into shapes. Place the biscuits on a well-greased baking sheet and bake at 180 °C for about 10 minutes or until they are lightly golden and firm. Remove at once and dust with icing sugar.

FLAX FLOWER CHOCOLATE SAUCE

Serves 6-8

This is spectacular over ice-cream, rice pudding or over a plain cake, and is probably my most talked about dessert!

250 g plain milk chocolate, broken into pieces
2 tablespoons butter
4 tablespoons water
4 tablespoons thin cream

Melt the chocolate in a double boiler, stirring occasionally. Add the butter and beat gently. Then add the water, mix well, and remove from the heat. Finally add the cream, beating all the time. While the sauce is still warm, pour it over the cake or pudding and immediately press in several flax flowers that have been pulled gently out of their calyxes. When they are cool and set, the flowers look like tiny blue cups and no one ever knows what they are.

CHOCOLATE MINT MOUSSE

Serves 4

Use the leaves and flowers of chocolate mint (*Mentha spicata* var. *piperita*) here. Pull the tiny flowers off their stems and break them up into tiny pieces.

250 g plain dark chocolate
1 tablespoon finely chopped chocolate
mint leaves and flowers
4 eggs, separated
1 cup cream, lightly beaten
1 tablespoon good instant coffee
mixed into 1 tablespoon hot water
½ cup thick cream, whipped for decoration
chocolate mint flowers for decoration

Break up the chocolate and melt the chocolate with the chocolate mint in a double boiler. Beat the egg whites into soft peaks. Beat the egg yolks and carefully stir into the melted chocolate. Add the cream and stir well. Add the dissolved coffee. Finally fold in the egg whites. Spoon into pretty dishes, decorate with the whipped cream and sprinkle with chocolate mint flowers. Serve chilled.

WATERMELON AND MINT DESSERT

Serves 6-8

This is one of my favourite summer desserts. It is so quick and easy and makes a refreshing end to a dinner party on a hot summer's night.

1 medium-sized watermelon
1 cup white sugar
¾ cup chopped spearmint leaves and flowers

Cut the watermelon in half with a zigzag edge. Scoop out the flesh in neat balls using a melon baller and remove the pips where possible. Keep chilled until ready to serve.

Meanwhile mix the sugar with the chopped spearmint leaves and flowers (pull the flowers off their stems and break them into tiny pieces). When you are ready to serve, layer the balls of watermelon with the mint and sugar mixture into one half of the watermelon shell. Pile the watermelon balls high and end with a layer of sugar and mint. Decorate with sprays of mint leaves and flowers.

MORINGA FLOWER FRUIT DESSERT

Serves 4

This recipe is much loved by children especially and is a nourishing standby for those who have no appetite. Add or substitute the fruit with fruit in season, such as peaches, nectarines, mangoes, litchis or grapes.

1½ cups sago
2 cups milk
¾ cup honey
stick cinnamon
2 apples, peeled and grated
2 pears, peeled and grated
2 bananas, thinly sliced
1 cup moringa flowers,
removed from their stalks

Simmer the sago in a double boiler with the milk, honey and cinnamon for about an hour, or until tender. Add more milk if necessary. Meanwhile prepare the fruit and keep it covered so as not to let it discolour. As soon as the sago is tender and transparent, remove the cinnamon stick and fold in the fruit with the moringa flowers. Serve hot with plain yoghurt or a little cream, decorated with moringa flowers.

STRAWBERRY AND MULLEIN MOUSSE

Serves 4-6

This delectable dessert is perfect for a summer lunch.

3 cups hulled, sliced strawberries
½-¾ cup castor sugar
2 eggs
¾ cup castor sugar
1 tablespoon gelatine
½ cup warm water
1 cup fresh cream, whipped
1 cup mullein flowers,
pulled from their calyxes

Sprinkle the strawberries with ½-¾ cup castor sugar and leave them to stand for 2 hours. Beat the eggs with ¾ cup castor sugar until creamy. Dissolve the gelatine in the warm water and stir into the egg and sugar mixture. Fold in the whipped cream. Gently add the strawberries and lastly the mullein flowers. Pour into a glass dish and set in the fridge, or pour into individual glass dishes. Serve decorated with a few fresh strawberries and mullein flowers.

APPLE AND MYRTLE STIR FRY DESSERT

Serves 4

This is a quick dessert that is always so enjoyed, I tend to make double. It is ready in 5 minutes, so the secret is to have all the ingredients ready before you start.

5 apples, peeled and coarsely grated
½-¾ cup sugar
juice of 1 lemon
½ cup sunflower seeds
½ cup crystallised ginger, cut into small, thin pieces
½ cup chopped pecan nuts
about 1 tablespoon butter
½ cup myrtle flowers, calyxes removed
about ½ cup apple juice

In a pan or wok heat the butter and add the apple. Stir fry quickly, then add the sugar and mix well. Next add the lemon juice and all the other ingredients and stir well. Should it become too dry, add a dash more of apple juice. Serve piping hot with whipped cream.

ORANGE BLOSSOM SAGO PUDDING

Serves 4

This is one of those absolutely delicious old-fashioned puddings that is perfect for a springtime Sunday lunch.

1 cup sago
2 cups hot water
3½ cups milk
¾ cup sugar
1 cinnamon stick
½ cup orange blossom, removed from the calyxes
250 ml cream, whipped
ground cinnamon

Soak the sago in the hot water for an hour. Strain. In a double boiler heat the milk, sago, sugar and cinnamon stick, and simmer on low for about 2½ hours, or until the sago is swollen and transparent and tender. When you are ready to serve, remove the cinnamon stick and lightly stir in the orange blossoms. Spoon into individual dishes, smother in whipped cream and dust with ground cinnamon. Decorate with orange blossoms.

ORANGE BLOSSOM FAIRY BUTTER

Fairy butter dates back to 1736, when it was all the rage for use on buns and cakes. This modern version of the recipe can be used as a cake filling or icing on top of a plain sponge cake. I have used it to ice a wedding cake (orange blossom is a traditional wedding flower) and found it superb.

2 eggs
2 cups icing sugar
juice of 1 lemon
1 teaspoon vanilla essence
dash of brandy or your favourite liqueur
½–¾ cup orange blossom, calyxes removed
fresh orange blossom, for decoration

Whisk the eggs well with the sugar until creamy. Add the icing sugar and the lemon juice. Beat well. Add the vanilla essence, and a dash of brandy or liqueur. Beat well. Lastly, lightly fold in the orange blossom. Spoon and spread the icing onto the cake. Decorate with fresh orange blossom.

STRAWBERRY AND PANSY GRANITA

Serves 6-8

A real party dessert that needs to be made the day before to freeze it well.

2 kg ripe strawberries, hulled
300 g castor sugar
juice of 1 lemon
250 ml thick cream
about 125 ml sweet sherry

Liquidise the strawberries with the sugar and lemon juice. Place in a measuring jug and top up with water to 1,5 litres. Taste and add more sugar if necessary. Pour into a shallow tray and freeze. Roughly every 30-40 minutes take it out and break up the ice crystals with a fork. Do this 4 or 5 times or until you have a tray of strawberry ice crystals.

The following day, when you are ready to serve, whisk the cream. Pile the strawberry crystals into individual glass bowls or glasses, push a pansy or two down the side, dribble a little sherry over each, top with whipped cream and decorate lavishly with pansies. Serve immediately.

ALMOND PANSY MACAROONS

Makes about 18

These are simple to make and delicious served with ice-cream, custard, as a tea biscuit or with after dinner coffee.

4 tablespoons castor sugar
4 tablespoons ground almonds
2 egg whites, stiffly beaten
1-2 drops vanilla essence
fresh pansy flowers

Line a baking sheet with greaseproof paper and paint it with a little sunflower cooking oil. Mix together the sugar and almonds and fold into the egg whites with the vanilla essence. Drop small spoonfuls onto the greased paper, well apart. Bake for about 10-12 minutes at 180 °C until faintly golden brown. Cool for a few minutes, then lift off with a spatula and cool on a wire rack. Store in an airtight tin.

SPRINGTIME PEACH BLOSSOM SUNDAE

Serves 1

Treat yourself to this exquisite treat as soon as the blossoms appear, as they are there so briefly. This is so pretty, it's almost a shame to eat it!

2 scoops vanilla ice-cream
1 banana
1 tablespoon chopped pecan nuts
glacé cherries
cinnamon
at least ½ cup fresh peach blossom petals

Place the ice-cream in a pretty glass bowl. Slice a banana in half lengthways and place the halves on either side of the ice-cream to form a little boat. Sprinkle with the nuts and dot with cherries. Dust with cinnamon and liberally sprinkle with the peach blossom petals. Add strawberries or mulberries and whipped cream for a variation.

PEACH BLOSSOM SPRING FRUIT SALAD

Serves 4

All winter long one yearns for a refreshing fruit salad. This one uses the first spring fruits.

4 pears, peeled and diced
2 cups strawberries, hulled and sliced
and sprinkled with sugar
2 cups mulberries, stalks removed and
sprinkled with sugar
2 apples, peeled and finely grated
2 bananas, peeled and thinly sliced
1 small pineapple, finely grated
½ cup pear juice
about ¾ cup peach blossom petals
1 cup cream

Mix the fruits and juice together. Whip the cream, place the fruit salad in pretty individual glass dishes, add a good dollop of cream and sprinkle lavishly with peach blossom petals.

PLUMBAGO FRUIT JELLY

Serves 6

This exquisite recipe comes from a farm in the hot, mountainous region of the Eastern Cape. For dessert on a summer's day it takes some beating.

4 cups peeled, sliced peaches or nectarines
2 tablespoons sugar
4 cups peeled, sliced prickly pears
2 tablespoons gelatine dissolved in 1 cup warm water
2 cups peach or orange juice or water
1 cup plumbago flowers, pulled
out of their sticky calyxes

Sprinkle the sugar over the peaches and arrange the fruit in a glass bowl. Mix the dissolved gelatine and fruit juice or water together. Tuck in the plumbago flowers between the fruit and gently pour the gelatine and fruit juice mixture over the fruit. Chill. Serve when set with thick farm cream and decorate with plumbago flowers.

PRICKLY PEAR SUMMER DESSERT

Serves 6

This exquisitely succulent fruit makes a party dessert that gets everyone talking!

20 multicoloured prickly pears,
some golden yellow, some light
green and some ruby red
whipped cream
icing sugar

Peel the prickly pears and chill them for at least 1 hour. Then slice into 1 cm thick rounds and arrange the slices on a glass dish. Dot with little blobs of whipped cream and dust with icing sugar. Serve chilled and listen to the compliments.

ROSELLE JELLY

Serves 4-6

Delicious with ice-cream, pancakes, waffles and rice puddings, or with cold meat and chicken.

1 kg fresh calyxes and flower petals
broken off their seed capsules
½ cup water
1 kg white sugar

Boil everything together briskly for about 70 minutes until it starts to gel. Test by spooning a small amount onto a cool saucer; if it sets it is ready. Pour into hot jam jars and seal immediately.

ROSE-SCENTED GERANIUM MOUSSE

Serves 6-8

This luxurious dessert is a party piece that is unforgettable. I make it for Christmas lunch, it goes beautifully with Christmas pudding.

2 tablespoons gelatine
6 tablespoons boiling water
8 rose-scented geranium leaves
and ½ cup flowers
2 large eggs, separated
4 tablespoons castor sugar
200 ml cream cheese
200 ml plain Greek yoghurt
200 ml cream, whipped

Dissolve the gelatine in a little of the hot water and pour the rest over the scented geranium leaves and leave it to cool. Whisk the egg whites until they are stiff. Whip the egg yolks with the castor sugar until light and creamy, add the gelatine and then add the cream cheese. Whisk it well, then add the yoghurt and the water from the soaked leaves. Fold in the scented geranium flowers and finally the egg whites. Pour into a glass bowl and refrigerate until set. Decorate with scented geranium leaves and flowers.

ROSE-SCENTED GERANIUM FILO BASKETS

Serves 6

Use whatever fruit is in season for this elegant dessert.

3 sheets filo pastry
1 tablespoon melted butter
1½ cups thinly sliced strawberries, raspberries or
peaches, sprinkled with sugar
1 cup plain Greek yoghurt
½ cup whipped cream
1 cup rose-scented geranium flowers
icing sugar

Preheat the oven to 200 °C. Cut the sheets of pastry into squares measuring about 10 cm (one sheet cuts into 6). Brush each square with a pastry brush dipped in butter. Arrange a single square at a time in a patty pan, layering them in threes so that it forms a pretty little basket. Bake for 6 minutes or until they turn golden brown, then turn them out and cool very carefully as they are fragile. When cool mix the fruit mixture into the yoghurt and spoon into the basket. Top with whipped cream, sprinkle with scented geranium flowers and dust with icing sugar. Serve on individual glass plates.

ROSE PETAL CREAM JELLY

Serves 6

This is an exquisite dessert for a summer party and so easy to make.

3 tablespoons gelatine
1 litre red grape juice
½ cup white sugar
1 cup red wine
2 cups fruit, e.g. strawberries, sliced peaches,
youngberries or mixed fruit

1 cup mixed rose petals
1 cup cream, beaten
icing sugar

Melt the gelatine in a little warm water. Add it to the grape juice, sugar and red wine. Pour into a pretty glass bowl or individual tall glasses and gently lower in the fruit and rose petals. Place in the fridge until set. Just before serving, spoon the cream on top, making a pretty pattern with more fresh rose petals. Dust liberally with icing sugar.

TIRAMISU WITH ROSEMARY

Serves 6

This is a delicious variation of this famous Italian dessert.

1 cup strong black filter coffee
2 tablespoons brandy
175 g sponge fingers
1 cup plain Bulgarian yoghurt
1 cup cream cheese
4 tablespoons castor sugar or honey
3 egg whites, well beaten
2 tablespoons rosemary flowers, pulled from their calyxes
3 tablespoons grated milk chocolate

Mix the coffee and brandy together in a flat bowl. Briefly dip half the sponge fingers into the mixture and line the bottom of a glass bowl with them. Mix the yoghurt, cream cheese and the sugar or honey and lightly beat until smooth. Fold in the beaten egg whites and the rosemary flowers. Spoon this mixture on top of the sponge fingers. Briefly dip the remaining sponge fingers into the coffee and brandy mixture and neatly lay these on top of the cream cheese mixture. Sprinkle with the grated chocolate and more fresh rosemary flowers. Cover and chill before serving.

MULBERRY AND SNAPDRAGON DESSERT

Serves 4

This is a real spring dessert and can be served in pretty glass dishes as a party piece.

4 cups mulberries, stems removed
1 cup water
2 cups sugar
1 cinnamon stick
1 cup snapdragon flowers calyxes removed
1½ cups whipped cream
½ cup chopped pecan nuts
½ cup desiccated coconut
few mint leaves

Simmer the mulberries in the water with the sugar and the cinnamon stick for exactly 4 minutes, no longer. Stir gently. Cool. Remove cinnamon stick. Spoon the mulberries into a glass bowl. Tuck the snapdragon flowers deeply into the syrup so that they soak it up. Dot with small spoonfuls of the whipped cream. Sprinkle over the pecan nuts and coconut and decorate with a few fresh snapdragon flowers and mint leaves. Serve chilled.

PINK PANDA PASHKA

Serves 6-8

This is the traditional Russian Easter cake or dessert that is made in a cheese cloth-lined terracotta flower pot. The secret is the hole that helps the cream cheese drain beautifully.

350 g (about 1½ cups) cottage cheese
1 cup plain Bulgarian yoghurt
3 tablespoons runny honey
1 cup fresh fruit, e.g. peaches, mangoes, nectarines, pears, strawberries, peeled and chopped finely
¾ cup sultanas that have been soaked in hot water
¾ cup strawberry flowers – Pink Panda is pretty but any strawberry flowers will do
1 teaspoons rose-water or vanilla essence

Tip the cottage cheese into a sieve and rub it through. Mix the honey and rose-water or vanilla into the yoghurt, stir until smooth, then add to the cheese. Add the sultanas and chopped fruit to the mixture. Line a new 12 cm unglazed clay flower pot with a square of fine muslin or cheese cloth. Spoon the cheese mixture into it, fold over the corners and put a weight on it. Stand it over a bowl to drain it. Leave overnight in the fridge or preferably for a day and a night. Open the corners, invert the pot on a pretty plate, decorate with the Pink Panda flowers and, if liked, add fresh slices of fruit. Dust with icing sugar and serve as a dessert with coffee.

TUBEROSE FRIDGE CAKE

Serves 6-8

Quick, easy, nourishing and delicious. Serve as a dessert with ice-cream or custard or as a teatime treat. It keeps well in the fridge.

4 tablespoons butter
1 teaspoon ground cinnamon
1 teaspoon ground pimento (allspice)
1 teaspoon ground nutmeg
3 tablespoons treacle or honey
3 tablespoons sherry
5 tablespoons sultanas, soaked for an hour in hot water
225 g digestive biscuits, coarsely crushed
4 tablespoons chopped glacé cherries
4 tablespoons candied peel
4 tablespoons chopped pecan nuts
3 tablespoons chopped tuberose flowers

Melt the butter with the spices in a double boiler. Add the treacle or honey and the sherry and mix well. Drain the sultanas and mix with all the other ingredients. Add the sherry, honey or treacle and the

melted butter mixture. Stir in thoroughly over and over. Line a loaf tin with greaseproof paper. Press the mixture hard down into the tin and cover with more greaseproof paper and weight it down. Chill for at least 2 hours. Turn out onto a flat plate and slice thinly. Decorate with tuberose flowers.

TULIP SYRUP

Serves 6

This unusual recipe dates from the seventeenth century and is delicious spooned over rice or sago pudding, custard and cream desserts. It keeps well in the fridge.

2 cups white sugar
3 cups water
6 cloves
1 cinnamon stick
juice of 2 lemons
petals from 8 tulips, cut into thin strips
(reds and pinks are prettiest)

Place all the ingredients in a pot and simmer gently for about 12 minutes, stirring occasionally. Allow to cool for 10 minutes, remove the cinnamon stick and cloves and stir in the tulip petal strips. Refrigerate when cool.

CHOCOLATE AND VIOLET CHEESE CAKE

Serves 6-8

Exquisite, unusual and unforgettable, this dessert or teatime treat is a no-fail favourite.

250 g ricotta cheese
250 g smooth cream cheese
6 tablespoons castor sugar
2 eggs, beaten until creamy
½ cup violet flowers cut off their stems
2 tablespoons cocoa powder
½ teaspoon ground ginger
1 teaspoon vanilla essence

Beat the two cheeses together well. Whisk the sugar into the beaten eggs and fold into the cheese mixture with the violets. Dissolve the cocoa and ground ginger and add to the mixture with the vanilla. Pour into a glass ovenproof dish and stand the dish in a pan of water. Bake at 180 °C for 30-40 minutes or until the cheese cake is firm and lightly brown. Remove and cool. Serve covered in fresh and crystallised violets and whipped cream.

WATER LILY AND APPLE DESSERT

Serves 4

6 apples peeled, cored and diced
1 cup water lily petals, pulled off their calyxes
¾ cup sugar
1½-2 cups water
½ cup sultanas

1 teaspoon ground cinnamon
½ teaspoon crushed cardamom seeds,
removed from their pods
½ cup chopped pecan nuts
1 cup whipped cream

Quickly cook the apples and water lily petals with the sugar and water, sultanas, cinnamon and crushed cardamom. Mash well or put through a blender. Spoon into individual bowls and pile a mound of cream on top. Spike with 5 or 6 fresh water lily petals and dust with more cinnamon. Serve either warm or chilled.

WISTERIA FRITTERS

Serves 4-6

These fritters have an oriental touch and would be beautiful served under a bower of wisteria for a spring luncheon.

8 flowering wisteria sprays

BATTER

2 eggs
¾ cup sugar
1½ cups flour
few drops vanilla essence
2-3 cups water
1 cup sunflower oil

Whisk the eggs and the sugar. Add the flour and water alternately, and the vanilla essence. Beat to a thin batter, adding more water if necessary. Heat the oil in a large pan on the stove. Holding the flowering sprays by their stalks, dip them one by one gently into the batter, and being careful not to splash, lower them carefully into the hot oil and fry for about 2 minutes or until golden. Drain on crumpled kitchen paper towel, snip off the stems and serve warm with whipped cream and a dusting of icing sugar.

YUCCA AND APPLE CRUMBLE

Serves 6

4-6 apples, peeled, cored and sliced
½ cup sultanas
2 cups yucca petals, broken off the centre
1 cup brown sugar
1 cup water
1 cup oats
½ cup sesame seeds
1 teaspoon cinnamon
½ cup honey
½ cup butter

Boil the apple slices, sultanas and yucca petals with the sugar and water for about 10 minutes or until tender. In a pan, melt the butter and stir fry the oats and sesame seeds with the cinnamon and honey, turning constantly, until they start to turn golden. Spoon the apples and yucca petals into a glass ovenproof dish and then carefully spread the crumbly oats topping over it. Sprinkle with a little cinnamon and keep hot until you are ready to serve. Serve with a generous helping of whipped cream and top with a fresh yucca flower.

DRINKS

... health teas, energisers, liqueurs and much more

ALMOND BLOSSOM MILK ENERGISER

Serves 1

Made with full cream milk and almonds as well as the blossom, this is a quick pick-me-up at the end of a busy day, or a lunch time energiser much loved by children.

1 glass milk
1-2 tablespoons roughly chopped almonds
1 peeled banana
1 dessertspoon honey
1 dessertspoon almond blossom petals
removed from their calyxes

Pour half the milk and all the almonds into a liquidiser and whirl briefly until the almonds disintegrate. Add the banana, honey, almond blossom petals and the rest of the milk. Blend until well mixed. Pour immediately into a glass and drink it slowly.

> **Cook's Note**
>
> ALL TEAS MUST BE MADE WITH YOUR OWN SEEDS AND FLOWERS BECAUSE YOU NEED TO KNOW THEY ARE ORGANICALLY GROWN AND NOT IRRADIATED OR SPRAYED IN ANY WAY.

ANISE HEALTH TEA

Serves 1

I find this tea superb after a heavy meal or when I've dined out, or eaten rich or spicy food. It also helps with cramps and coughs and every other ailment mentioned above. I even travel with a little jar of anise seed and some dried flowers to ensure I have a good night. Leave out the honey if you prefer it unsweetened.

2 teaspoons anise seeds
1 tablespoon fresh flowers and leaves

Pour over this 1 cup of boiling water. Stand for 5 minutes. Stir well. Strain, sweeten with a touch of honey, and sip slowly.

ANISE HYSSOP PARTY PUNCH

Serves 12

I make the most delicious party punch with anise hyssop over the Christmas festive season when it grows so prolifically.

juice of 4 lemons
2 cups white sugar
2 litres boiling water
2 cups anise hyssop leaves and flowers
2 litres mango juice or mango and orange mixed

Mix the lemon juice with the sugar and leave to stand for an hour or two. Pour the boiling water over the anise hyssop leaves and flowers and leave to stand until cool. Strain. Add the lemon and sugar mixture and the fruit juice, mix well and chill. Just before serving add crushed ice and sprinkle with a few anise hyssop flowers and tiny leaves.

> **Cook's Note**
>
> I USE ANISE HYSSOP FLOWERS TO DECORATE EVERYTHING FROM DRINKS TO PASTA, DESSERTS TO CAKES AND EVEN ROASTS, AS IT CLEANSES THE PALATE SO BEAUTIFULLY.

BERGAMOT HEALTH TEA

Serves 1

If you enjoy the taste of Earl Grey tea, you can make your own by adding a leaf or two and a flower of bergamot to a pot of ordinary Ceylon tea. This will infuse, giving it that typical Earl Grey taste. (Commercial Earl Grey tea is not made with bergamot, however, but the dried rind or the essential oil of the bergamot orange, *Citrus bergamia*, an evergreen tree native to tropical Asia that produces these small fragrant oranges.)

1 bergamot flower, calyx discarded
1 bergamot leaf
1 tea bag of your favourite tea
1 cup boiling water

Pull the petals out of the calyx and infuse with the leaf and your favourite tea for a few minutes in boiling water. Strain. Sweeten with honey and add a slice of lemon. Serve either hot or cold and sip slowly. It will relax and help you to unwind and clear a stuffy head.

BORAGE SANGRIA

Serves 6-8

I was once lucky enough to find an ancient recipe made by monks in England, who called borage the Good Herb. My modern version of this ancient drink draws many a favourable comment, especially when served warm on a cold winter's night.

2 cups borage leaves, stems and flowers
roughly chopped
3 thumb-length sprigs fresh rosemary
4 tablespoons honey
4 cups good red wine
2 cups pure apple juice
2 lemons, thinly sliced
1 naartjie, thinly sliced
borage flowers

Crush the rosemary and borage leaves, stalks and flowers and pour over them the honey and the wine. Stir well and leave to stand for about an hour. Add the apple juice and the fruit and stir well. Cover and refrigerate for a day and a night. Strain the following day. Keep chilled. Serve either hot or cold before dinner and float several borage flowers on it as you serve.

Burdock Bud Syrup

Makes 2 litres
A most refreshing drink either hot or cold.

20 very young burdock buds
2 cups stems peeled and cut into 3 cm lengths
4 cups dark brown treacle sugar
2 teaspoons ground cinnamon
½ teaspoon ground cloves
1 cup thinly sliced ginger root

Trim the buds with a sharp knife to remove all the rough bits. Place the buds in 2 litres of cold water, bring to the boil and simmer for 10 minutes. Discard the water and boil up again with another 2 litres of cold water, again simmering for 10 minutes. Add the sugar, cinnamon, ground cloves and thinly sliced ginger root. Keep the lid on and simmer gently for another 10 minutes. Remove from heat and cool. Strain. Bottle the syrup and keep in the fridge. Dilute ¼ glass syrup and top up with iced water and crushed ice and a thin slice of ginger. Sip slowly.

Burdock Flower and Leaf Tea

Serves 1
This is excellent as a cleansing, rejuvenating tea, also good for acne and boils. The Chinese add a few seeds.

1 burdock flower
1 piece burdock leaf, about 3 cm square
1 cup boiling water

cinnamon stick
honey
powdered ginger

Pour the boiling water over the flower and piece of leaf. Stir with a cinnamon stick and let it draw for 5 minutes. Then strain, sweeten with a touch of honey and a pinch of powdered ginger and sip slowly. Add 1 dandelion flower if you're taking it for acne or boils. They combine exceptionally well.

Calamint or Emperor's Mint Tea

Serve this in place of after dinner coffee in small cups, or add fresh sprigs to filter coffee. The same tea cooled and mixed with equal quantities of fresh unsweetened fruit juice, particularly litchi juice, served with crushed ice and a sprinkling of calamint flowers, will refresh and revive you after a long day. With a little dash of white wine it's a party time treat and a tonic as well!

¼ cup fresh calamint sprigs, leaves and flowers
1 cup boiling water

Pour the boiling water over the calamint sprigs and allow to stand for 5 minutes, then strain. Serve hot and sip slowly. This is particularly soothing when you have overeaten, or when you feel nauseous or very chilled.
Caution: Avoid if you are pregnant as both calamint and emperor's mint are very strong herbs.

Carnation Tonic Wine

Makes 1 litre

3 teaspoons crushed coriander seeds
2 teaspoons powdered ginger
2 teaspoons powdered nutmeg
½ cup honey
4 cups good white wine
½ cup carnation petals, white heel removed
½ cup lemon balm leaves (*Melissa officinalis*)

Mix the spices into the honey. In a double boiler warm the wine with the carnation petals and lemon balm leaves for 5-10 minutes. Add the honey and spice mixture and warm for a further 5 minutes. Strain. Pour into a wine bottle and cork well. Refrigerate. Take half a cup at a time and sip it slowly. For sensitive stomachs dilute with a little water. It can be served warm on a winter's night, or cool in summer. It keeps well in the fridge.

MANGO NECTAR WITH CARNATION PETALS

Serves 1

This exquisite drink is a magical midsummer experience. I have it every year as a party drink and no one can ever get enough! Serve it chilled.

1 mango, peeled and sliced
1 cup unsweetened mango juice
3 mint leaves
carnation petals, heel removed

Blend the mango flesh, juice and mint together in a liquidiser, adding a little water if it is too thick. Serve chilled in a tall glass, with carnation petals and mint leaves sprinkled on top.

CARPET GERANIUM COMFORT TEA

Serves 1

For those rushed, tense and harassed days, this pleasant tea is a real comfort. For iced tea on a hot day, cool the infusion and add about ¾ cup of fresh fruit juice – grape or litchi is wonderful – and an ice cube.

1 thumb-length sprig peppermint
¼ cup carpet geranium leaves and flowers
1 cinnamon stick
2 teaspoons honey
1 cup boiling water

Pour the boiling water over everything. Stand for about 5 minutes, then strain. Sip slowly.

CHAMOMILE TEA

Serves 1

This old-fashioned tea is an age-old remedy for insomnia.

1 teaspoon dried or 2 teaspoons fresh
chamomile flowers
1 cup boiling water
1 clove

Place dried chamomile flowers in a little sieve and pour the water through them until level with the edge of the cup. (Fresh flowers can be added straight to the water.) Add a clove to the water and stand for 5 minutes. Remove the flowers and the clove. Sweeten with a touch of honey and sip slowly.

CHAMOMILE SYRUP

This is a superb cough mixture for tight chests or a soothing drink for restless children. It makes a delicious drink hot or cold.

4 cups fresh chamomile flowers or 2 cups dried flowers
4 cups sugar (I use brown treacle sugar)
1 stick cinnamon

10 cloves
juice of 3 lemons
a few thin slivers lemon rind
1 large sprig lemon balm mint (*Melissa officinalis*)

Simmer everything together for 20 minutes in a covered pot. Remove from heat and allow to cool, then strain. Pour into clean bottles, cork well and label. To drink it, dilute ¼ cup syrup to 1 cup warm or ice cold water and sip slowly. For a cough syrup, dilute 2 teaspoons in a little hot water and take frequently.

CRAB APPLE VERJUICE

Make this in autumn and store sealed, until spring, when the crab apple blossom is at its most glorious. That is the secret ingredient! The crab apples need to be soaked overnight in apple cider vinegar beforehand.

2 cups ripe crab apples
1 cup apple cider vinegar
2 cups soft brown sugar
½ cup grated ginger root
2 cinnamon sticks
10 cloves
1 bottle good brandy
1 cup runny honey

Clean and slice the crab apples, cover well and soak overnight in the apple cider vinegar with a weight on them. Next morning sprinkle the sugar over them and leave to stand for 2 hours. Meanwhile add the ginger root, cinnamon and cloves to the brandy and leave it to stand.

After the sugar has dissolved and mingled well with the crab apples, add the honey and stir in well. Now add the brandy and spices and pour into a wide-mouthed jar with a tight-fitting lid. Shake it up well and store in a dark cupboard all winter, giving it a daily shake and inspection. In spring, add 1 cup crab apple blossom and seal again, giving it a gentle daily shake for 14 days. Finally, strain it and bottle in a pretty decanter.

Serve well diluted with chilled apple juice as it is potent! In each glass put 5 raisins soaked in brandy overnight. Taken as a liqueur at the end of a meal, it is a remarkable digestive and a very little goes a long way! Let me know if you see fairies!

MEXICAN CERIMAN (DELICIOUS MONSTER) DRINK

Serves 4

ripe pulp from 1 delicious monster
flower, scales removed
(about ¾ cup mashed)
2 cups hot water (not boiling)
1 litre iced water
about ½ cup honey

1 litre granadilla or mango juice
sprigs mint

Mash the pulp and cover with the hot water. Leave it to stand and cool, then put it through a liquidiser with a little of the iced water. Strain if you prefer it. Add the honey, fruit juice and mint, and chill. Serve in tall glasses with a sprig of mint. Sip slowly and relish every magical mouthful.

ELDER FLOWER LEMONADE

Serves 8
This is an exquisite summer cordial and keeps well in the fridge.

4 cups elder flowers, pulled off their stems
juice of 8 lemons
1 tablespoon lemon rind
6 cups white sugar
2 litres water

Simmer everything together for 10 minutes. Add a little extra water if necessary. Cool, then strain. Pour the lemony syrup into a decanter and keep in the fridge. To serve, pour ¼ glass syrup and top up with iced water and crushed ice, or ice cold soda water with a sprinkling of elder flowers floating on top.

FALSE ACACIA SYRUP

Makes 2 bottles
This is most refreshing on a hot day, or alternatively served with hot water and a dash of brandy, it makes a superb winter chill-chaser.

4 cups flowers and buds, stripped off their stalks
4 cups sugar
2 litres water
1 cup lemon juice
1 cinnamon stick

Boil up the flowers and sugar with the water, lemon juice and cinnamon stick for 20 minutes. Set aside and cool. Strain. Pour into clean wine bottles, cork and refrigerate. Serve ¼ of a glass of syrup topped up with ¾ of a glass of iced water and add an ice cube.

FALSE ACACIA LIQUEUR

The recipe for this rather potent liqueur was devised by a historian after studying ancient manuscripts from monasteries where *Robinia pseudoacacia* was grown in the physic gardens for its medicinal properties. The recipe varied from monastery to monastery. A little goes a long way, so it should be drunk sparingly!

1 tablespoon grated lemon rind
6 allspice berries, crushed
6 cloves, crushed
1 cinnamon stick, roughly broken
1 bay leaf
2 cups false acacia flowers and buds,
stripped off their stems

1 cup dark rum
1 bottle good brandy
1 cup brown sugar

Soak the lemon rind, spices and flowers in the rum for 3-4 hours. Mix in the brandy and the sugar and pour everything into a large jar with a well-fitting lid. Give it a good daily shake and keep it in a dark cupboard for 1 month. Then strain, bottle and drink diluted with ice water.

FENNEL TEA

Serves 1
This is the world's favourite slimming drink and it is also a superb detoxifier.

¼ cup fresh fennel leaves and flowers
1 cup boiling water

Pour the boiling water over the fennel leaves and flowers, stand for 5 minutes, then strain. Two cups taken during the day is the standard dose during a time of infection, followed by 1 cup a day thereafter for about 10 days.

FENNEL HOT TODDY

Serves 1
In monasteries in the seventeenth century this hot toddy was used to cure everything from rheumatism to the ague, bites from a mad dog to fainting fits. On a winter's night it is like a magic potion. It warms you up, lifts your spirits and chases stiffness and chills away.

1 cup boiling water
½ cup fennel flowers
4 cloves
1 teaspoon crushed cinnamon
(not powdered cinnamon)
juice of 2 lemons
1 tablespoon honey
dash of good brandy

Pour the boiling water over the fennel, cloves and cinnamon. Stand for 5 minutes. Keep it covered to retain its warmth, or place it in a pot on the stove. Turn the stove down low and cook for 5 minutes. Strain. Add the lemon juice, honey and brandy and sip slowly. Watch your mood change radically!

GARDENIA MILK SHAKE

Serves 1
Energising and nourishing, this exotic milk shake is a meal in a glass and very refreshing on a hot day. Children love to drink it with a straw.

1 glass milk
1 ripe banana
1 egg, well beaten
1 tablespoon honey

about 6 gardenia petals
1 teaspoon cinnamon

Blend all the ingredients except for the cinnamon together in a liquidiser. Pour into a glass and sprinkle cinnamon over the frothy top. Drink immediately and feel your energy levels rise!

GOLDEN ROD HEALTH TEA

Serves 1

As a general tonic a cup of this marvellous tea taken once a day for a few days is wonderfully soothing. The honey and the cayenne pepper can be left out if preferred.

1 cup boiling water
3 cups flowering golden rod sprigs
2 cloves
1 mint leaf
honey to taste
tiny pinch cayenne pepper

Pour the boiling water over the golden rod flowers and mash well with a teaspoon. Add all the other ingredients and stir well. After 5 minutes strain and sip slowly.

GOLDEN ROD AND CELERY HEALTH DRINK

Makes 3 glasses

This is a superb drink for any bladder or kidney ailment, and for cystitis I know no better drink. It is also excellent as a general health builder and detoxifier. It can also be served chilled with freshly squeezed orange juice. As with any herbal remedy, remember to discuss it with your doctor first.

2 cups boiling water
1 cup golden rod flowers
½ cup chopped parsley
1 cup chopped celery
2 cups barley water
juice of 1 lemon

Make the barley water by boiling 1 cup pearl barley in 2 litres of water for 40 minutes. Keep topping up and simmer gently with the lid on, then strain.

Pour the boiling water over the golden rod flowers, parsley and celery. Leave it to stand for 5 minutes, then quickly put through a liquidiser. Strain, add the barley water and the lemon juice. Drink slowly warm or cold. During acute infections, like an acute cystitis attack, drink three times a day and add extra water.

PASSION FLOWER NECTAR

Serves 4-6

At the end of a hot day there is nothing nicer than this relaxing, exotic fruit drink.

1 cup granadilla pulp
2 cups granadilla juice
about ½ cup sugar
1 cup granadilla flowers, roughly broken
3 cups chopped watermelon, seeds removed

Whisk the sugar into the granadilla pulp. Put everything into the liquidiser and blend for 2 minutes. Pour immediately into glasses with crushed ice, and add a dash of soda or iced water if desired. Top each glass with a luscious granadilla flower and let your guests savour its delicate fragrance while you tell them the story about those ancient Spanish monks who first ascribed mystical qualities to the passion flower (see p. 41).

HAWTHORN FLOWER TEA

Serves 1

This is a marvellous tea to help you unwind, easing tension and anxiety as well as lowering high blood pressure.

1 tablespoon fresh hawthorn flowers and a leaf or two
1 cup boiling water

Pour the boiling water over the flowers, stand for 5 minutes and strain. Sweeten with honey if liked.

HONEYSUCKLE ENERGY DRINK

Serves 1

This is an excellent exam time drink that will give energy and a feeling of well-being. It is also nourishing for invalids and for those who are overworked and overtired. Make it fresh every time and do not let it stand.

1 egg
1 tablespoon honey
1 tablespoon sunflower seeds
1 banana
1 cup milk
1 tablespoon chopped almonds
½ cup honeysuckle flowers

Whisk everything together in a blender for 3 minutes. Pour into a glass and drink immediately, sipping slowly.

HONEYSUCKLE SYRUP

I have made this for many years and keep it as a standby for coughs, chills, sore throats, runny noses, tight chests and exhaustion. It is an old-fashioned recipe but works as well today as it did in our grandmothers' day.

2 cups honeysuckle flowers and buds
1 tablespoon aniseed
1 tablespoon fresh lemon thyme
juice of 2 lemons
2 teaspoons lemon zest
1½ cups soft brown sugar
500 ml water

Put everything together in a pot and simmer gently for 15 minutes with the lid on. Remove from heat and allow to cool. Strain, and discard the herbs. Pour into a bottle with a tight-fitting lid and keep in the fridge. Take 1 tablespoon in about ¾ of a cup of hot water twice a day, the second dose preferably just before going to bed.

JASMINE SYRUP

Jasmine flowers have been used in cooking for centuries. I was intrigued to find recipes in ancient herbals using the flowers in syrups and cordials to soothe anxiety and calm restless children, of which the following is one. Use only *Jasminum officinale* for this.

2 cups white sugar
2 cups jasmine flowers,
pulled from their calyxes
juice of 1 lemon
1 teaspoon lemon zest, finely grated
1 teaspoon freshly grated nutmeg
1 litre water

Simmer everything together for 15 minutes. Remove from heat and allow to cool. Strain, discard the flowers and bottle the syrup. Take 1 tablespoon of syrup in a glass of chilled water with crushed ice and sip slowly. As a nightcap, take 1 tablespoon of syrup in 1 cup of hot water, stir well and sip slowly.

JASMINE TEA

Serves 1

Use *J. officinale*, Arabian jasmine (*J. sambac*) or yellow jasmine (*J. nudiflorum*) or Chinese jamine (*J. polyanthum*), or our own indigenous jasmine (*J. multipartitum*). Use a tin or glass container rather than plastic.

250 g loose Ceylon tea
2 cups fresh jasmine flowers
pulled out of their calyxes
1 airtight cake tin or large
glass jar with a good lid

Mix the flowers into the tea leaves in the tin or glass jar, covering the flowers completely with the tea leaves. Seal and leave undisturbed for 5 days. Open and check that the fragrance is as strong as you like it, adding more fresh jasmine flowers if necessary. By now the flowers should be almost dry. Spoon the tea and the jasmine flowers into smaller tins or bottles with lids that seal well, to lock in the fragrance. To make the tea, place 1-3 teaspoons in a tea pot, cover with about 2 cups of boiling water and let it draw. Use a tea strainer and serve either black with lemon or add a little milk.

LUCERNE ENERGY DRINK

Serves 1

For a quick pick-me-up and a boost for the immune system, this can take the place of a meal when you are very tired.

1 banana, peeled
½ cup lucerne leaves and flowers
1 apple, peeled and cored
1 tablespoon sunflower seeds
½ cup stoned dates, cut into pieces
½ cup sultanas, soaked
1 cup fresh fruit juice, e.g. mango, orange, litchi

Whirl everything in a liquidiser, then sip slowly straight away, adding a little water if it is too thick.

ICED TEA WITH ORANGE BLOSSOM SUGAR

Serves 4-6

Served in tall frosted glasses on a summer afternoon, this takes some beating.

1 litre boiling water
1 tea bag
1 tablespoon orange flowers
1 litre iced water
juice of 1 lemon
orange blossom sugar to taste
(see recipe below)
1 lemon or orange, thinly sliced

Pour the boiling water over the tea bag and leave to stand for just 3 minutes. Remove the tea bag and allow the tea to cool. Float the orange blossom in the iced water. Add the iced water and lemon juice to the tea and sweeten to taste with orange blossom sugar. Pour into a glass jug, float the lemon or orange slices on top and several fresh orange blossoms. Serve chilled with a little crushed ice. Individual flowers can be frozen into individual ice cubes and served with the iced tea.

ORANGE BLOSSOM SUGAR

This wonderful old-fashioned recipe with its lingering, haunting scent and taste would have been kept in a silver sugar casket in days gone by and used with iced tea, jasmine tea, or in eggnogs, custards or cream.

1 kg white sugar
1 cup orange or lemon blossom
1 whole nutmeg, cracked with a
mallet or using a pestle and mortar
1 stick cinnamon
1 tablespoon roughly crushed
allspice berries (pimento)

Mix together all the ingredients and store in a large, sealed screw-top jar. Shake daily.

PINEAPPLE SAGE AND PINEAPPLE DRINK

Serves 4

This is a delicious drink for hot summer days. Ring the changes with litchi juice, apple or mango juice. If using mango juice add 1 peeled ripe mango cut off its stone to the pineapple puree.

1 large, very sweet pineapple or 2 small ones
½ cup fresh mint leaves
3 cups plain white grape juice
honey to sweeten
pineapple sage flowers for decoration

Peel, chop and liquidise the pineapple. Add the mint leaves and grape juice and whirl until smooth. Chill until ready to serve. Just before serving, taste for sweetness. If it is not sweet enough, add a little honey and whirl again. Pour into tall glasses and sprinkle with pineapple sage flowers.

POPPY BRANDY

Makes 750 ml

This potent brandy is based on a medieval recipe and can be served as a liqueur, on ice-cream or on sponge cake with cream. It makes a divine present for a special person. It is also delicious made with rum instead of brandy.

½ cup seedless raisins
1 tablespoon fennel seed
1 tablespoon coriander seed
1 tablespoon anise seed
2 tablespoons thinly sliced ginger
1 cup dark treacle sugar
1 bottle good brandy
1 cup lightly packed poppy petals
and a few stamens

First pack the raisins into an empty bottle, followed by the spices and the sugar. Add about 2 cups brandy and shake well. Leave to stand for 2 hours, shaking every now and then until the sugar has completely dissolved. Add the poppy petals and stamens and the rest of the brandy. Shake well. Store in a dark cupboard for 1 month, giving it a shake every now and then. Resist tasting it before it is ready! Strain and pour into a pretty bottle. Discard the spices and petals.

CHINESE PLUM BLOSSOM TEA

Serves 1

In China around the sixteenth century plum blossom tea with its almond overtones was considered a great delicacy. The buds were picked in spring and dried and stored in caddies for the winter months. Fresh blossoms are far nicer, and remember, the Chinese tea drinking ceremony is unhurried and peaceful, which is when this delicious tea will do you most good.

1 cup boiling water
1 tablespoon fresh plum blossom
1 small sprig spearmint (or any other mint)

Pour the boiling water over the plum blossom and mint. Allow to draw for 5 minutes. Strain and sweeten with honey. Sip slowly. This is an excellent after dinner drink too, and can be added cold to jellies and jams.

ROSE HIP SYRUP

This delicious, health-giving syrup keeps well in the fridge in hot weather.

2 cups ripe rose hips, trimmed of stamens
and stalks and finely chopped
2 cups brown treacle sugar
1½ cups water
1 cinnamon stick

Simmer everything together in a covered pot for about 20 minutes. Pour into hot sterilised jars and seal well. Take 2 teaspoons at a time, chew well and follow it with a little hot rose petal tea (see p. 67).

ROSE PUNCH

Serves 8-10

This light and refreshing punch looks magnificent served in a glass punch bowl with whole roses set into a big block of ice or several ice cubes, which keep it beautifully chilled.

2 litres white wine, chilled
4 tablespoons Kirsch
1 cup rose petal syrup (see p. 144)
1 litre water
juice of 2 lemons

Gently mix everything together and serve in a glass punch bowl with frozen roses (see below).

TO FREEZE THE ROSES

The day before the party, choose perfectly formed pink rose buds that are just opening and trim them of their stalks. (I find the old-fashioned Margaret Roberts rose exquisite here as it never loses its shape and is tender and sweet to the taste.) Select a bowl that holds about 2 cups of water and fill the bowl with the rose buds. Fill the bowl with iced water and freeze it overnight, keeping it in the freezer until you are ready to serve the punch. (Alternatively, freeze rosebuds in individual ice cubes.) Just before serving the punch, dip the bowl in hot water, then turn it upside down to release the block of ice. Slide it into the punch.

Rose Petal Syrup

Serve on ice-cream, rice or sago puddings or add to drinks.

4 cups red and pink rose petals
2½ cups water
2 cups white sugar
1 cinnamon stick

Simmer the petals in the sugar water with the cinnamon stick for 15 minutes. Stand aside to cool, then strain.

Roselle Health Tea

Makes 2 litres

Hibiscus sabdariffa is the species used in hibiscus tea, not the bright-flowered species commonly grown in the garden. Hot roselle tea taken with honey is an excellent remedy for a hangover.

1 cup fresh or dried roselle calyxes
2 litres water

Break away the five pointed calyxes from their marble-sized seed capsules, and use only those bright red pieces in the tea. Boil in the water for 10 minutes, stand aside and let it steep. When pleasantly hot, discard the calyxes, sweeten with honey and stir with a cinnamon stick. Cool the rest and chill. Mix in equal quantities of grape juice or litchi juice for an energising cold drink. Add sliced strawberries and mint leaves and a dash of good red wine for a party punch and as a bonus you'll feel no alcohol build up.

Sage Flower Eggnog

Serves 1

This is a refreshing 'quick fix' that is excellent for all age groups, particularly students during exam time. It immediately energises and revitalises.

1 egg
1 glass milk
1 tablespoon honey
1 teaspoon finely grated nutmeg
1 banana
2 teaspoons sage leaves and flowers

Blend everything together in the liquidiser until it froths. Pour immediately into a glass and sip it slowly.

Strawberry Tonic Wine

Makes 1 bottle

This one of the most loved tonic wines from the seventeenth century. It is said to ease all stomach ailments, fevers and coughs, to comfort the liver and to make the heart merry!

1 bottle good red wine
2 cinnamon sticks
3 tablespoons honey

1 cup strawberry fruits
½ cup strawberry flowers
½ cup strawberry leaves

Choose small strawberries or cut the fruits in quarters. Remove some of the wine and press all the ingredients into the bottle. Cork well and shake. Leave to stand at least 1 week before opening. Sip half a small glass of wine slowly.

Pink Panda Pink Punch

Serves 8

For a party drink that is delicious and healthy!

juice of 6 lemons
2 teaspoons lemon zest, finely grated
1½ cups sugar
1½ litres water
2 tablespoons finely grated ginger
2 cups thinly sliced strawberries
1 cup Pink Panda strawberry flowers

Mash the strawberries with half the sugar and leave to stand about 2 hours. Squeeze the lemons, dissolve the rest of the sugar in them, add the ginger and the zest and leave to stand about 2 hours. Mix everything together, pour into a jug, float the flowers on top. Optional: Add 1 litre of rosé wine. Serve chilled.

Tuberose and Pineapple Cordial

Serves 6-8

For a party time treat that will long be remembered!

2 well ripened pineapples, peeled and chopped
2 litres white grape juice
about ½ cup runny honey
2 teaspoons ground ginger
10-15 fresh tuberose flowers

Put the pineapples through a liquidiser with a little of the grape juice, the ground ginger and the honey. Whirl until smooth. Mix in the rest of the grape juice. Toss in the flowers (the Chinese chop them, I like them kept whole in all their beauty), refrigerate for at least 2 hours before serving. Taste for sweetness, add more honey if needed. Serve in wine glasses and tuck in a tuberose in each glass.

Violet Liqueur

Makes 750 ml

I had a thriving business making this delicious and unusual liqueur from rows of violets I grew in my farm gardens as a young mother. People came from far and wide to buy it and the violet jam I made each spring. It is delicious served over ice-cream or cream cakes and it makes a superb present for a special person.

Rose petal syrup, p. 144

Roselle health tea, p. 144

Nasturtium salad vinegar, p. 148

750 ml good vodka
100 violet flowers, picked off their stalks
1 stick cinnamon
6 allspice berries (pimento)
250 g white sugar
a small piece fresh ginger root

Mix everything together and pour into a large, sterilised glass jar with a well-fitting lid. Shake it well and leave in a dark cupboard for 2 weeks, giving it a daily shake for a minute. Strain first through a muslin cloth, then through a coffee filter. Pour into a pretty glass decanter, add a few fresh violets, and serve just a little at a time in a tiny liqueur glass with a splash of fresh thin cream.

Violet Syrup

Makes about 20 servings

This delightfully calming and soothing syrup is an old-fashioned remedy for winter coughs and colds.

It is delicious in hot water to soothe a chill, and equally delicious in iced water to cool you down on a hot afternoon. It is also good over ice-cream and oat porridge.

4 cups violet flowers, cut off their stems
4 cups white sugar
1 cup runny honey
juice of 4 lemons
1 tablespoon thin ginger slices
2 star anise
2 teaspoons finely grated lemon zest

Gently simmer everything together in a saucepan with a tight-fitting lid for 15 minutes. Stand aside and cool, then strain and carefully pour the syrup into a sterilised glass bottle. Discard the rest and cork well. Allow it to stand for 3 or 4 days before serving. Pour about 2 tablespoons into a glass of water, mix well, float a violet or two on top and sip slowly. Feel the tension drain away!

PRESERVES

... jams, pickles and condiments

PICKLED ARTICHOKES

Makes 1 large jar
Serve with cheese and salads or finely chopped over mushroom dishes.

6 young tender artichoke buds
sprig of origanum
2 bay leaves
2 sprigs parsley
2 cups brown grape vinegar
1½ cups brown sugar
½ cup mustard seeds

Select young tender buds, cut off the tough outer leaves and pare away the tops of the leaves, leaving the base. Scoop out any of the fluffy flower parts, the thistle's 'choke', and cut the heart into quarters. Pack into a glass jar, add the origanum, bay leaves and parsley. Boil up the vinegar with brown sugar and mustard seeds for 10 minutes. Pour the hot mixture over the artichoke hearts, seal and label. Leave it to mature for at least a month before eating.

CARNATION PICKLE

This enchanting recipe dates from 1629, from a book called *The Garden of Pleasant Flowers*. It ends with the charming line: 'This pickle now draws the highest esteem with Gentlemen and Ladies of the greatest note.' I make it as a sweet and sour pickle to serve with cheese.

6 cups carnation flowers
brown sugar
a few cloves
2 teaspoons coriander seeds
2 cups brown grape vinegar
2 bay leaves
1 stick cinnamon

Strip the flowers out of their calyxes and remove the bitter white heels from the petals with a sharp knife. Lay a thin layer of petals in a wide-mouthed jar and sprinkle with brown sugar. Add another layer and sprinkle with sugar and a few cloves and the coriander seeds. Add more layers and more sugar. Warm the vinegar with the bay leaves and cinnamon for 10 minutes. Pour the hot vinegar over the carnation petals. Seal and stand for 2 weeks before eating it. A peeled, sliced cucumber, or pickling onions, or green peppers and even sweet corn cut off the cob, can be added to the recipe, alternating layers with the carnation petals.

PICKLED CHICORY FLOWERS

Makes 2 jars
This is an old-fashioned recipe made with hot spicy vinegar and onions which may be used in the stir fry recipe above instead of fresh chicory flowers. Keep this pickle close at hand for a quick tasty addition to soups, stews and stir fries.

4 cups chicory flowers
4 cups onion rings
2 cups good grape vinegar
1 cup honey
2 tablespoons coriander seeds
bay leaf

Fill wide-mouthed glass jars with chicory flowers and onion rings. Boil up the vinegar with the honey, coriander seeds and bay leaf. Pour this over the chicory flowers, seal and leave for 10 days.

CHIVE BLOSSOM VINEGAR

This pretty pink vinegar is delicious as a salad dressing or add a dash to stir fries, grills, braais or stews. Make it in spring when the blossoms are abundant. You can also add peeled garlic cloves, chopped onions, coriander seeds and a bay leaf, or even a fresh cayenne pepper.

1 bottle white grape vinegar
chive flowers, including garlic chives

Fill the bottle of vinegar with chive flowers and place it in the sun for 5 days, shaking it daily. Strain out the vinegar and discard the chive flowers. Pour into a pretty bottle and add fresh chive flowers for identification. **Note**: The pungent taste of the chives means you need do it only once in the sun, whereas for other herb vinegars the process is repeated two or three times for optimum flavour.

Cook's Note

CHIVE, GARLIC CHIVE OR WILD GARLIC FLOWERS CAN BE USED INTERCHANGEABLY IN THE RECIPE ABOVE. CHIVES HAVE A TONIC EFFECT AND IMPROVE THE APPETITE, SO USE LAVISHLY IN SAVOURY DISHES.

LEMON AND CRAB APPLE BLOSSOM JELLY

Makes 3 jars

This is a delicious jelly – a more delicate version of marmalade – to serve on toast, or topping a steamed pudding, or as a cake filling. With the crab apple blossom, it is so pretty that it makes a charming gift.

1 kg fresh lemons
1 kg white sugar
3 litres water
3-4 cups loosely packed crab apple blossoms

Scrub the lemons, then peel them. Shred the peel finely and simmer with 1½ litres of the water for 1½-2 hours. Keep it covered and gently simmering. Roughly chop the lemon pulp and simmer it in another pan with the rest of the water for 1½ hours. Strain this pulp through a fine sieve and add the juice to the lemon peel mixture. Bring to the boil and boil briskly for 10 minutes, then lower the heat and add the sugar. Stir well and gently simmer until it sets (usually about an hour). Pour a little into a saucer and let it stand. If it sets it is ready. Finally add the crab apple blossoms and mix well. Pour into hot sterilised jars, seal while hot, and label the jars.

JUDAS TREE PICKLE

Makes 2-3 jars

This old-fashioned recipe was popular long before commercial pickles were available for sandwiches and with cold meats and cheeses.

2 cups water
3 cups brown grape vinegar
2 cups brown sugar
½ cup mixed coriander seeds,
peppercorns and caraway seed
2 cups thinly sliced small young cucumbers
4 cups pickling onions, peeled and sliced in half
2 cups sliced green pepper
2 cups Judas tree flowers

Boil the water, vinegar and sugar together with the spices for 10 minutes. Meanwhile, pack bottles that have well-fitting lids with the vegetables and flowers. Pour over the vinegar and sugar mixture until each bottle is full. Seal immediately while hot. Wipe down the bottles and label.

HOMEMADE MUSTARD

Makes 1-2 bottles

Use as a spread on cold meat, sandwiches or with chicken, meat and fish as a delicious condiment. It makes a superb gift too.

2 tablespoons whole mustard seeds
4 tablespoons honey
1 cup white grape vinegar
2 tablespoons dry mustard powder
(or crush your own seeds in a food processor)
2 tablespoons olive oil
2 tablespoons fresh mustard flowers
2 tablespoons chopped fresh tarragon

Soak the whole mustard seed with the honey and vinegar overnight. Next morning add all the other ingredients and mix well. Spoon into a glass jar with a well-fitting lid and keep refrigerated.

MUSTARD FLOWER PICKLE

Makes about 4 bottles

Keep this delicious pickle for at least 3 weeks before eating. Serve it with cold meats, salads, sandwiches and pasta. The vegetables can be varied according to what's in season.

4 cups peeled, thickly sliced cucumbers
2 cups cauliflower florets
4 cups small pickling onions
4 cups green peppers cut into strips
1 cup red peppers cut into strips
2 cups mustard flowers
2 tablespoons mustard seeds
2 cups brown sugar
4 cups brown grape vinegar
about 1 tablespoon sea salt

Wash the vegetables thoroughly in salted water and pack them attractively into glass jars with the mustard flowers. Boil the mustard seed with the sugar, vinegar and salt for 15 minutes with the lid on. Pour the hot mixture over the vegetables until the bottle is full. Seal immediately. Store in a dark cupboard.

MYRTLE PEPPER

Makes 2 bottles

This is a deliciously spicy pepper that is very easy to make and makes a superb gift for the keen cook.

1 cup dried myrtle flowers
1 cup dried myrtle flower buds
½ cup coriander seeds
½ cup peppercorns
½ cup dried paprika pieces
or ¼ cup powdered paprika
½ cup powdered nutmeg
½ cup dried thyme

Mix everything together well and store in a screw-top jar. Shake well. Spoon small, well-mixed quantities into a pepper grinder, leaving a bit of space to be able shake the mixture every now and then. Grind onto savoury dishes such as pasta or egg, cheese and potato dishes.

Nasturtium Salad Vinegar

Makes 1 bottle

This is a delicious, easily made salad dressing with an almost addictive bite. It can also be used in stir fries and the pickled flowers are delicious as well. Some cooks make it in a wide-mouthed jar tightly packed with nasturtium flowers so that the flowers can be easily fished out for flavouring soups, sauces, stews and gravies. It makes a superb gift.

several nasturtium flowers and buds
nasturtium leaves
about 10 nasturtium seeds
1 tablespoon mustard seed
2 tablespoons sesame seed
2 tablespoons runny honey
brown grape vinegar

Pack the nasturtium flowers and buds and a leaf or two into a pretty 750 ml bottle. Add the nasturtium seeds and sesame seed. Dribble in the honey and finally top with a good-quality brown grape vinegar. Shake gently, store out of the sun and leave to mature for about 1 month before using. Give it a gentle daily shake in order to disperse the ingredients. It will keep for several years in a cool place.

Thyme Salt

Having a cannister of thyme salt at hand is so useful while cooking. For added zest and flavour it takes some beating.

2 cups coarse sea salt
¾ cup fresh thyme leaves and flowers
1 tablespoon coriander seeds
1 tablespoon black peppercorns
1 tablespoon mustard powder
1 tablespoon paprika

Mix everything together well. Store in an airtight screw-top jar. Have a pestle and mortar next to the stove; or have a large pepper grinder nearby. Grind the mixture before adding to the cooking or have it in a small grinder at the table.

Cook's Note

THIS MIXTURE IS PERFECT FOR ALL SAVOURY DISHES, MEAT, EGGS, PASTAS, CASSEROLES, SOUPS, SAUCES, ETC. FOR FISH AND CHEESE DISHES SUBSTITUTE THE FRESH GARDEN THYME WITH LEMON THYME LEAVES AND FLOWERS AND INCLUDE 1 TABLESPOON OF SESAME SEEDS AND 2 TEASPOONS OF LEMON ZEST. ALL THE OTHER INGREDIENTS REMAIN THE SAME.

Ailment chart

abscess	burdock, crab apple blossom, echinacea, hollyhock, pumpkin flowers
aching joints	anise, bergamot, chicory, coriander, cornflower, dandelion, day lily, false acacia, fruit sage, St John's wort
acidity	anise, caraway, chamomile, fennel, hollyhock, mint, orange blossom
acne	burdock, calendula, Cape sorrel, coriander, crab apple blossom, dandelion, echinacea, fennel, myrtle, roselle, rosemary, tuberose, waterblommetjie
aids	echinacea, St John's wort
allergic rhinitis	echinacea, elder flowers, hollyhock, mullein, sage
anaemia	dandelion, Judas tree, lucerne
analgesic	anise, Californian poppy, day lily, rosemary, St John's wort, water lily
angina	chamomile, hawthorn
anorexia	anise hyssop, lucerne
anti-allergenic	chamomile, echinacea, yarrow
antibacterial	calendula, lavender, mint, roselle, rosemary, sage, strawberry flowers, thyme, winter savory
antibiotic	burdock, chives, echinacea, myrtle, nasturtium, sage, St John's wort
anti-cancer	burdock, clover, lucerne, strawberry flowers, violet, water lily
anticoagulant	evening primrose, mullein
antifungal	burdock, calendula, echinacea, Judas tree, sage, thyme, winter savory
anti-inflammatory	calendula, chamomile, echinacea, fennel, golden rod, hyssop, mint, rosemary, rose-scented geranium, yarrow
anti-oxidant	burdock, calendula, chamomile, golden rod, hawthorn, mint, mullein, mustard, myrtle, nasturtium, rosemary, rose-scented geranium, thyme, winter savory
antispasmodic	anise, Californian poppy, caraway, chamomile, coriander, evening primrose, false acacia, fennel, hawthorn, honeysuckle, hyssop, mint, mustard, orange blossom, roselle, rosemary, St John's wort, yarrow
antiviral	anise hyssop, calendula, echinacea, hyssop, sage, St John's wort, strawberry flowers
anxiety	anise, borage, calendula, Californian poppy, carnation, chamomile, coriander, evening primrose, gardenia, granadilla flower, jasmine, lucerne, orange blossom, rose, sage, snapdragon, St John's wort, tuberose
aphrodisiac	water lily, winter savory
appetite stimulant	caraway, chives
arteriosclerosis	buckwheat, hawthorn
arthritis	buckwheat, burdock, clover, elder flowers, golden rod, mustard, rose-scented geranium
asthma	anise, chamomile, echinacea, evening primrose, gardenia, honeysuckle, hyssop, sage, winter savory
astringent	calendula, myrtle, orange blossom, prickly pear, roselle, rosemary, sage, St John's wort, strawberry flowers, yarrow
athlete's foot	sage, thyme
backache	lucerne, St John's wort, thyme
bad breath	almond blossom, anise, caraway, coriander, fennel, mint, plum blossom, rosemary
bedwetting	Californian poppy, rose-scented geranium

bladder ailments	carnation, carpet geranium, chives, cornflower, echinacea, Judas tree, nasturtium (*see also* Urinary tract ailments)
bladder tonic	dandelion, garland chrysanthemum, pumpkin flowers, strawberry flowers
bleeding	calendula, gardenia, yarrow
blisters	banana flower, fruit sage, fuchsia, gladiolus
bloating	anise, anise hyssop, artichoke, bergamot, caraway, carpet geranium, chamomile, coriander, fennel, garland chrysanthemum, hawthorn, mint, yarrow
blocked nose	calamint, mint, orange blossom, pineapple sage, roselle, sage, winter savory
blood pressure	evening primrose, hawthorn, moringa
blood sugar levels, regulate	artichoke, burdock, rosemary
blood tonic	borage, chives, dandelion, evening primrose, garland chrysanthemum, Judas tree, moringa, nasturtium, orange blossom, peach blossom, roselle
boils	burdock, Cape sorrel, coriander, crab apple blossom, dandelion, echinacea, hollyhock, linseed, pumpkin flowers
bronchitis	anise, bergamot, borage, clover, echinacea, elder flowers, mullein, mustard, nasturtium, sage, thyme, violet, winter savory
bruises	buckwheat, calamint, day lily, delicious monster, evening primrose, fruit sage, gardenia, hollyhock, myrtle, peach blossom, rocket, waterblommetjie, wisteria
bunions	dahlia
burns	banana flower, Cape sorrel, feijoa, plumbago, prickly pear, St John's wort, tulip, water lily, waterblommetjie, yucca
callouses	banana flower, fuchsia
calming	anise hyssop, borage, Californian poppy, chamomile, coriander, fruit sage, jasmine, lavender, rose-scented geranium, sage, tuberose, violet
catarrh	chamomile, elder flowers, golden rod, hollyhock, hyssop, mullein, orange blossom
chest pains	anise, chamomile
chicken pox	St John's wort, chamomile
chilblains	buckwheat, calendula, echinacea, hawthorn, linseed
chills	anise, anise hyssop, false acacia, linseed
cholesterol	artichoke, buckwheat, chives, evening primrose, linseed, sunflower
chronic fatigue	buckwheat, mint, rosemary
circulation, aid to	anise hyssop, burdock, elder flowers, hawthorn, hyssop, lucerne, rose, rosemary
circulatory ailments	buckwheat, calendula, hawthorn, linseed, fennel, mustard, orange blossom, rose
cold sores	echinacea, elder flowers, St John's wort
colds	anise, bergamot, borage, calamint, chives, crab apple blossom, echinacea, elder flowers, evening primrose, gladiolus, hollyhock, hyssop, lucerne, mullein, mustard, nasturtium, pansy and viola, pineapple sage, roselle, sage, St John's wort, thyme, violet, winter savory
colic	anise, bergamot, calamint, caraway, carpet geranium, chamomile, coriander, false acacia, fennel, fruit sage, hollyhock, mint, prickly pear, sage, winter savory
colitis	calendula, honeysuckle, prickly pear
conjunctivitis	clover, linseed, rose
constipation	carnation, chicory, dandelion, false acacia, hyssop, linseed, mustard, orange blossom, plum blossom, violet

corns	banana flower, dahlia, dandelion, fuchsia
coughs	anise, bergamot, borage, calamint, caraway, chives, clover, cornflower, crab apple blossom, echinacea, elder flowers, evening primrose, gladiolus, hollyhock, honeysuckle, linseed, mullein, nasturtium, pansy and viola, pineapple sage, rose, roselle, sage, St John's wort, thyme, violet, winter savory, wisteria
cracked heels	elder flowers, lavender, rose-scented geranium, yucca
Crohn's disease	chamomile, mint
cuts and grazes	banana flower, calendula, Cape sorrel, dahlia, fuchsia, gardenia, gladiolus, linseed, peach blossom, prickly pear, pumpkin flowers, St John's wort, tulip, waterblommetjie, yucca
cystitis	carpet geranium, chicory, gardenia, garland chrysanthemum, golden rod, hollyhock, strawberry flowers
dandruff	carpet geranium, sage
deodorant	artichoke, fruit sage, garland chrysanthemum, lavender, rosemary, rose-scented geranium
depression	buckwheat, jasmine, lavender, orange blossom, rose, rosemary, rose-scented geranium, St John's wort
detoxifying	anise hyssop, artichoke, burdock, calamint, calendula, chicory, dandelion, echinacea, fennel, fruit sage, garland chrysanthemum, lucerne, peach blossom, thyme
diabetes	artichoke, strawberry flowers
diarrhoea	carpet geranium, crab apple blossom, feijoa, gladiolus, golden rod, hawthorn, hollyhock, moringa, prickly pear, sage, strawberry flowers
digestive aid	anise, artichoke, bergamot, caraway, chives, fennel, fruit sage, mint, mustard, roselle, rosemary, sage, thyme, tuberose, winter savory
digestive ailments	anise, anise hyssop, bergamot, calamint, chamomile, calendula, coriander, cornflower, evening primrose, false acacia, fennel, gladiolus, golden rod, hollyhock, hyssop, linseed, mint, prickly pear, sage, strawberry flowers, tuberose, winter savory (*see also individual ailments*)
disinfectant	day lily, sage, thyme
diuretic	anise, burdock, caraway, dandelion, fennel, garland chrysanthemum, golden rod, hawthorn, Judas tree, moringa, mustard, roselle, rose-scented geranium, sunflower
diverticulitis	hollyhock, mint
dizziness	lavender, mint, rosemary
dry skin	almond blossom, bergamot, calendula, carnation, carpet geranium, dahlia, delicious monster, elder flowers, fruit sage, honeysuckle, lavender, mint, sage, tulip, yucca
dysentery	crab apple blossom, feijoa, gladiolus, mint, moringa
earache	echinacea, elder flowers, mullein
eczema	borage, burdock, calendula, carnation, chamomile, clover, elder flowers, evening primrose, honeysuckle, mullein, pansy and viola, peach blossom, thyme, violet, water lily
energising	almond blossom, lucerne, rosemary, St John's wort, thyme
expectorant	anise, calamint, caraway, fennel, honeysuckle, hyssop, mullein, sunflower, thyme
eye ailments	calendula, chamomile, clover, cornflower
fainting fits	lavender, rosemary, yarrow

fear	anise hyssop, borage, evening primrose, gardenia, granadilla flower, lavender, orange blossom, tuberose
fever	anise hyssop, bergamot, borage, calendula, dandelion, elder flowers, gardenia, hawthorn, moringa, mullein, yarrow
fever blisters	echinacea, elder flowers (*see also* Cold sores)
flatulence	anise, artichoke, bergamot, caraway, carpet geranium, coriander, fennel, fruit sage, mint, prickly pear, rosemary, winter savory
flu	anise hyssop, borage, calamint, chives, cornflower, echinacea, elder flowers, gardenia, lucerne, mustard, nasturtium, thyme, winter savory
freckles	elder flowers, fuchsia, water lily
fungicidal	anise hyssop, echinacea, rosemary, rose-scented geranium, sage, thyme
gall bladder ailments	artichoke, calendula, chicory, crab apple blossom, dandelion, mint, rosemary, St John's wort
gout	buckwheat, chicory, clover, dandelion, moringa, pansy and viola
gripes	anise, caraway, coriander, fennel
gum disease	almond blossom, caraway, hollyhock, mint, moringa, plum blossom, rosemary, sage, strawberry flowers
haemorrhoids	buckwheat, calendula, linseed, mullein, snapdragon
hair loss	banana flower, nasturtium, rosemary, sage, yucca (*see also* Scalp problems)
hayfever	chamomile, echinacea, elder flowers, hollyhock, honeysuckle, mullein, thyme
headache	anise, chicory, gardenia, jasmine, lavender, moringa, rosemary, violet
heart palpitations	anise, gardenia, hawthorn, mint, orange blossom, tuberose
heart problems	hawthorn, pansy and viola
heart tonic	buckwheat, hawthorn, honeysuckle, lucerne
heartburn	anise, caraway, coriander, fennel, mint, prickly pear
hiatus hernia	chamomile, mint
high blood pressure	chives, gardenia, hawthorn, pansy and viola, rosemary
hives	borage, evening primrose
homesickness	honeysuckle
hot flushes	golden rod, mint, sage
hyperactivity	chamomile, evening primrose, lavender, mint, rose-scented geranium, tuberose
hypochondria	dandelion, lucerne
immune system booster	borage, chives, echinacea, elder flowers, mustard, rose, roselle, sage, sunflower, thyme
indigestion	anise, artichoke, calamint, caraway, carpet geranium, coriander, fennel, pansy and viola
inflammation	pansy and viola, sage, snapdragon, thyme
insect bites	almond blossom, borage, calendula, clover, coriander, crab apple blossom, dahlia, echinacea, false acacia, feijoa, fruit sage, fuchsia, gardenia, hollyhock, mint, peach blossom, pineapple sage, poppy, prickly pear, St John's wort, thyme, tulip, waterblommetjie, yucca
insomnia	Californian poppy, chamomile, dandelion, granadilla flower, lavender, orange blossom, St John's wort

irregular heartbeat	anise, caraway, hawthorn
irritable bowel syndrome	chamomile, evening primrose, hollyhock, prickly pear
kidney ailments	carnation, chives, cornflower, crab apple blossom, dandelion, echinacea, fennel, golden rod, nasturtium, peach blossom, sunflower
kidney stones	burdock, clover, fennel, golden rod, hawthorn, Judas tree, sunflower
kidney tonic	burdock, chicory, fennel, garland chrysanthemum, linseed, peach blossom, pumpkin flowers, strawberry flowers
lice	sage, thyme
liver ailments	calendula, caraway, cornflower, dandelion, fennel, St John's wort, strawberry flowers
liver tonic	artichoke, burdock, chicory, gardenia, Judas tree, strawberry flowers
low blood pressure	rosemary
malaria	hawthorn, sunflower
menopause	evening primrose, golden rod, hawthorn, lucerne, mint, sage, St John's wort
menstruation, irregular	calendula, carpet geranium, hawthorn, hollyhock, lucerne, sage
menstruation, painful	anise, calendula, caraway, chamomile, mint, yarrow
milk production, stimulates	anise, carpet geranium, fennel
morning sickness	anise hyssop, chamomile, mint
mouth infections	day lily, mint, plum blossom, rosemary, sage
mouth ulcers	almond blossom, elder flowers, plum blossom, sage, snapdragon, strawberry flowers
mucous, excessive	borage, cornflower, mullein, sage
multiple sclerosis	evening primrose
muscle spasms	burdock, calendula, caraway, false acacia, jasmine, St John's wort, thyme
muscular aches	anise, anise hyssop, bergamot, chamomile, day lily, fruit sage, jasmine, mullein, rose-scented geranium, St John's wort, thyme
nausea	anise, anise hyssop, artichoke, bergamot, coriander, fruit sage, mint, tuberose
nervousness	anise hyssop, calendula, carnation, coriander, evening primrose, granadilla flower, mint, rose-scented geranium
neuralgia	rose-scented geranium, St John's wort
nightmares	Californian poppy, mint, rose-scented geranium
nose bleed	yarrow
oestrogenic	calendula, hawthorn, lucerne, sage
oily hair	banana flower, carpet geranium, rosemary, sage
oily skin	bergamot, calendula, Cape sorrel, coriander, fennel, garland crysanthemum, myrtle, orange blossom, plumbago, roselle, rose-scented geranium, strawberry flowers, tuberose
over-exhaustion	chamomile, lavender, lucerne, rose-scented geranium

panic attacks	Californian poppy, chamomile, evening primrose, granadilla flower, lavender, lucerne, mint
peptic ulcer	calendula, chamomile, hollyhock, mint, rose-scented geranium
pimples	Cape sorrel, dahlia, delicious monster, elder flowers, garland crysanthemum, linseed, moringa, poppy, strawberry flowers, waterblommetjie, wisteria
pleurisy	borage, hollyhock, hyssop, mullein, mustard, sage
pneumonia	echinacea, mullein, mustard, thyme, violet, winter savory
post nasal drip	chamomile, elder flowers, violet
postnatal depression	buckwheat, lucerne, mint
post-viral fatigue syndrome (ME)	Californian poppy, echinacea, St John's wort
premenstrual tension	borage, evening primrose, hawthorn, orange blossom, rosemary, yarrow
prostate problems	dandelion, pumpkin flowers, prickly pear
psoriasis	borage, burdock, calendula, carpet geranium, clover, elder flowers
rashes	banana flower, borage, burdock, calendula, chamomile, clover, coriander, dahlia, feijoa, fruit sage, fuchsia, hollyhock, honeysuckle, Judas tree, linseed, mint, myrtle, pansy and viola, peach blossom, plumbago, poppy, prickly pear, snapdragon, St John's wort, strawberry flowers, tulip, violet, water lily, waterblommetjie, yucca
respiratory ailments	bergamot, borage, burdock, calamint, chives, cornflower, evening primrose, honeysuckle, Judas tree, moringa, mullein, sage, thyme, winter savory (*see also individual ailments*)
restlessness	anise, chamomile, lavender
rheumatism	chicory, coriander, cornflower, dandelion, day lily, honeysuckle, lavender, linseed, moringa, mullein, mustard, pansy and viola, rosemary, thyme, waterblommetjie
ringworm	anise hyssop, thyme
scabies	elder flowers, thyme
scalp problems	banana flower, carpet geranium, rosemary, yucca
sciatica	St John's wort
scurvy	Cape sorrel, nasturtium
sedative	bergamot, Californian poppy, chamomile, hawthorn, jasmine, orange blossom, rose, St John's wort
shingles	chamomile, St John's wort
shock	anise, anise hyssop, mint
sinus problems	bergamot, calamint, elder flowers, golden rod, linseed, mullein, violet, winter savory
skin ailments	almond blossom, anise hyssop, banana flower, borage, burdock, calendula, carnation, chicory, dahlia, delicious monster, echinacea, elder flowers, evening primrose, feijoa, fennel, fuchsia, hollyhock, honeysuckle, Judas tree, lavender, mint, moringa, mullein, myrtle, pansy and viola, plumbago, poppy, prickly pear, snapdragon, rocket, rose, roselle, rosemary, violet, wisteria, yucca (*see also individual ailments*)
sore nipples	calendula, chamomile
sore throat	anise hyssop, bergamot, calamint, echinacea, elder flowers, fuchsia, lavender, moringa, nasturtium, plum blossom, roselle, sage, thyme, wisteria, winter savory

sprains and strains	burdock, calamint, day lily, delicious monster, fruit sage, myrtle, rocket, St John's wort, snapdragon, waterblommetjie
stiffness	burdock, cornflower, false acacia, jasmine, pansy and viola, rosemary, rose-scented geranium
stimulating	anise hyssop, lucerne, mint, rosemary
strained throat	anise, chamomile, sage, snapdragon
stress	anise, borage, chamomile, gardenia, hawthorn, jasmine, Judas tree, lucerne, orange blossom, St John's wort, tuberose
sunburn	almond blossom, banana flower, bergamot, borage, calendula, delicious monster, feijoa, fuchsia, honeysuckle, linseed, mint, pineapple sage, plumbago, snapdragon, water lily, waterblommetjie
tension	anise, anise hyssop, hawthorn, jasmine, lavender, lucerne
thrush	calendula, golden rod, sage, thyme, winter savory
tight chest	anise, bergamot, borage, calamint, honeysuckle, Judas tree
tired feet	banana flower, dahlia, fruit sage, gladiolus, lavender, linseed, mint
tonic	almond blossom, borage, buckwheat, cornflower, mustard, sage, St John's wort, thyme, wisteria, yarrow
tonsillitis	echinacea, fuchsia, sage
tooth decay	anise, moringa, sage
toothache	anise, Californian poppy, day lily, echinacea, Judas tree, yarrow
tranquillising	lavender, rose-scented geranium, water lily
tremors	cornflower
urinary tract ailments	chicory, chives, fennel, golden rod, hyssop, linseed, mustard, myrtle, peach blossom, strawberry flowers (*see also individual ailments*)
vaginal itching	buckwheat, clover, elder flowers
varicose veins	buckwheat, mullein, wisteria
verrucas	dandelion
vertigo	cornflower, lavender, mint, rosemary
vomiting	anise hyssop, bergamot, caraway, fennel, tuberose
warts	dandelion, poppy
weak nails	Judas tree, pineapple sage, tuberose
weight loss	evening primrose, fennel
whooping cough	anise, borage, caraway, clover, mint, thyme, violet
worms	pumpkin seeds, thyme
wounds	banana flower, bergamot, calendula, crab apple blossom, evening primrose, mullein, prickly pear, pumpkin flowers, yarrow, yucca

Flower index

RECIPE INDEX